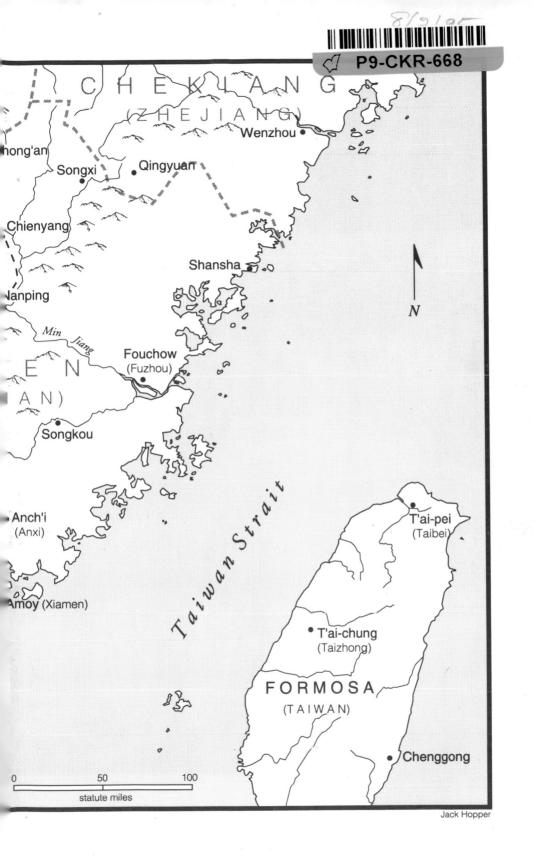

Jack Hopper

# Sampan Sailor

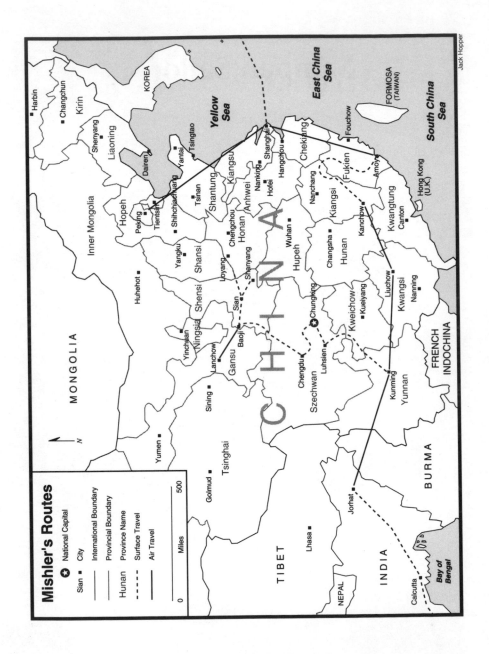

**Mishler's Routes**

⭑ National Capital
Sian ▪ City
—— International Boundary
—— Provincial Boundary
Hunan Province Name
- - - - Surface Travel
—— Air Travel

Miles
0        500

Jack Hopper

# Sampan Sailor

## A Navy Man's Adventures in WWII China

## Clayton Mishler

Brassey's (US)
A Maxwell Macmillan Company
Washington • New York • London

BRASSEY'S (US)
*A Maxwell Macmillan Company*
Washington • New York • London

Brassey's (US)

| Editorial Offices | Order Department |
| --- | --- |
| Brassey's (US) | Brassey's Book Orders |
| 8000 Westpark Drive | c/o Macmillan Publishing Co. |
| First Floor | 100 Front Street, Box 100 |
| McLean, Virginia 22102 | Riverside, New Jersey 08075 |

Brassey's (US) is a Maxwell Macmillan Company. Brassey's books are available at special discounts for bulk purchases for sales promotions, premiums, fund-raising, or educational use through the Special Sales Director, Macmillan Publishing Company, 866 Third Avenue, New York, New York 10022.

Library of Congress Cataloging-in Publication Data

Mishler, Clayton, 1908–1992.
    Sampan Sailor: a navy man's adventures in WWII China / Clayton Mishler.
      p.  cm.
    Includes index.
    ISBN 0-02-881073-2
    1. Mishler, Clayton. 1908–1992. 2. World War, 1939–1945—Commando operations—China. 3. World War, 1939–1945—Personal narratives, American. 4. World War, 1939–1945—Military intellegence—China. 5. United States, Navy—Biography. 6. Seamen—United States—Biography. I. Title
D794.5.M57    1994
940.54'25—dc20                        93-9963
                                           CIP

10 9 8 7 6 5 4 3 2 1

Printed in the United States of America

*To Craig, my son, who persuaded me to write my China experiences.*

*To Audrey, my wife, who assisted and encouraged me in my efforts.*

*To my friends, who had faith in me.*

# Contents

# Preface

My adventure in the U.S. Navy began in Washington, D.C., on October 20, 1943, and lasted the next two years of my World War II tour of duty in provincial China, until my return to the States on January 3, 1946. This book is based solely on my memory and on brief notations in a small notebook, since diaries were strictly against U.S. Navy regulations. I also consulted some of the many letters I wrote home to my wife, Audrey. She, my son Craig, and several friends persisted for years in efforts to get me to write about my secret mission in mainland China.

One day several years after I retired from the Veterans Administration, I was shopping in a discount department store and noticed 500 sheets of loose-leaf paper on sale for sixty-eight cents. It was too good a bargain to pass up. On the first day of spring in 1980, I sat down at the typewriter and began to tell my story.

I began to remember lots of little things—the unexpected but joyous, tinkling pony bells on a remote Chinese mountain road somewhere near the Old Silk Trail, the night I spent in a 2,000-year-old Chinese temple where the monks prepared an elegant dish of Lion's Tongue from the pheasants I shot, and the time I walked through a rainbow of dragonflies while traveling a well-worn path along the Nine Dragons River.

Once a person has lived in a foreign country, he can never dissociate himself from what goes on there. He has traveled its highways, eaten its food, met its people. He may or may not recognize that, right or wrong, attractive or otherwise by his own values, people there do what they do because that's the way they like it. And, whether he realizes it or not, something of that country rubs off on him.

After all these years, China still remains vivid in my mind. I think that's because of the friendships I developed there.

This book relates the details of the Sino-American Cooperative Organization's (SACO's) day-to-day military operations; but it is much more. It recounts many of my life's rarest and most cherished moments.

*   *   *   *   *

I wish to extend a very special thanks to Mary Mae Hartley of Clifton, Texas, who helped edit and reshape the original manuscript. Her tireless dedication and enthusiasm did much to guide this story into print.

# Introduction

One of the best-kept secrets of World War II was an intelligence operation between the United States and China. Its objective was the defeat of the Japanese war machine occupying the coast of mainland China, and the unit was known as SACO (the Sino-American Cooperative Organization). It was directed jointly by Adm. Milton E. Miles, U.S. Navy, and Lt. Gen. Tai Li, Chief of Chinese Intelligence and the right-hand man of Gen. Chiang Kai-shek. At one time the Japanese offered several million dollars to anyone killing either of these leaders. No one knows how many attempts were made on Tai Li's life.

The agreement between these two countries provided that the Chinese and Americans would work together, with the Americans providing technical experts and materiel, and China supplying recruits. Under this mutual plan, China and the United States operated what was probably the most closely integrated allied organization that ever surmounted a major language barrier.

SACO was an amazing military achievement made possible only by the natural and basic friendship of Americans and Chinese and by their unwavering determination to defeat a common enemy. From its inception, "Friendship" was the code name that protected members of SACO. High adventure, tragedy, and terror packed the SACO files, and the role of the U.S. Navy men was among the most dramatic. Few of us were familiar with China, and we ventured into occupied territory with a vocabulary of only about fifty Chinese words. We learned to eat with chopsticks, live off the country, and be satisfied at mealtimes with a bowl of rice and a few boiled vegetables or bean curd.

Following the unprovoked Japanese attack on Pearl Harbor on December 7, 1941, the United States was forced into war in the Pacific. While the United States was recovering from the Pearl Harbor disaster and planning defensive actions, the Japanese were moving rapidly, taking island after island in the Pacific, and were also invading the Chinese mainland, from Shanghai to Hong Kong.

SACO began in 1943 as a U.S. Navy weather reporting project from about a dozen weather stations in China. One such camp was located in the Gobi Desert to the far north, but the others were scattered in the southern part of the country. Headquarters was in a closely guarded valley in the mountains outside Chungking (Chungching). This nerve center tied together 600 field units operating in remote areas with hand-cranked and battery-powered transmitting equipment.

SACO weather observers and other agents equipped with radios sent the intelligence information promptly to headquarters in Chungking, where it was analyzed, condensed, and flashed directly to the Pacific Fleet Headquarters and to listening air, surface, and submarine units at sea. Fleet operations in the Western Pacific made the most of these China weather reports, especially in planning and executing hazardous carrier strikes despite the treacherous weather conditions prevailing near Formosa and the Japanese home islands.

SACO coastwatchers played an important role in the submarine campaign against Japanese shipping. So, most of the work was concentrated along the China coast, where Japanese sea operations were kept under constant surveillance. To obtain the weather reports from the areas of China occupied by the Japanese, we worked with select Chinese soldiers and Chinese guerrillas. The valuable weather information and other essential intelligence reports we collected contributed significantly to the defeat of the Japanese. We SACO men affectionately called our secret unit "The Rice Paddy Navy."

I enlisted in the wartime navy because, as a married man with a child, they would not draft me. I felt a great compulsion to be a part of our nation's fighting forces. Audrey, my wife, understood. After reporting to the Great Lakes Naval Training Station, where I went through boot camp training and aptitude testing, I was sent to storekeepers school in Toledo, Ohio, where I learned naval supply and procurement procedures. Shortly before graduation from the storekeepers school, our company was requested to "stand fast." An officer asked for volunteers for hazardous duty, and twenty-five of us stepped forward. After a round of interviews, twenty of us were selected.

After the war, the statistics on the effectiveness of the Rice Paddy Navy were as follows: from June 1944 to July 1945 Chinese guerrillas killed 23,540 Japanese military personnel, wounded 9,166, and captured 291. They destroyed more than 200 bridges, 84 locomotives, 141 ships and river craft, and 97 depots and warehouses. Official estimates indicated that 30,000 Japanese were killed during the last eighteen months of the war. At its peak, SACO personnel numbered 3,000; but just 5 Americans were killed.

The Chinese in the project at one time numbered 100,000, of whom approximately 10,000 were killed and an equal number wounded. Among the Chinese guerrillas working in SACO were pirates turned patriots who roved from island to island in their junks, plotting the course of Japanese shipping for U.S. planes and submarines. Teams of one or two Americans and sixteen Chinese comrades, hidden at vantage points on the Japanese-held shore, provided information that killed Japanese operations.

It was SACO information that led to the U.S. submarine *Barb*'s famous feat of destroying an entire eleven-ship Japanese convoy. The *Barb*, by itself, sank a total of twenty-six enemy ships during the war in the Pacific. SACO troops helped in the liberation of the ports of Foochow (Fuzhou) and Wenchow (Wenzhou) and many Japanese-held islands along the China coast. In October 1944, during Gen. Douglas MacArthur's invasion of Leyte, SACO supplied the first word that a Japanese carrier task force was approaching for the crucial battle of Leyte Gulf.

There were four specific tasks for SACO.

1. Naval specialists collected weather reports from all Asia and radioed forecasts to the headquarters of Fleet Adm. Chester W. Nimitz. These forecasts were essential for naval and B-29 strikes against Japan. More than 1,000 Chinese weather observers, including women, were trained by the United States for this duty. Fifty weather stations were established in unoccupied China, and observers were placed in areas as remote as Malaya and Burma.

2. U.S. submarines off the China coast surfaced twice daily to listen to direct radio broadcasts from Chungking, which told where and when Japanese convoys were expected.

3. U.S. Navy men, hiding under Chinese coolie hats, photographed every

important anchorage and inlet along the Chinese coast. Navy teams, working often with guerrillas such as the pirates, mapped every feature of the China coast from below Shanghai to Amoy, and finally to Hong Kong.

4. Twelve SACO training camps were set up to train Chinese Nationalist guerrillas in such areas as sabotage, underground fighting, and handling weapons and explosives.

SACO worked with guerrillas to rescue Chinese and American flyers shot down in Japanese territory. One of these was Don Bell, a U.S. war correspondent who was plucked from the Japanese by SACO men. He wrote, "Imagine our gasps of amazed delight when told that there was a U.S. naval station just about twenty-seven miles away. We had been shot down less than a mile from a Japanese garrison, and here was a man telling us that we were within a few hours of safety."

The friendship pact between the United States and China paid off because the specially trained Chinese guerrillas, who lived and worked with SACO operatives, trimmed the size of Japanese forces in China and terrorized others so much that they were afraid to venture from their strongholds.

# CHAPTER 1

# The Japanese Patrol

*June 1945—The Allied forces win a decisive naval battle against the Japanese in the Philippine Sea.*

July 5, 1945. This was a day to remember! Early in the morning our camp radio announced that the Philippines had been liberated by the United States! The few of us left at Camp Six were excited, but we had work to do. Nearly all of our SACO unit personnel, some thirty men, had already moved down to Changchow (Zhangzhou), Fukien (Fujian) Province. With me were two radiomen and two experts for the direction finder. The weapons and supplies in nearby Hua'an, where our Chinese guerrillas camped, had dwindled to almost nothing. As storekeeper first class, I had been left in camp to see that requested supplies were shipped downriver to Changchow as needed. So on this special day I needed to check on the availability of sampans for the river shipments. I would find that performance of this duty would make the day even more memorable.

"Alnav," I called. Within seconds, the small, twelve-year-old Chinese boy, classified as a soldier but assigned to me as a houseboy, appeared at my side, smiling, as usual.

Seeing I was prepared for travel, with my rifle and musette bag (backpack), he fell right into step behind me. We passed through the main gate of the bamboo fence that surrounded the camp compound and set out on the down-

1

river trail, which went over the mountain to our south, leading to a small village on the Nine Dragons River. There we could obtain information about
sampans we could hire to take the supplies to Changchow as necessary.

I had become very accustomed to this route, as I had traveled it many times
in the past several months, going for supplies for the camp, making arrangements for camp necessities, and obtaining valuable information.

The weather was hot, and flies and bugs were with us along the trail, as
usual. Alnav never seemed to mind. This day, as usual, he was wearing the
black pants and shirt I had bought, the Chinese Army cap with some sort of
insignia and, for a change, shoes.

As we walked, I nodded to some of the people we passed on the trail to the
village, and Alnav called out, "Ni hao ma?" as a greeting. When we reached the
ridge where the 500 stone steps down to the Nine Dragons River and the village began, we were alone. Suddenly Alnav stopped dead in his tracks.

"Summat?" (What?) I asked. He grabbed my arm and placed a finger on his
lips for silence. Then he whispered in my ear, "Nippon! Nippon!" (Japanese!
Japanese!) and motioned that we should turn back on our trail.

As best I could, I quickly whispered back in Chinese, "Are you sure?"

Alnav nodded. "Sidi! Sidi!" (Yes! Yes!)

My thoughts were spinning, but I instinctively motioned for him to follow
me as I climbed the bank on the left side of our trail. Here we were in knee-
high grass with taller weeds all around us. For some reason I turned and
looked back up the trail from whence we had come. There, padding along in
his old green Chinese uniform, was my p'eng-yu (good friend), Sergeant
Chen! One of the Chinese officers had assigned Sergeant Chen the detail of
safeguarding me. I never really knew if he was my bodyguard or not, but he
always showed up when I needed him.

I motioned to him to be quiet and waved for him to follow me into the high
grass. By the time he reached me, the smile on his face had changed to concern. He had heard the Japanese voices, and he looked at me with a question in
his eyes.

"Chen," I whispered, "I want to see how many there are." I bellied myself
to the edge of the bank where I could see down the steps. Cautiously I peeked
over. There was the Japanese patrol—seven soldiers sitting on a resting ledge
about forty-five steps from the top.

They were talking loudly and laughing. They were in uniform and armed.
The one who seemed to be the officer in charge wore a revolver in a skeleton

holster. The only other weapon I readily identified was an automatic rifle carried by one soldier.

I thought quickly and whispered to Alnav to run back to camp for some Chinese soldiers to help us. I knew, however, that they would not come in time. It would be up to Sergeant Chen and me.

Alnav wriggled backwards in the grass and was gone in a hurry, but it would take him at least twelve to fifteen minutes to get back to camp. It was mostly downhill, which would allow him to make good time, but it would take at least another forty minutes for the Chinese soldiers to assemble, double-time their march on the trail, and arrive to help us.

So, it was up to Sergeant Chen and me! These thoughts had taken about a minute to pass through my head. I felt the patrol would likely continue climbing the steps toward our hiding place. They would get winded and slow down the closer they got to the top of the steps, and to us.

I whispered to Chen, "When the patrol starts up the steps, wait until they nearly reach the top. Then I'll shoot the one with the automatic rifle (he was third in line) and you shoot the officer (second in line). I'll shoot the first one next, and you take the fourth . . . got it?"

I repeated, "Dung bu dung?" (Do you understand?)

He answered, "Dunga." (Yes, I understand.)

We waited in the heat and tall grass, tense and ready, for the patrol to make its move. Bugs were buzzing around my ears and eyes, but I couldn't risk swatting at them. I had to be ready. Fortunately, Chen and I had a grandstand seat, in belly position, for what was to come.

It must have been a full five minutes before the officer stood up and barked out a command. The point, or lead, soldier started up the steps, then the officer, then the soldier with the automatic rifle. It was working just as I had planned. The others strung out single file about five steps behind one another. They were climbing the steps, slowing as they got closer to us. They could have seen us in the tall grass if they had known where to look.

I was afraid to breathe. Two of us! Seven of them! Our carbines had fifteen round clips. I looked at Chen and sensed that he felt my apprehension.

The patrol was quiet now, and getting even slower as they approached the top of the 500 steps. Just as I suspected, a few of the Japanese had fallen behind, but the point man was now standing on the top step looking around and back down the steps as the officer joined him. They were all in the clear now. The first men were less than 150 feet from us!

From my flat position, I carefully touched Chen with my foot; we looked at each other a second, and he nodded. I aimed for the chest of the rifleman and squeezed off my shot.

The surprised Japanese soldier stopped for a moment, grabbed his chest and then slumped to the ground.

Chen's shot, a bare split second after mine, hit the officer, who turned halfway around and fell forward.

The rest of the men stopped for a second, wondering what was happening. As they did, I shot the point man. In another moment Chen's second shot dropped the fourth soldier, but not before he managed to fire his rifle in a wild direction.

We had taken them entirely by surprise. The last two men began running back down the steps and another one momentarily stood with his rifle pointed in our direction. Then he jumped over the edge of the stone steps on the far side of the trail. As he did I shot him in the shoulder. He managed to turn and run behind the steps into the steep canyon, toward the waterfalls I knew were there.

Chen and I stood up and fired several shots at the two retreating soldiers. One pitched forward headlong and lay halfway off the steps. There was now only the wounded man somewhere behind the steps and the one running down the steps. I knew we had to get both of them. We approached the fallen men cautiously. Both my Chinese friend and I were now breathing heavily from excitement.

Chen pointed his carbine at the head of the fallen point man and pulled the trigger. Then, in quick succession, he put bullets into the heads of the other two that lay at the top of the steps. I picked up the officer's Luger and stuck it in my belt. We hurried down the steps and looked over the steep side of the hill, but we did not see the last fleeing soldier. There was blood on the steps where he had stood. I knew I had wounded him.

Chen ran down the steps, while I returned to the top where the four bodies lay. A strange, eerie quietness settled on the hilltop, and I stood there for a few minutes, watching flies and insects gather. Their hum interrupted the silence. These Japanese were the first men I had ever killed.

It was war!

I picked up the automatic rifle, as well as the point man's rifle, and pitched them into the grass just above the trail where I stood. I began searching the bodies. I grabbed a white towel in one dead man's pack. Bold red letters on it said, "Philippines General Hospital!" In a flash I realized that this dead man might have been one of the Japanese who had invaded the Philippines and overrun our American forces, taking this towel as a trophy.

Chen was coming back up the steps. He told me he had seen no evidence of the soldier who got away. "Wait until our help comes from camp before searching for the wounded Nippon," I said, still in low tones. What if the soldier was still near by? I kept listening for any kind of sound that might indicate his whereabouts. All I heard were the rushing waterfalls in the canyon.

I motioned for Chen to go back down the steps to where the fifth soldier lay. The man had not moved. He appeared to be dead, but I needed to be sure. When Chen reached the body, he picked up the man's head and then shot him through the back of his neck. He picked up the dead man's rifle and slowly climbed the steps. I took it and pitched it into the grass with the others.

Both Chen and I relaxed a little. We looked at each other in relief, forcing weak smiles. "Ding hao!" (very good), he said.

We sat on the steps and waited and listened. We heard only the waterfalls, the buzz of the flies, and the occasional cry of a bird. Suddenly, far below on the steps we detected movement and heard shouts of "Wai! Wai!" (Hello, or Your attention!) Instantly, we were on our feet, our carbines trained on the two people who came into view. They looked like two Chinese farmers, but who could be sure? I beckoned them forward, the barrel of my gun still on them. They approached slowly, with fright in their eyes.

When they were within reasonable talking distance Chen began questioning them in Chinese. Did they see a Japanese soldier? Yes. Did they see two Japanese soldiers? No. Only one. What was he doing? Where was he going? They replied that he had come running into the small village, yelling to a boatman who had brought the Nippon patrol up the river. Did the boatman and the Nippon start down the river? Yes. Where are you going? Hua'an, our home. Chen motioned for them to come up the steps. They passed the bodies with peering looks but did not stop. They were anxious to leave.

Above us several vultures had appeared and were soaring in circles. The flies and insects had increased to a swarm, and loud buzzing sounds came from all about us.

"I wish the men from camp would come," I told Chen. We waited. I examined the Japanese officer's Luger, a small bore, maybe a .25. I had some second thoughts about the pistol. It was really not mine to keep, since Chen had shot the officer. Rightfully he should have it, so I handed it to him. "It's yours,"

I told him. At first he hesitated, but after he accepted it, he thanked me many times. "Shi, shi." It gave him a great deal of pleasure. Maybe these were the first soldiers he had killed, too.

The air was stifling on the steps near the top of the lofty mountain. The sun was out in full force, and the sky was clear except for the increasing number of vultures. There were about fifty sailing around now. The blood on the bodies and all around where they lay had dried. It was almost black in color.

I was restless, so I told Chen I was going to look around. When I reached the plateau, I was surprised to find several Chinese travelers calmly waiting there. They must have known a fight had been going on below them. Perhaps the two farmers had told them. One of the travelers was an old Chinese woman in a curtained sedan chair. Four Chinese men who carried the chair were sitting beside it. I told them to continue waiting. This worn trail over the mountains to the river village was always well traveled. Perhaps Alnav had warned them of the Nippon soldiers on the trail as he sped past.

"Dinge! Deng!" (Wait!), I told them, then went back down to join Chen.

Soon our support arrived. The waiting had seemed long to me but, indeed, probably had not been much more than an hour. Chen explained to the Chinese officer, Captain Pao, all about our ambush, gesturing firmly. He showed him where the wounded Japanese had jumped over the wall and offered to help look for the escapee. But Captain Pao shook his head. He picked eight men to search the area and asked Chen and me to return to camp to explain to General Lui what had occurred.

Before we left, I pointed out the rifles I had thrown into the weeds, and he told a soldier to gather them. "Take the Nippon prisoner," I suggested, with the idea that we might be able to find out what plans the Japanese had for our camp if, indeed, they knew about it. If not, why was the Japanese patrol on the same trail leading to our camp near Hua'an? Why had they come up to that particular village in the sampan?

A surprising thing had happened a few weeks before this day. Our radio transmission was being continuously disrupted by a Japanese radioman. Sometimes we heard him distinctly. He called himself "Joe" and spoke a little English. His shrill voice interrupted many of our transmissions to tell us that the Japanese knew the location of our camp and that there was a minimum price of 5,000 CN on each of our heads.

Chief Newell got teed off one day and answered Joe. "Get off the air, you little yellow bastards, and let me send my message!" From then on the jamming and voice interruptions became more frequent. We were more than surprised one day during all these interruptions when Joe said he knew our

names and then rattled off the names of seven SACO men at our camp. One
of them was mine!

Up on the mountain, everyone was busy. Captain Pao agreed to try to capture the Japanese soldier, and about thirty men stayed behind to search the
area thoroughly. Pao called out instructions to his men, directing a sergeant to
take care of the burial detail. He signaled the waiting travelers back up the trail
to come ahead. Chen and I watched the carriers of the curtained sedan chair.
They were very cautious and quiet until they passed us and the bodies, whereupon they began chattering like magpies.

Alnav met us at the gate of the bamboo fence around our compound. "Good
job," I told him, commending him for his swift trip back to camp for help. He
asked a dozen questions, which we answered. The rest of the day he wore a
smile on his face and told everybody all the details.

Our Chinese soldiers never found the wounded soldier, as far as I know. He
might have fallen over the canyon's edge and been swept downriver by the
waterfalls.

While Alnav proudly stalked about camp, Chen and I went into Hua'an to
report to General Lui, who also wanted to know every detail: how we had set
up the ambush and how we had carried it through. He, too, was full of smiles,
and very effusive as he asked question after question. The general spoke some
English, but as long as I worked with him and his men I never saw him without an interpreter by his side. He was a very thorough general.

Chen showed him the Japanese officer's Luger and the general
expressed great interest in it. After a while, Chen offered it to him, and
General Lui accepted it, a little more readily than I thought he should have.
At least he needed no coaxing. Up until now our specific SACO Camp Six
had had few skirmishes with the Nipponese. I still wondered what prompt-
ed their trip to our area.

Upon my arrival back in camp, Alnav searched me out and touched my arm.
He gestured that there was a message for me. I found that the Changchow
unit had sent orders for me to start packing all military supplies and gear
stored in our three "godowns" (storage points) and make plans to move the
rest of the camp to Changchow.

"I'll hate to leave here," I said to one of the radiomen.

"Yeah, we built it from scratch. Home sweet home," he replied. That had
been only ten months ago.

The message had said our new location would be in the administrative
building and classrooms of a large school two miles north of the center of
Changchow, where our coastwatcher's unit was stationed. I delivered this

piece of news to the direction finder's crew and other personnel, six all told, including Mr. Yip and the Chinese assistant to our cook.

We decided to celebrate our success in bringing down a Japanese patrol and our farewell to Unit 6 on the Nine Dragons River. I sent Alnav to Hua'an for red wine. "Quity en!" (Hurry!), I told him.

The label on the wine bottle proclaimed its properties in a very interesting way. Before we had a chance to get too bleary-eyed, I read out loud the words on the label. In addition to some 130 Chinese characters, there was in English the following translation, which, somehow, at that moment, seemed appropriate:

LITCHI WINE

LITCHI IS THE BEST KIND OF FRUITS IN CHANGCHOW, FUKIEN. WHEN IT IS HARVEST IN THE SUMMER TIME, WE TAKE ITS SNOWY AND SWEET MEAT, WHICH, AFTER CHEMICAL WORK, MAY BE FERMENTED INTO SUCH KIND OF WINE.

THE LITCHI WINE IS THE MOST NUTRIMENTAL, SANITARY AND VIGOROUS LIQUOR. THAT EVEN OLD OR YOUNG MEN OR WOMEN DRINK SOME OF THIS ANY TIME WILL MAKE THEIR BODIES HEALTH AND SPIRIT; AND IS ESPECIALLY EFFICIENT FOR THE WOMAN AFTER BRINGING FORTH.

WE FERMENT THIS WINE WITH OUR OWN PARTICULAR METHOD: AFTER TRYING, YOU WILL SAY "OH! THIS WINE IS THE BEST QUALITY I EVER DRINK."

Warmed up, the wine tasted very good, and we sat around drinking and talking until chow time. My buddies quizzed me about the day's activities regarding the enemy patrol and wanted to know all that happened on the trail. How do you feel about shooting another human being? Do you have any guilt feelings?"

My answer was "No," but that night it was difficult for me to sleep. I relived the day over and over again before I could fall asleep, and when I finally did, it was time to get up.

My hard days of training back on the Potomac River had proved their worth, for I had been well prepared for hazardous duty. My assignment as naval store-keeper should have kept me away from the lines of combat, but here in faraway China, with strangeness all about, the grim prospects of war had finally come to pass.

# CHAPTER 2

# A Secret Mission

*August–October 1943—Munda, New Georgia, is captured by
the U.S. Army, and troops occupy Bairoko Harbor, ending
the Central Solomon campaign. A U.S. amphibious force
invades Vella Lavella, Lavella Island; and a U.S. task force
attacks Marcus Island.*

The twenty of us who had volunteered for hazardous duty two weeks earlier
awaited our orders in Washington, D.C. Although the days dragged by, they
weren't really boring because we had the opportunity to tour the city and to
lounge in the naval barracks. We speculated among ourselves as to what we
had volunteered for and where we might eventually end up for our war
assignment.

Finally the words we waited for came. On Saturday evening, October 23,
1943, we were told to report to a certain point behind the Navy Department
Building on Constitution Avenue promptly at 8:00 A.M. Sunday.

We were there on time. Pretty soon a canvas-covered, stake-body truck
pulled up and stopped. The driver and a navy lieutenant emerged from
the cab.

"I am Lieutenant Smith of the Naval Station," said the officer, who was
dressed in fatigues. "Get in the truck and secure the canvas endflaps. It would
be best not to attempt to look out."

We tossed our duffle bags, containing all our worldly possessions, into the
truck first, then scrambled in. Just before I closed the flap, he said tersely, "It

will take about two hours to reach your destination, which is a secret camp. Again, gentlemen, do not try to locate yourselves."

We made ourselves as comfortable as possible, not realizing that this would probably be the most comfortable truck ride we would have for a couple of years. Regardless of the lieutenant's warning, occasionally one of us couldn't resist. We peeked out. After leaving the city, we did not recognize the road or area, but soon we entered a thickly wooded area. We traveled through it for at least an hour, and shortly before 11:00 A.M., the truck came to an abrupt stop. The flaps were opened and the lieutenant snapped, "O.K. This is as far as you go."

In a clearing in the forest was a crude camp composed of three principal and three minor frame buildings. Running past the camp was a very wide river, which I found out later was the Potomac. I did not know it at the time, but this makeshift camp was be the first leg of my long journey to China.

We carried our gear inside one of the larger buildings as the lieutenant instructed. The structure was entirely empty except for two long rows of cots. I counted them. There were 100 cots. For the next three weeks, the twenty of us were its only occupants, and we were there only to drop exhausted into bed. We never saw the lieutenant again, but soon another one took his place, also dressed in fatigues. "Sunday dinner is ready in the mess hall. Follow me."

The twenty of us filled a couple of tables. Eight other navy men, our trainers, were eating at a third table. This comprised the entire training camp. At first the food was good. There was an excellent cook with three assistants. But after ten days, the cook left, and the quality of the food left with him.

One of the officers, a Lieutenant (j.g.) Salter, concluded the meal by introducing himself and the others and by telling us not to leave the campgrounds. He said our first day of work would begin the next morning at 5:00 A.M.

He didn't tell us that each day at 5:00 A.M. we would be awakened for a mile run before breakfast. He didn't tell us any additional details about our labors for the next three weeks, but the training never let up.

The first thing we learned was every detail of the Colt .45 automatic. We learned to take it apart and put it back together with our eyes shut. It was the same with the carbine and the Thompson submachine gun. Each piece of each gun had a name; we learned them all.

Sometimes my buddies and I discussed what the training might be for: an invasion force? a rescue mission? But where? When we learned to use a compass, snowshoes, kayaks, and dynamite, we were stumped. Most of the time, we were too tired to discuss anything at all. They drove us intensely and almost mercilessly every day of the week, morning to bedtime.

We were paired off one day and assigned a collapsed kayak to assemble, quickly. Then for about a week we had upriver and downriver exercises. We were lucky to get a downriver problem the first day, because the tide was running out, and we turned with the tide. However, we worked our arms and backs to the limit later when we had to paddle against the tide going up, and against the incoming tide on the return trip to camp.

One day at lunch on the banks of the Potomac, I said to Gerry, "We're storekeepers. What does that have to do with all this?"

"Got me, Clayt, but one of these days we're gonna find out."

Duties of a storekeeper might include those of a disburser of equipment, procurer of supplies, paymaster, and custodian. We kept striving; the instructors kept driving.

In one class we learned how to use a malleable plastic explosive that came in pieces about the size of a quarter-pound of gray butter. This was Composition C, a compound we just called Comp C. In addition to the prima-cord, it took two #8 detonating dynamite caps to set it off. Hitting the plastic with a carbine bullet or one #8 cap did not provide enough impact to explode it. We learned its power and predictability by exploding cut-down trees and torn-up sections of a railroad track, which had been brought to the camp specifically for us to experiment on. We also blew up two small frame buildings on a deserted farm near the camp.

We had evening classes right up until bedtime. They were cramming skills into us. Then came the night exercises, where problems were approached by teams of two, four, six, or eight men. Teams were dropped off by jeep or truck at some distant point in the forest, and then, by using only a compass, we were to find our way back through the dark woods to a predetermined rendezvous. Each time we signaled our arrival by clicking two stones together.

"Wouldn't you think they'd give us a whistle or something?" laughed Bill. Later we were to learn that making do and living off the land would be two of the most important lessons we learned. The darkness became our ally in these endeavors. Our compasses had luminous dials that allowed us to see their numerals in the densest woods at midnight even with no moon. When it was dark we would open one hand in a fanlike spread, moving it back and forth in front of our eyes to feel for obstructions in front of our faces. Then we moved the brush and branches in order to pass quietly. The holly leaves that abounded in the area, as well as other scrub trees, continually scratched and scarred our faces.

A doctor joined our group at the beginning of the third week; and during his first day of judo training, he broke his arm. He left us for a day and returned with his arm in a sling. Evidently, he was supposed to give us immunization shots. What he did was choose me and another man to give the shots under his supervision. All went well with the exception of one shot I gave where the needle broke. I had to pull the broken piece out with tweezers.

We knew we had completed this phase of our training when a lieutenant ordered us into another truck, secured the flaps, and told us to keep our eyes within the closed vehicle. A few hours later, we were unloaded back in Washington, D.C.

It was nice to lounge a couple of days in the old barracks and sleep on a bunk bed whose mattress was pure luxury. One by one, the twenty of us were summoned to the Executive Office Building next door to the White House. I was told to report to an office on the first floor. This might be it, I thought, and hoped, as I entered the reception area. The secretary ushered me into a large, well-furnished office where a man in civilian clothes introduced himself as Mr. Milford, who worked for the State Department. He was easy to talk to and asked a number of questions. One was whether I had feelings as to whether I could get along with Chinese people. I told him I was sure I could get along fine.

From a desk drawer he pulled out a little book and handed it to me. It was my passport!

"Mr. Mishler," he said. "Your orders call for you to report to Chungking, China. As soon as possible. Your lieutenant will give you a transportation schedule. Good luck!"

I was given two weeks leave and I traveled to Kansas City to visit my wife and year-old son. In conversation with Audrey, I left out most details of the training on the Potomac and any reference to my destination except that I was going to China. She understood. Of course, I hated to leave them. But this was war, and the surge of a secret mission and an adventuresome journey excited me, I must admit.

When I returned to Washington, I received another series of immunization shots, which resulted, this time, in a very fat swollen arm. I felt I was surely immunized against any disease that might come along in China.

In fourteen days, the twenty of us assembled in Room 2732 for the last time. A Chinese colonel, who spoke excellent English, and two U.S. Navy lieutenants spoke to us for a total of two hours. It was here we learned that we would be part of a secret, vital weather-gathering and information network system in the interior of China, behind Japanese-held China coastal areas, and working sometimes in disguise with the Chinese Army or Chinese guerrillas. The name was new to me: Sino-American Cooperative Organization. I was to be a part of a unit called SACO! It sounded very far away. My mind was running full blast. SACO would eventually acquire other nicknames, like the Rice Paddy Navy, but it would create a bond between Americans and Chinese in an offbeat sort of way.

The lieutenant emphasized that our Pacific Fleet would be depending upon weather forecasts that originated in Asia and moved eastward toward the Pacific Ocean. We also would be gathering information about Japanese military movements, he explained, and passing this information to the Chinese as well as to U.S. military personnel.

An important thing for us to remember, he said, was that we would be working close to Japanese military operations and we must be ever on the alert. "Do not permit yourselves to be captured, OR SHOT!"

With these words and others ringing in our astounded, interested, and anticipating ears, we boarded a special, private Pullman train car. We were joined by two junior-grade lieutenants. One, Lieutenant Mastenbrook, a specialist in aerography, was in charge of our draft. Mastenbrook became a good friend.

When we reached Chicago, the nation's great train center, our conductor announced that we would not be changing trains, as most other travelers were required to do. "The only through cars nowadays are those carrying pigs," he explained. We burst out laughing, relieving the tension that had begun for most of us at that last meeting in Room 2732.

My buddy Gerry Gebraad said, "You can't get much more prestigious than a pig!" Our car was shunted back and forth on Chicago tracks for the better part of that day, until we found ourselves attached to one of the Chief trains, which, we were told by our friendly conductor, was headed for San Francisco.

We reached San Francisco, the Gateway to the Orient, just before Thanksgiving and were quartered in the naval barracks downtown on Market Street. The friendly people of the city invited naval personnel for Thanksgiving dinners, and Gebraad and I went to the home of a shipyard worker and his family. The special day was sunny and pleasantly cool, and the family made us feel right at home. We played with their four small children and ate a wonder-

ful dinner. When we started to leave, our host presented each of us with a five
dollar bill and a bottle of liquor. Gebraad and I declined both, but thanked
him. "The finest thing you could have given us," I said, "was a Thanksgiving
dinner complete with mother, father, and children."

During our week's stay in San Francisco, we were free as the gulls. We
had no extra duty to perform and no watches to stand; we were granted liberty every day and soaked up all the sights and sounds of the unusual and
beautiful city of San Francisco. Our Army-style uniforms and Marine-style
seabags were objects of curiosity and conjecture by other sailors. Naturally,
we haunted the docks, viewing ships from many countries and talking with
their sailors.

At the end of the week we were advised that we would be boarding a British
aircraft carrier, one we had observed in the harbor for several days.

"Like it's been sitting there waiting for us," remarked Gebraad.

After two false boarding alerts, we went aboard His Majesty's Ship (HMS)
*Patroller* and entered a new naval world. We were quartered with the British
radio and radar crews near the bow of the ship directly under the flight deck.
Our bunks were four-tiered and so close above each other that I could not turn
over on my side without exerting pressure on the sagging bunk above me. I
was in the bottom bunk and only six inches above the deck. Our two lieutenants were quartered with the lesser officers of the ship's staff.

We spent two boring days on the ship, mostly watching the San Francisco
bayside activities from afar. The second evening, we put to sea with a U.S.
pilot guiding the *Patroller* out of the harbor. When he had accomplished this,
he was picked up by a small motor launch. We hit the long low swells of the
ocean, and I felt I would soon become seasick. Within an hour, I did.

We now had only the broad blue Pacific ahead of us, and we saw no other
ship for the next two weeks.

The HMS *Patroller* was an American-built British auxiliary aircraft carrier.
Lashed down on the flight deck were twenty U.S. Air Force P-40 planes evidently being delivered to the Far East.

"Just enough for all of us," I remarked.

And, indeed, each of us twenty storekeepers was assigned a plane, which we
checked twice a day for taut lashing and saltwater erosion. The latter was
caused by salt spray coming in contact with the metal surfaces of the plane.
This problem was remedied by daubing the spots with paralcatone, a clear
plastic-like liquid, a solution whose name we learned from the British seamen.
I named my plane *Li'l Audrey* in honor of my wife, and it was the only place

around where I found peace and privacy. I spent many hours sitting in the cockpit, reading and writing, thinking and wondering what lay ahead for me.

Our two officers, the twenty planes, and we twenty storekeepers were all classified as "super cargo" by the British navy men.

The captain of the ship, who privately afforded Gebraad and me much laughter, frequently lost or misplaced his personal possessions. When this happened, it upset the entire crew of His Majesty's Ship. All hands were alerted by the boatswain's pipe on the public address system, saying, "Do y'hear there?" Then there would come an order for all hands to turn to and search for the captain's binoculars or raincoat or swagger stick. I can't say I really liked the old captain. He had his private Coke machine, which was off limits to everyone in the ship's crew, no exceptions. The damned machine was located just outside our bulkhead door and handy to the pilot house.

The carrier cruised in a constant zigzagging, southwesterly direction after leaving San Francisco. Nights on the ocean were spectacular. A steady phosphorous light hung on the surface, and the waves sparkled. During the day we could see porpoises dart from one wave to another; and, if lucky, they cleared a first wave and continued on to a second. Many times we saw a single shark, with its dorsal fin showing clearly as it followed our ship.

One day when I was leaning on the rail on the fantail, I was surprised to see several of the ship's crew dumping open crates of oranges overboard. None of us Americans had had any fresh fruit on the trip so far. I think none of the lesser British crew had either. I asked one of the crew why they were dumping them overboard.

"Spoiled," he grumbled.

The crates bobbed in the turbulence of the ship's wake, and I watched as long as I could see them. I knew that dumping or throwing anything overboard was forbidden on the ship; not even a cigarette butt was to be thrown overboard.

The first land we saw was when we passed through Cook's Strait, and viewed New Zealand's north and south islands on both sides of the *Patroller*. Once we were zoomed at by a New Zealand patrol plane. After identifying himself, the daring pilot dove and then skimmed across our flight deck. He made a second pass at us, and we ducked our heads—he was that close.

At sea again, we ran into a heavy storm that caused waves to heave up and break over the flight deck. My concern was for *Li'l Audrey*. I checked her every two hours to see that her lashings were holding. This storm at sea, I decided, was the most ferocious storm I had ever encountered.

Members of the British crew, for the most part, were a sad lot but very capable seamen. They were required to enlist for nine years, more than double the U.S. four-year enlistment period. Their pay scale was far below ours. They looked bedraggled, unkempt, and sort of hopeless.

One day while I was reading quietly on the flight deck above the fantail, a five-inch gun just below me let out a devastating roar. I jumped straight up! A big black shellburst broke the tranquil sky. In less than five seconds several of the antiaircraft crews were firing into the black blob in a gunnery exercise. This turned out to be one of the random exercises that were held unannounced from time to time. Their tracer shells showed they were pretty much on target. But I was cured forever of sitting aft on the flight deck; you couldn't trust those British gunners.

We skirted the southeast coast of Australia, which in places was sheer stone cliffs hundreds of feet high. Here and there in the water stood immense rocks like sentinels protecting the downunder continent. We were on course to Melbourne.

# CHAPTER 3

# Going In
## Australia and India

---

*November–December 1943—U.S. Navy, Marine, and Army
forces land on Tarawa and Makin in the Gilbert Islands. The
3rd Marine Division lands on Cape Torokina, the Battle of
Empress Bay, Bougainville.*

It was a warm and sunny Christmas Eve day when our carrier was pushed and pulled into a Melbourne dock by three panting tugboats. We had been on the ship for two very long weeks, so we gathered at the rails, watching the docking and looking at the people and their city.

"Look at the sharks," exclaimed one of our men. They were swimming all around the carrier.

That evening we viewed an impressive Christmas ceremony in Melbourne. Over 5,000 people gathered at one of the public parks, carrying lighted candles and singing Christmas carols. From a distance, and against a dark sky, it was a stirringly beautiful observance; and in the clear air, we could hear all the words they sang.

Early Christmas morning, Lieutenant Mastenbrook played Santa Claus and opened a large cardboard carton that had been brought aboard in San Francisco. Inside were twenty packages, one for each of us, from various people in central California. A young lady who lived in Salinas had packed mine with needed articles such as toothpaste, shaving lotion, candy, writing paper, and several books. It made the day a bit more festive, and we were all very grateful to these wonderful people.

The lieutenant advised us that we had shore liberty for the next three days, but before we had a chance to disembark, tragedy marred the holiday mood. Two young English seamen had been assigned the punishment duty of working on a swinging scaffold over the side of the ship. They were busy chipping loose paint when one end of the scaffolding gave way, plunging the two men into the water. The crew on deck heard their cries and immediately threw life preservers. The sharks reached them before the preservers, and the water turned red. We watched in horror as more and more sharks came into view and the water was lashed into a terrible frenzy. One of the victims grabbed a life preserver, and the men tried to pull him clear of the water, but a vicious shark literally tore him from the life preserver. The other man was never seen among the bloody waves and sharp fins.

There was almost complete silence on the ship. Then the crew disbanded, muttering angrily among themselves about the officer-of-the-day permitting punishment details on Christmas Day.

It felt good to be on land. I had become close friends with Gerald Gebraad, who was from Grand Rapids, Michigan. We got along well in just about every situation. He was a quiet, easygoing guy with a good sense of humor and a deep-rooted religious background. From Washington, D.C., until we received different assignments in China, Gerry and I were to be almost constant companions.

On this Christmas Day we rode a shuttle passenger train from the dock area to downtown Melbourne. We walked up and down the streets, relishing our first visit to a foreign land. We knew gasoline was in short supply, and wondered how they could operate so many cars. I asked a fellow on a corner about this, and he explained a remarkable achievement. The Aussies used charcoal to generate gas, which was then fed into a large vertical metal tank. This tank looked much like the old gas-heated hot water tanks that stood in the corners of most kitchens many years ago.

Even on Christmas the shops and restaurants were open. All were buffered by sandbags piled high in front of the doors and display windows. The people were ready just in case the Japanese paid Australia a visit. We ate wonderful steaks, drank milk at the milk bars, and bought fresh fruits, which were plentiful because this was summertime "Down Under." Beer in the pubs was served warm. All pubs closed sharply at 6:00 P.M. Five minutes before closing, the bartenders called out, "Drink up, laddies, and go home to your wives."

Each of us twenty U.S. Navy men found our own excitement in Melbourne. Several went to the horse races. Bill Sharrard found an Australian pound note, so he figured it was his lucky day. It was, because he picked six winners in a row. Tony Rutz rented a horse to ride near the park of the Christmas Eve celebration. The horse evidently became scared and, because Tony couldn't control her, she didn't stop running until she hit a wall at the end of the bridle path. Tony arrived back at the ship with a broken arm and numerous bruises. Everybody liked Tony. A shoe salesman in Germantown, Illinois, before the war, he was tall, quiet in manner, and physically fit. His round face always wore a smile.

Melbourne residents were in an all-out war effort, which included feeding and entertaining servicemen. At one club we met several members of the Women's Royal Australian Naval Service (WRANS). One day Lieutenant Mastenbrook asked Gebraad and me if we'd like to accept an invitation to have dinner in the beach home of a man who lived in Melbourne. Our answer was yes. After swimming in the waves, we ate an elaborate meal. This was the kind of war we could live with.

On our last afternoon on shore we visited the zoo, where I was fascinated by the kangaroos. The big red kangaroos, called jerries, were more than six feet tall; the grays were smaller, and the rat kangaroos were the smallest. "Roos" was the common name for all members of the kangaroo family, we were told by a couple of "diggers," who were also visiting the zoo. A "digger" was an Aussie soldier. They were friendly, in spite of bemoaning the fact that the American servicemen were taking their "sheilas" (girls) away from them.

"Why is that?" I asked.

"You make so much more money than us diggers! But you're a good lot, anyway, you know."

From Melbourne we sailed, in the company of an escort destroyer, to Fremantle, a southwestern port of Australia. We docked beside a U.S. Navy submarine tender. One of the submariners invited me to dinner at the Prince Edward Hotel, which the U.S. Navy had leased as a rest center for sub men coming in from weeks or months of sea duty.

The hotel dinner tasted wonderful, mainly because food on the *Patroller* was as bad as could be imagined. It lacked both flavor and quality, but one of the main reasons we detested mealtime was the men who dished up the mess. They were a dirty lot! They were unshaven and unbathed; they wore the dirtiest aprons I ever saw. We were served some kind of potatoes at every meal, mashed, fried, baked, boiled, or oven browned. If a man in line jokingly asked for potatoes or voiced a complaint, one of the greasy food crew would reach over and ladle hot grease onto his potatoes. They were a discredit to His

Majesty's Service, and I wondered how the superior officers permitted the dirty kitchen situation to remain. More and more I lost respect for the majority of British officers.

We had a shore leave one day and toured the nearby city of Perth, a true colonial city. It was beautiful, with buildings that resembled those in New Orleans's French Quarter; and government buildings that were constructed of dark stone and looked very imposing. I was delighted to find a Red Cross center that served delicious hamburgers and milk shakes, the last I would eat for more than two years. They also had coffee—a rarity on any British vessel—ice cream, and fresh fruits. Every man in our group bought fresh fruits to take on board. We also picked up some empty bottles and glass jars, and then bought powdered milk so we could make our own milk. The *Patroller* had several kinds of American dry cereals, which we could buy at the ship's store, but there was no milk available. I became chummy with the ship's storekeeper and gave him razor blades in return for sugar. We had our breakfast problem solved. Tea and biscuits served once a day were the best of the ship's fare. We managed to survive with breakfast and tea most of the time.

January 4, 1944, we sailed from Fremantle with the Dutch escort, *Tromp*, keeping us company. Somewhat bigger than the U.S. destroyers, the *Tromp* usually stayed just within sight. One day the *Tromp* notified the *Patroller* that it had just made contact with a submarine, and the *Tromp* took off like a hound after a rabbit. An hour later we learned that it dropped depth charges in the area where the sub had been sighted. Since our group was quartered with the ship's radar, radio, and communications specialists, we were informed of the latest news. After this incident, our carrier assumed battle stance. Hatches were dog-eared (closed and secured) with heavy timbers braced against the bulkheads. For two days we ate only sandwiches (not too bad) and no one was permitted to pass from one deck to another. Two more destroyers appeared and joined us for escort duty. They heeled way over when making turns ahead of us, and the entire group of ships followed a new zigzag pattern.

The weather was good but increasingly hot, so that our fruit ripened rapidly and we were forced to eat it ahead of our planned schedule. Lime water was the order of the day. Everyone was required to drink a cupful, to protect against scurvy, before getting into the chowline. No one got by the monitor of the lime water, who was a real cockney and a good enforcer. He made everyone dip a cupful of the lime water out of a large barrel; this is why English sailors are called Limeys.

Our carrier had picked up eighty Tasmanians at Melbourne, who soon challenged the English seamen to a boxing match. For the event, an airplane elevator was depressed to the storage level or hangar level below deck. We sat around the edge of the opened well, and watched the RANS (Royal Australian Navy Service, the Tasmanians) whip the RNS (Royal Navy Service) nineteen matches to thirteen. There was never any love lost on the English by the Tasmanians, who constantly made derogatory remarks to the English sailors, unmindful of consequences. They had come aboard with no cots or berths, so the rough-and-tough Tasmanians slung their hammocks at night in the mess hall area. In the mornings, they lashed up their hammocks and stowed them in a corner of the sleeping area. Thus, they never had the few extra sleeping minutes the rest of us enjoyed.

We were in the beautiful, crystal-clear Indian Ocean and could see fish and sea snakes swimming close to the ship.

Once a PBY aircraft approached us from the north, circled the carrier twice, and then returned in the direction from whence it came. Immediately all antiaircraft crews were at the ready until the plane vanished. The incident passed.

The *Tromp* left us just south of the tip of India, and the two destroyers slipped away into the night. We sailed on alone, each day gliding nearer our destination.

One day a large frigate bird appeared and landed on a cross section of the carrier's superstructure. Then we passed a few small fishing boats with limp sails. We saw a few birds on the wing, and in the distance we sighted a thin, dark line.

"Land!" several of us said simultaneously.

On January 14, 1944, the *Patroller* slipped into the small harbor of Cochin, India, and was pushed and warped into place against the dock. Within half an hour, one of the British officers announced over the loudspeaker, "All Americans and all P-40 planes will leave this ship at this port."

The British officers immediately changed into their formal uniforms and lined up on deck. They made it clear that only officers remained above deck. I wanted to watch everything, so I stood my ground from my position on the flight deck by our airplanes.

"It's all right, my man; I'm permitted to stay on deck," I said to the ship's senior chief bosun's mate. He walked away to make sure all the full-dressed men were standing at attention. They never knew whether I was an officer or not, as I wore a khaki shirt and trousers with no insignia or sign of rank. This was to be our dress the entire time we were in India and China. Our officers wore the same "uniform." No one could tell us apart; nor did they know just who we were or what we were. In the months ahead, we confused the Chinese military and inhabitants, as well as our own various military personnel.

I watched the ship's captain, dressed in white uniform, including white shorts, and a scrambled-eggs visor, walk down the gangway and across the loading docks to an administration building. He returned in about two hours with three gallants (smartly dressed young sailors) in tow.

The captain was bowlegged, Churchillian, and feisty, and I always wondered why he wanted to show off those gnarled legs. Upon approaching the ship, he ostentatiously whipped a riding crop across his right leg. He backed away a couple of steps, turned around, and said a few words to his newly acquired entourage. Then he turned to the gangway again and laid his hand on the guideline. After a pause, he shouted up to his men, "Pipe me aboard, you Goddamned fools." The bosun's pipe sounded the boarding signal, which we had never heard before, although we had grown accustomed to hearing the pipe for lots of other commands. Every morning we heard it blown three times at 6:00 A.M., followed by calls of "Heave ho, heave ho, lash up, lash up and stow!"

A crew member told me that the captain had lost two ships in the war so far. "He's a bad luck skipper." One night someone raided the skipper's private Coke machine, which was located near my quarters. Oh, there was hell to pay the next day when he made a search for the culprit. No one was ever caught, but I know this: there is nothing so good as a cold Coke on a hot night at sea!

After the captain returned, we received the word to disembark. It was good-bye to the *Patroller* and the friends we had made among the men. When we stepped ashore, five U.S. Army Air Force men were there, and they assured us they would handle the unloading of the planes the next day. We went on to the customs house. I was the first in line. The Indian customs inspector reached for the six cartons of American cigarettes I had bought from the ship's store, as each of us had done. Although I did not smoke, we had been told they were good bargaining items. The Indian obviously was going to confiscate them. American cigarettes were worth a lot of money.

"No," I yelled, and drew my hunting knife. My buddies backed me up, so the inspector replaced my cartons in my bags and cleared us without further inspection.

Lieutenant Mastenbrook went with us outside the customs office where a truck was parked. "Get in, Gentlemen." The truck bumped along a very dusty road until it stopped at a group of plaited rattan buildings. There was one new sheet metal building, and that was where we were taken to bunk for the night. It was empty of people, but had about eighty bare cots with rope-mesh springs.

We slept without blankets or sleeping bags. About midnight, we were awakened by a British lieutenant who turned on the lights and started hollering about the fact that we were not permitted to sleep in this building. We began answering in angry words, and a ruckus developed. Finally, Lieutenant Mastenbrook told the Britisher that his men would sleep where they were "come hell or high water." We slept through the remainder of the night as best we could. This was our first encounter with the British lend-lease program.

In the morning we washed and shaved in a long lean-to type of shed. Long troughs running from one end to the other were equipped with water taps about every four feet. Only cold water came out. We saw a number of snakes on shelves and ledges in both this washroom and the latrine. This was India all right!

The flat and uninteresting land was already hot; waves of heat shimmered in the sunlight. Near our barracks some Indians were building a small house. As the son of a brick mason, I marveled at their very creditable performance in laying bricks with antiquated tools. They used the old-style plumb line for corner work.

Lieutenant Mastenbrook soon called us together and advised us we would leave by railway for Calcutta at 4:24 P.M. He told us to sign the papers at the depot and put "lend lease" by our names, so that this program would take over our transportation expenses. The train pulled out of the station precisely on schedule, which was the only time it accomplished this feat during the entire trip to Calcutta.

Our car, which was divided into compartments for two to four passengers, had doors on both sides. The beds were folded against the sides, with hooks to hold them in place. In every cabin was a fold-up metal wash basin and toilet. We were not allowed to pass from one compartment to another when the train was moving. About noon, we stopped at a small village and ate in the railroad station. Our table was covered with white linens and held sparkling silverware. We ate our first curried rice.

The train made many, many stops during the five days it took us to reach Calcutta.

Once we traveled through a heavily wooded area where we saw elephants working, carrying logs and tools with their trunks. When we passed villages, we saw monkeys on housetops and the carcasses of animals hanging from hooks at shops. People bought pieces of the meat cut by a butcher. In rice fields we watched water buffaloes pulling plows. Natives threw buckets of water over the buffaloes, and then threw water over their own heads.

At one twilight, I saw a sight that made me forget the terrible heat and the swarms of mosquitoes always with us, even in the moving train. From the east appeared a long line of slow-moving people and ox carts. The line was coming our way and stretched so far I could not see the end of it. As the migrant line came tediously forward, I could see the fully loaded carts had solid wheels that were heavy, and the oxen didn't seem to exert much energy in pulling them. The wheels glugged and clunked as they turned.

The long procession made a soft dust that hugged the ground like a low-lying fog; and with no breeze at all, the dust enveloped the lower parts of the people. I saw gold rings in one nostril of some of the girls. The round faces of the youngsters were sometimes expressive, but the faces of the older men and women were heavy-lined and devoid of any emotion. Very few people rode, only ones who looked very old and ill. The others walked close to their carts, sad and forlorn. Their dusty and ragged clothing looked soft, lightweight, and light-colored, which emphasized their dark skin. Sometimes the carts traveled two abreast, sometimes single file. Our train slowed down until we barely moved as we intersected the cavalcade. I looked out the other side of the train and again, as far as I could see, the silent line continued into the west.

I felt strange. There was a weird sensation inside me. Although I had never been to India, somehow this sad procession was familiar to me. I had had dreams as a youth in Pennsylvania in which I saw just such a migration. It was such a strong feeling that I wondered if there really was such a thing as rein-carnation. The feeling continued long into the night. Am I already dead and reliving a moment of history? I asked myself. Or did I have a premonition of this scene many years ago? I was glad when sleep came.

One of our stops along the railroad was the large city of Madras, where we ate in the railroad's dining room with a draft of WRANS who were on their way to Ceylon. Back on the train, I counted thirty-one stops in the next six hours. At noon on this day, we stopped at a small station for lunch, prearranged by the conductor. Twelve waiters hurried out of the station, each bearing a tray of food held high above his head by one hand. The trays were covered with large white cloths. Suddenly, from out of the sky, several large hawks dove like bullets and struck the coverlets with their talons and flew away with anything they could clasp. They regained a good altitude very quickly, and we could see at least two white cloths sailing in the air. Several of the waiters had to return to the restaurant and bring out a second tray. This time they were more careful

about how they carried their trays. Two station stops later, several railroad
employees boarded the train and gathered up the trays, silverware, and other
items. They were very careful to count and itemize everything they collected
from each person.

We passed over many dry riverbeds. At one point, we saw great masses of
people carrying on their heads wicker baskets filled with small stones. They
were part of a dam-building crew. Hundreds of the skinny, barefoot, scantily
clad people followed one another in a single file to the large breastwork of the
dam site. When I smiled at them filing by our train, their dark eyes lighted up
for a moment, and then quickly faded back into a nothingness. God, what an
existence!

About the third night out, we began having trouble. Two of our men, Andy
and Holly (short for Hollenbach), came down with malaria and had to be left at
a small hospital in Waltair, India. A few of the men developed dysentery. Water
tanks in our compartments ran dry. We had no dinner that night.

North of Cuttack the land lay stark and dry, and all the world looked dead.
The slow train ride made everything a bore.

The few houses we saw were whitewashed. Hanging outside on their walls
were large pie-shaped brown things, which we were told was animal dung,
being dried to use for starting cooking fires. The hard dung was a substitute
for wood in this unfruitful land.

Calcutta's railway station was large, noisy, and busy when we arrived at
6:00 A.M., and the most welcome sight was a military information desk where
we obtained a number to call for U.S. Navy assistance. When we were
squared away at a building identified as Navy Hostel #2, an aide brought us
mail! Thank goodness I had a letter from Audrey. It was always a relief during my travels in remote sections of the Far East to hear that all was well
back at home.

On this stop, we were assigned duties. At one time I was ordered to count
bombs being unloaded from a U.S. freighter at the King George Dock. They
were being taken to storage sheds. The Indian laborers who unloaded them
were so skinny I wondered how they managed to even get around, let alone to
carry the heavy bombs, which were encased in wood crates. Poor fellows that
they were, they did not shirk their turn to carry the heavy loads.

Calcutta was a vast melting pot of people, including many from Tibet to the
north and the mountain regions to the northeast, plus natives of Europe,
Africa, and various other parts of the world. I guessed some were descendants
of the barbarous Genghis Khan and the warlords of China who had intermixed

with the soft, affable people of Burma. The locals resembled the short heavy people of Nepal and Bhutan in their skin tone and bone structure. Their eyes were black and sunken to the depths of dark tunnels. Hindus, Jains, Sikhs, and Muslims were easily identified by their dress, mannerisms, markings on their foreheads, and rings in their noses or ears. I learned that the light-skinned people were generally from the north. Very few white women were to be seen. The higher their caste, the cleaner they were, and the more European they dressed.

Because India was still trying to recover from its great famine, thousands of people lay dying on the downtown streets of Calcutta. There was a continual stream of litter bearers carrying bodies barely covered with light shifts. The feet of the dead were painted in various pastel colors, which denoted their religion. When litter bearers became tired, they lowered the burden to the street, sat on the curb and lit a piece of a cigarette. One would take two puffs, then pass it along to the other bearers for two puffs. The last man pinched it out and wedged it behind his ear. Some kind of signal then would be given; the litter would be lifted in two movements to shoulder height, and they would disappear into the antlike procession of other bearers.

The Jains placed their dead on rooftops and other open areas where the vultures tore away at the remaining shreds of flesh left on bodies. It took a rich person to buy wood to build a funeral pyre, and I saw only two such cremations during my time in the big city. The streets were incredibly dirty, with no apparent drainage; dirty puddles abounded.

Beyond the Chowringee Road (which was so pitiful), I found, to my horror, conditions were worse, in unutterable squalor. This was "The Black Hole of Calcutta" that I had read about many years ago. Around Dalousie Square were cripples and diseased people by the thousands who begged for food or money. I was amazed at the cases of elephantiasis. These victims had legs that were five to six times the size of a normal leg, and the skin was coarse and checked like an elephant's hide.

Sacred cattle wandered freely everywhere in Calcutta, and their dung was deposited on the streets, sidewalks, and paths. This added considerably to the overall stench that hung over this large and historic city. More than three-fourths of the people lived in crowded rooms with no running water or toilets.

Gebraad and I ate lunch one day at the Grand Hotel; and I was very much surprised to see a girl acquaintance of mine. She had worked in the V.A. hospital in Dearborn, Michigan, where I was employed. In India she was with the Red Cross in offices in the hotel.

Several of us were invited to the fabulous home maintained by an Army Air Force pilot. Later we learned he became very rich operating a smuggling business when he was on official flights in and out of China. He had six servants and a beautiful mistress. When he made his flight and was gone for several days, he rented out the girl and the house at astronomical rates, which added to his fortune. And a soldier of fortune he was. He was a short, cocky guy; and after knowing him only a few hours, I strongly disliked the waxy son-of-a-bitch.

Gerry and I visited Jimmy's Kitchen one evening, reputedly the best restaurant in Calcutta for servicemen. We sat by a window; and if we looked out, we saw starved, dead bodies being carried along the street. Eating our big meal made me feel rotten. How unfortunate to be born to poverty, for life. Money could buy the right to live; money could buy anything.

It was rumored at our "bash" (British name for barracks) that soon we would meet our commanding officer and depart for China. I was anxious to be on my way, as Calcutta was not to my liking. We all looked forward to the next move, but I wondered if we were jumping out of the pot and into the fire.

# CHAPTER 4

# Over the Hump to Kunming

*January 1944—The 7th Amphibious Force lands on Saidor, New Guinea. Our forces also strike the Marshall Islands.*

**O**utfitting SACO men in Calcutta was not like selecting gear in a sporting goods store. We were taken one by one to an old warehouse near the dock district that was jam-packed with all kinds of U.S. Navy equipment. It was almost "old home week" meeting the driver of my truck. His name was Warren Higby, and his dad had owned the corner drugstore just two blocks from where I had once lived in Wyandotte, Michigan. Warren helped me select the items of army clothing that were to stay with me for the next two years.

My Indian-made sleeping bag was poorly constructed of low-quality materials; I later discovered it was less than adequate in cold weather. But it was the best available. I was issued two white wool medical blankets, a Colt .45, and more khaki shirts, pants, sox, shoes, and towels. I still carried the hunting knife I had brought from the States.

Higby mentioned that I would be the first of the twenty-two men scheduled out for China the next day; but when I finally did leave, Tony Rutz went with me.

The night before we left, our commanding officer, Capt. Milton Edward Miles, threw a party for all of us and wished Tony and me luck on our trip north to Assam and our flight over the Himalayas, better known as "the Hump." There was not a man in SACO that didn't admire and respect

Captain Miles, nicknamed "Mary" by his officer friends. He later became a commodore and then a rear admiral. After the war he wrote a book about the SACO operation entitled *A Different Kind of War*. He died before finishing it, and a writer named Hawthorne Daniel completed it for Doubleday and Company in 1967. We all thought Admiral Miles was a great man and a real war hero.

On January 24, 1944, Tony and I left Calcutta via third-class rail service at 11:45 P.M. We were responsible for mounds (approximately a ton) of aerological equipment (packaged in eight heavy wooden crates) as well as some other supplies. The only water we had was in our canteens, and we usually had only C rations for food. All the equipment was loaded with us into a rickety old railway car that had a bare wooden bench running along one side and a potty, called a "poophole," at the back. Two marked footprints indicated where a person should stand, then squat over the poophole. All of this was out in the open, as there were no enclosures of any kind for privacy.

"Tony, we now know what they mean when they say 'squatters' rights,'" I said.

Rail traffic was a farce. One day we covered about a hundred miles in sixteen hours, which was an astounding accomplishment for the puffing old train; the next day we traveled six miles in three hours. Several Indians in our car seemed as uncomfortable as Tony and me trying to sleep on the wooden bench.

At one stop a small Indian boy of about nine years, accompanied by a very tiny, shy girl of about seven or eight years, got our attention. He then went through a few movements of a military drill he had learned, and ended by kicking one leg outward, then stomping it firmly on the ground and saluting. He said, "No mama, no papa, no food, no per diem." After extending his hand and receiving several annas from us, he then offered his little sister for the price of two rupees. We told him we were not interested and he dropped his price to one rupee (worth about thirty-two cents). When our train started to move, he looked both disappointed and offended.

Among our fellow passengers was a Burmese courier named Percy Tresham, a friendly and interesting traveling companion who also had a shipment of freight under his supervision in our car. We became friends and shared a pack of Camel cigarettes with him. We spent two days and two nights on the train, finally arriving at Parbatipur near the Indian border, where Percy helped us secure coolies to unload our gear from the train, carry it down a sloping bank of the Ganges River, and load it aboard a ferryboat.

The large ferryboat had a surprisingly nice restaurant, complete with white tablecloths. Percy ordered for Tony and me. Other diners included three junior British army officers at one table, two senior British officers at another, and numerous other travelers. The Indian waiter seemed to have a hard time understanding the junior officers, and one of them loudly called him "stupid and stinking."

Our food came and it tasted delicious, but when the junior officers were served, the loudmouthed one stood up and started cursing the waiter. He raised his riding crop, and I pushed my chair back and rushed to stand between the man and the waiter.

"You hit that man and I'll beat the hell out of you; you're a poor excuse for a British officer and a discredit to your country." By now the headwaiter had taken the other waiter away.

The other officer stood and said, "Keep yourself under control, or we'll take care of you," whereupon the two senior officers (majors) came over and made them sit down. One major told me in a soft and kindly manner that he was sorry for the conduct of the junior officers. They knew Tony and I were American soldiers, but without insignia of any sort the British major did not know how to address me. I did not enlighten him by identifying myself as a third-class storekeeper. Even Captain Miles wore only khaki shirts, pants, and hats; no identifying insignia. This was to be a help many times during my China tour of duty.

Our ferry took a long time to cross the Ganges River. Then Percy hired coolies again to unload our equipment and carry it over a wide, sandy shoreline to another train, this one bound for Pandou. The coolies worked hard, and we were glad to pay them more than the standard rate, for which they appeared very thankful. This train was better than the last; we sat in a coach with real seats! The other passenger in our car was evidently a high-caste Indian. He was quite friendly and shared his fresh fruit with us.

We reached a small town with a railway station, and again had help to unload our freight and gear, move it across the depot platform, and reload it into a narrow-gauge railway car. The move had just been completed when an air raid warning sounded, and Tony and I dove under the station platform. A few minutes later a Japanese plane flew over the rail yards and dropped two bombs which exploded several hundred yards from where we lay.

I had survived my first air raid!

The smaller, narrow-gauge train took until 4:00 A.M. to chug into Marianne, Assam, where the conductor told Tony and me that we had arrived at our destination near Jorhat. It had taken three days and two nights to get here from Calcutta.

"Please unload your shipment," the conductor said.

Since Tony's arm was still in a sling, healing from the fall off the Australian horse, it was up to me to unload everything. I opened the freight compartment and looked around for coolies. I saw only one poor old man beside the tracks. He could hardly stand up. Finally the train fireman came to help, and as I was lowering the heavy 300-pound crate from the train to the ground, something snapped in my back. I couldn't even straighten up properly, the pain in my lower back was so severe. The fireman went for help and returned with the engineer, conductor, and another person. They managed to get the other crates unloaded while I sat on a crate watching helplessly.

When the station agent arrived at his office about 6:00 A.M., I asked him to contact the U.S. Navy observer in Jorhat for me. Tony and I sat on the crates for a couple of hours. Finally a six-by-six truck arrived with a navy man behind the wheel. He left us for a few minutes and reappeared with eight coolies, who loaded our freight into the truck. Some twelve miles of driving brought us to a navy bash composed of four tents and a large, tin-covered warehouse. We had been told back in Washington that operations in the Far East were no-frills affairs. We knew that was right! Two navy radiomen and two Indian army men maintained a communications center in one tent, slept in another, and ate in a third. The fourth tent, with four cots in it, was for transients like us.

Since I was in great pain with my back, one of the navy men took me by jeep to see the doctor at the U.S. Army Air Force (AAF) headquarters two miles away. This field was the departure point for all planes flying the Hump into Kunming, China. The doctor gave me pain pills and taped my back from my buttocks to my neck. He ordered me to spend all my time in a padded pilot's seat that had been salvaged from a wrecked plane and come back in two days. This back injury, which I learned later was a ruptured disk, followed me for years, until I underwent surgery in 1955.

A sergeant arranged for Tony and me to eat in the AAF mess hall before returning to our navy bash, and I enjoyed my best dinner since leaving Melbourne.

When I returned to see the doctor two days later, I used the air force facilities to take a good, hot shower. It was a happy surprise when I met in the shower room an old schoolmate from Johnstown, Pennsylvania, Henny Schneider. He had been in India for some time, and he walked around with a small pet monkey perched on his shoulder, its tail half-wrapped around Henny's neck.

That evening he picked me up in a jeep and took me back to the AAF base to see a movie, which was shown in a hangar. Henny said the nearby town of Jorhat had been half-leveled by an earthquake a couple of weeks earlier.

Fellows at the navy bash had built a small chicken coop and, in Chinese fashion, covered it with stones and dirt except for a small opening. During the day the eight chickens were tethered with strong strings tied to their legs and fastened to stakes in the ground. At night they were put in the coop and a heavy stone leaned against the closed door. The chickens provided the men with a few eggs.

My first morning at the bash I was awakened at daybreak by a faint yipping sound. The sound got stronger and louder until it seemed to be within a few feet of our tent. It was a pack of jackals coming after the chickens. Suddenly, there was a lot of yipping and scurrying around, and two jackals came right up to our open tent.

The second morning, I was ready with my flashlight; and when they came to our tent, I flashed the light into their eyes, which lit up like gold sparks. I yelled at them and they ran off. The third morning I stood in the tent's opening with my carbine ready. In the half-light of day I saw the forms coming nearer across the field, their yipping getting louder and louder. Suddenly the jackals made a rush for the chicken coop, digging at the rock at the door. I could just make out the frenzied forms, now whimpering, all around me. I could see one jackal coming directly toward my tent. He stopped abruptly and I shot him. Like magic, the rest of the jackals disappeared.

"Did you get him?" asked Tony from his cot.

"Yep," I replied and crawled back into my sleeping bag for another twenty winks.

At breakfast one of the radiomen said that since I shot the jackal, I would have to bury him.

"That's the rule around here and that's why we don't shoot them," he added.

My back would not allow me to dig, so I paid a native a rupee to do the job for me.

The next day we were told that Tony and I were scheduled to fly the Hump. Before we could leave, two more navy men of our draft (unit) arrived. I traded names with one of them, so he could go in my place and give me another few days to rest my back. The other newcomer who remained with me was a like-able fellow from Kansas City named Tadlock. What I remember most about

him was his ears, which stuck out from his head like two halves of large clam-
shells. He grinned a lot and talked a lot. I thought he looked kind of frail and
wondered why he had been selected for the tough SACO mission, but I sup-
pose, actually, he was just a wiry guy. He had been a salesman for a greeting
card company in Kansas City. Tadlock did not believe our story about the jackals and their continued early morning attempts to get our chickens.

"Mish, you are just feeding me a bunch of crap," he said.

On his first evening in camp, one of the radiomen took him to the movies at
the air force base. While he was gone, I spread a can of C rations under
Tadlock's assigned cot. I was still awake when he came in, so I said, "Tad,
leave the bottom of the tent flap open so we can get some fresh air."

As usual, I awoke before dawn, and soon heard the familiar yipping in the
distance. It got closer and closer. In a little while they were at the chicken
cellar, and a couple of minutes later they got wind of the beans and made a
rush for our tent. The brazen and hungry jackals rushed in, barking like
crazy and heading straight for Tad's cot. Somehow Tad got out of his sleeping bag and stood on his cot yelling at me. "Mish! Mish! For God's sake,
shoot them, Mish!"

By this time I had my flashlight on and was yelling at the jackals, too, swip-
ing at them with my carbine. I had ruled out shooting, since I didn't want the
responsibility of burying them. Somehow, in all the bedlam, the jackals
became frantic and managed to escape from the tent. We could hear their yipping for some time. I did not know if Tadlock suspected how the early morning fracas had erupted; but about six months later I received a terse note from
him saying only, "I'll get even with you some day, old buddy!"

I rode into Jorhat one day with one of the radiomen and found that Henny
was right when he said the earthquake almost leveled the town. We bought
bread, salt, and two dozen eggs, because the camp's chickens were not laying
enough for the increased demand. The Indians sold eggs by weight, and the
way the merchant weighed them showed great ingenuity. He took the eggs
from a large basket placed at the elevated end of a channel or sluice. Along the
bottom of the sluice was a series of weighted trap doors about three inches by
four inches, delicately balanced with weights which reacted to the weight of
the egg passing overhead. If the egg was heavy, it would trigger the first
weighted mechanism and the trapdoor would drop open, depositing the egg in
a padded compartment below. If the egg was not heavy enough to trip the first
trapdoor, it would continue rolling down the sluice until it found a trapdoor of

lesser weight, and then it would drop. There were five trapdoors and five sizes of eggs. We bought the eggs that dropped through the first trapdoor, the largest ones. During the entire selection process, not one egg was broken.

I rode about the countryside, which was barren of trees, as much as possible. The land looked like some of that found in our dry western states, only supporting low, bushy plant life. I heard that rainfall was abundant at certain times of the year, but there were no lakes or running streams. There were many small birds, and there seemed to be plenty of wildlife. I saw a dead twenty-one-foot king cobra, and once an army guy killed a 400-pound tiger.

On February 1, 1944, two more SACO men arrived, and I had as my new flying partner, Minnie Perril, the quietest man I had ever met. It almost took an act of God to draw him into a conversation. He had a round face, was on the plump side, and looked older than he was. His dad was a psychiatrist back in Chicago.

When we were readying for the flight over the Hump, crew members advised us that we would experience severe cold in the plane. We took off in the wee hours of the morning, loaded with bombs, and were the second of fourteen planes scheduled for the flight to Kunming, China, that day. We climbed to 26,500 feet, where we had to wear oxygen masks. I watched the little round ball in a glass tube move up and down, indicating the level of oxygen intake. Jeez! It was cold! I wrapped myself up in both of my blankets and wore most of the clothing I owned. Minnie Perril was shaking like an autumn leaf on a windy day. When I looked out the portholes I could only see white fog, but after about an hour, the skies around us cleared. Two hours and twenty minutes later I felt the plane descending. We were landing! I couldn't believe it because the air force guys had told me it took three hours and fifteen minutes to reach Kunming, our destination. When we landed I was amazed to see we were back at Jorhat. The weather was too bad for flying the Hump that day. Only one of the fourteen planes made it to Kunming.

For some reason my back felt better, or perhaps I was getting used to the pain and inconvenience. Or maybe it was the cold in the aircraft that helped ease the pain. Minnie was sick and had to see a doctor. I think it was the cold that got him, but he was ready when we left the next morning.

The young pilot warmed up the engines and away we went down the runway. We took off, circled the airfield, and landed! One of the two lugs of the gasoline cap on the wing had broken off when the cap was tightened and had fallen into the gas tank. It worked itself into the pipeline leading to the engine, so the pilot was aware as soon as we were airborne that the engine was not getting a sufficient flow of gasoline at full throttle. Minnie and I hung around the plane for a couple of hours while they fished the broken piece of metal out of the tank and secured a new cap.

Then, for the third time, we took off! The air was clear, the scenery breathtaking, and the flight over the Himalayas was one I will never forget. The tallest mountains in the world were cloaked in deathly white and shades of gray, while the sky formed a roof of brilliant blue. I smiled at the beauty of it all, but thought sadly how only death could await anyone unlucky enough to crash in the Himalayas.

I pointed out to the crew chief that one landing wheel was not fully recessed into the wing. He immediately went forward, then returned to say the pilot was going to lower the wheels, then raise them again, which might cause noticeable jolts. Soon there was a jolt, but the wheels were recessed correctly and the plane soared ahead smoothly. The crew chief also explained how to fasten parachutes to our bodies and exit, if necessary, through a trapdoor in the floor. I had no feeling of excitement or apprehension about the possibility of having to jump, but Minnie looked pale and his lips were blue. He hadn't prepared any better for this flight than for the previous one and he was now frigid. Fortune was with us this time, and we made excellent time, arriving in Kunming in two hours and fifty minutes.

Kunming was the capital of the huge Yunnan Province and the main receiving point for Allied war personnel and supplies flown from India into China. Chiang Kai-shek's Chinese National Air Force Command (CNAC) also was centered here. The city was seething with activity. Planes were coming and going like a disturbed nest of hornets. We checked in with the U.S. Naval Operations Base Commander and were assigned quarters in a building that once was occupied by the Flying Tigers, Claire Chennault's famous mercenary pilots.

We joined a number of our original group that we had left in Calcutta, including my buddy, Gerry Gebraad, whom I was glad to be with again. Most of them had flown into Kunming direct from Calcutta, and they reported a very rough ride. Every one of them had been airsick. I told them my train ride had been every bit as rough.

Chinese merchants were selling everything imaginable everywhere we went in Kunming. Money and items passed through many hands, and everything was very expensive. For some reason, the Chinese wanted American fountain pens and toothbrushes. I bought a lightweight metal footlocker made in India to carry some of my clothing, writing paper, and other miscellaneous things that I wanted to keep dry. My money was now in short supply and I was informed that I would have to wait until Chungking to obtain funds from the naval disbursing officer. I sold a carton of cigarettes for twenty-five hundred Chinese dollars, the equivalent of about twenty-six U.S. dollars.

The money exchange rate on the black market was ninety Chinese dollars to one American dollar. Two days later it was ninety-five to one; and as we were leaving the city natives desperately seeking U.S. money offered one hundred twenty CN (Chinese National) for our U.S. dollar, a real black market bargain. At that time I exchanged all the U.S. money I could scrape up.

During my second day in Kunming, two Japanese planes dropped several bombs just outside the city, then flew off, pursued by two American fighter planes.

Our commander held a conference with each of us to explain our special SACO assignments. My orders were to proceed to Loyang (Luoyang), Honan (Henan) Province, which was on the Yellow (Huang He) River far to the north of Kunming and had once been the capital of China. It was the most distant destination for any of us. In addition, I was to go it alone. Most SACO assignments were for two or three men together, and I wondered why I was singled out for this lone placement so far to the north.

I had secured a good map of China while I was in Melbourne; it was a page from a *National Geographic* magazine, and the only map available in our group. All the men borrowed it to locate their respective destinations, but even on this map, only a few of us were able to locate our mission's secret positions accurately.

On the third morning in Kunming, I loaded my gear into one of the two trucks that was to form the entourage to Chungking. The men on the trip included the Chinese truck drivers and their assistants, a Chinese Army captain, eight U.S. Navy personnel, and me. We were transporting a lot of supplies, and took one case of C rations for the entire group. We were told it would be a four-day trip.

All my SACO buddies were there to say goodbye. We shook hands and wished each other luck. I hated to leave Gebraad. His orders would send him east, while I traveled north. Our chances of seeing each other in the future would be rather slim. Partings with buddies were part of war, I knew, but they also were always sad occasions.

# CHAPTER 5

# Of Bandits and Lepers

*February 1944—The Allies attack Truk and make their first strike against the Japanese-held Marianas.*

Traveling was easy for a while after we left Kunming because the road was hard-topped and fairly level; then the terrain became abruptly hilly. In the distance we could see faint blue mountains. The road was the usual dirt road, two lanes wide, and recently conditioned. We made good time and found the countryside void of anything interesting. There were no trees near the roadway, but a copse could be seen in the distance now and then. We passed a few very small villages, even too small for a wayside tea stand. When night came we camped by the roadside, with one of the truck drivers standing guard.

Whoever said one case of C rations would do for our trip to Chungking must have been out of his mind. It was completely gone by the second day, so we went without supper the first evening and without breakfast the next morning. I almost shouted when we arrived at Shangri-la! It was not a mystical city, but a U.S. Air Force base set up as a supporting operation for Kunming. We requested food and received an excellent, hot dinner. One of our trucks needed repairs, so we spent the night, and set out early the next morning.

In a couple of hours we realized the other truck was no longer with us. We pulled over on the road and waited for an hour. Still no truck, so we returned to the last small town of Kutsing. There we found our truck, being repaired by some English Friends (Quakers), missionaries living in Kutsing. We spent the night in several of the Friends' houses.

Before falling asleep, I heard a huckster hollering his wares of steamed bread. I couldn't resist going out to see all this in the middle of the night. He carried the bread on a little tray equipped with a tiny charcoal fire. The gray-colored loaves were the size of a small roll but had no crust. I bought one, but found it too doughy to eat. I would soon learn to consume this type of bread with relish. After I went back to my room, I could hear the huckster walking up and down the three-block street, calling what sounded like, "Oh yee! Oh yee! Oh yee!"

Truck travelers in China would find primitive sleeping accommodations in the small inns along the highways. In larger cities the furnishings were a little better. There were no linens. Sometimes the beds were solid wood and very narrow. Many pillows were solid, about four inches square on the ends and twelve inches long. They were heavily varnished and hard as a rock. Some beds had a rope netting that served as springs. Many times the truck was more comfortable than the accommodations in the small inns or private homes open to travelers.

Our two-truck fleet left at 7:30 in the morning and began climbing a mountain road immediately. It seemed we were destined to meet the sky, flanked by great precipices that dropped thousands of feet. We passed through a small village at an altitude of 10,000 feet. Toward evening, we reached the pass, and like a roller coaster, sped downward. We skirted a Chinese military camp, but slowed down to watch a squad of soldiers carry out an execution. An officer gave a command, and the prisoner was led to a designated position by two soldiers, who then returned to their squad. Another command, and the squad shot the prisoner, who fell to the ground. His arms continued to move, so the officer walked to the fallen man and shot him in the head with a revolver. The threshing stopped. When the squad left, a girl who had followed the death squad ran to the body and lifted the bloody head into her arms and then to her bosom. She began rocking back and forth on her knees, still holding the slain man. This was the first execution I witnessed, but it would not be my last.

We continued to travel into the night. Eventually it became so cold in our open truck that the five of us, plus the Chinese captain, got out and walked up the next mountain. The dirt road we were traveling later became an extension of the Burma Road. After a while we got back into the truck, but when we reached another mountain, we had trouble. A fine mist was freezing as it hit the ground. Again, we vacated the truck, this time because it was slithering about on the narrow road in the dark. It was difficult keeping our footing on the ice. We slipped and fell a lot, but we could see the steep edge of the road and none of us wanted to take a chance riding on the truck. Walking helped keep us a little warmer and also lightened the load for the truck, which barely chugged along. Our drivers were very good, but I would not recommend the 8,000-foot-high mountain roads of China in February to anyone.

Toward morning we came down into a valley and stopped at a farmhouse. We pulled out strands of stacked straw that was under a shelter and built a fire to warm ourselves. The Chinese captain went into the farmhouse and came back with the news that the farmer would boil water for us to make tea, or coffee, if we had coffee. The captain, who only knew a few words of English, was always anxious to please us, so he served as a willing, but poor, interpreter for us. At least he took care of everything at Chinese inns and restaurants, so we were happy to have him.

I remembered all the movies I had seen about China, which had probably led to my erroneous assumption that China was crowded with people. Not so. At this point in our journey, I found people were strangely missing in this desolate land. The few trees we saw were in the mountains. The cold valleys were barren.

Once we came to a walled city, but the captain said, "Bu Hao!" and waved the trucks on. This was the first common Chinese expression we learned. It meant "no good" or "don't want."

We drove by what looked like a nice farm, with a large barn and land that looked all neat and orderly. Across the road was a smooth area about the size of a basketball court. In the middle of it was a stocky, well-built Chinese man naked to his belly and barefooted, carrying a large broad sword. We stopped to watch and heard him exclaiming in a cadence as he swung the sword this way and that, with swift, flashing strokes. He was so fast with the sword I could hardly keep my eyes on the blade. His feet and leg movements were as light as a ballet dancer. He seemingly paid no attention to us; but as we pulled away, he made several half turns, jumped, and then stopped. He gave us a half bow and calmly walked across the road to the farmhouse. Our Chinese captain held up his thumb in a gesture of triumph and said, "Ding hao" (Very good). We began to pick up some of these common words and phrases; I knew I needed to learn as much of the language as possible.

My seat on the truck was over the left rear wheel and behind one of the three drums of alcohol lined across the back. I kept my carbine at the ready at all times. A chief bosun sat directly behind the cab and carried a tommy gun in his lap. I couldn't help being a little apprehensive, afraid he might become careless and forget the safety button sometime. Most of the time he seemed to be dozing, but we never had an accident on the trip.

As we rode along I noticed repetitive markings on telephone poles that ran along the roadway. China had a telephone network; and, as in the United States, it ran along the highways. The long ride gave me plenty of time to think, and I finally figured out that the poles were repetitiously marked in units of ten and by a preceding number. When I pointed to the numbers, the captain became pleased and pronounced the digits for me in Mandarin, the national Chinese language. This was how I learned the ten digits in Chinese.

On the third day the other truck slid off a slippery section of the road into a ditch, which, fortunately, was not deep. We all got out and pushed, but to no avail. The men from the other truck climbed in with us, and we headed for Weining, a small, walled city we could see in the distance. The driver went back with a crew of Chinese from the city and pulled the truck back onto the road with heavy ropes.

It was noon when we arrived in Weining, and the captain set about securing accommodations for the night. They turned out to be a vacant two-room schoolhouse some distance from the city's walls. I suspected the cold winter had kept the school closed. Captain Chui and I walked into town, where we bought a smoke-cured ham, which by U.S. standards would be the size of a goat leg, and a lot of frozen carrots that looked like small, white turnips. We were happiest at finding twenty-five eggs for sale. Since I was on mess detail, I made a fire in one of the schoolrooms and cooked a dinner of boiled ham and carrots. The ham swelled up as it boiled, and the whole dish turned out fine.

"Say, this is good," said one of the military men. I was proud of myself, though I believe anything would have tasted good that cold night.

We spread our sleeping bags over the dirt floors in the two rooms. It was rare to find anything but dirt floors in the China countryside. My back was hurting again, so I did not sleep well and it was painful to get in and out of the sleeping bag. The next morning I woke up scratching at little red pimples that had popped out all over my body.

The next morning the valley was covered with a glaze of ice. It was so slippery we couldn't walk, much less drive a truck into the high mountains. Weining itself was approximately 7,500 feet above sea level. In town the day before we had heard of a nearby lake, which not only was supposed to be filled with ducks, but had also had an airplane crash into it.

"Let's go have a look," I suggested to another storekeeper, so we grabbed our guns and set out across the valley. By now, the ice had melted a little, but there were still patches of it all across the valley. We neared the low-lying hills and started into a pass when a flight of what I thought were geese flew over in V formation. I picked out the leader, led him by a yard, and fired my carbine. I was lucky with my shot and he fell straight down, hitting the ground with a thud. I picked him up.

"This is no goose," I said, wondering what it was. It must have weighed twenty-five pounds. I threw him over my shoulder, and we started back to the schoolhouse. On the way, we approached a farmhouse, and three vicious chow dogs charged at us. I shot at their feet, and a farmer came from the house, waving his arms and shouting. Finally he got the dogs back into the yard. He came to look at my bird and smiled. I thought of my back, and offered him twenty-five CN to carry the bird to the schoolhouse. He was happy to do it.

Then we turned back to the pass because we wanted to see the lake. It took about an hour to cross the pass, and when we got our first glimpse of the lake, it was almost covered with ducks.

"Wow!" I shouted and began walking toward the lake to get closer to the ducks. The shore of the lake was marshy, and the mud nearly pulled my shoes off, so both of us just fired into the thousands of birds. They took off like a cloud and circled the lake. When they passed over us, we shot and killed two, but they dropped so far out in the waters we couldn't retrieve them.

Back at the schoolhouse the others in our party had been busy. They were cooking the bird, called an ibis, in a five-gallon vegetable oil can, along with carrots, turnips, and onions they had bought in town. However, we learned that the townspeople would no longer sell us "foreign devils" anything. This happened frequently during my stay in China.

That old ibis, after cooking for over six hours, was just as tough as when he was dropped into the pot. The next day we cooked him another four hours. He was still tough, but this time we ate him anyway.

The next morning was a repetition of the first. The valley spreading before us was enveloped in ice and looked like it was covered with brilliant diamonds. It was so slippery we couldn't even walk the 200 feet to the trucks, which were also covered with ice. Around noon, when the sun had melted some of the ice, our chief bosun's mate took off for the lake with his tommy gun.

"I'll get us some of those damned ducks."

He was back in about three hours with another ibis, about half the size of mine. We thought this one would not be so tough, so we cleaned it and hung it

outside on a roof rafter for the night. In the morning the bird was gone; fourteen men had slept through the burglary.

When I got up, I was again covered with those damned little red pimples,
which I had scratched all through the night. Someone suggested they were
caused by sand fleas living in the hard-packed earthen floors. I got some alcohol from a drum on the truck and doused it liberally on the seams in my sleeping bag. By nighttime, perhaps the fleas would be out of my bag.

We started for the mountains around noon, in spite of patches of ice on the
road. Ascending the first mountain was fine; it was a wild ride going down. It
was the custom when driving in the mountains for Chinese drivers to turn off
the ignition or take the truck out of gear to save gas, letting the vehicles coast
down the hills. At one point, our driver dozed off. His assistant noticed it and
whipped the steering wheel toward the inside lane, sending the truck into the
bank. We all clambered out and berated the driver for his carelessness. It was
even scarier when we rounded the next turn and saw a wrecked truck in a
ravine. More than once that day we careened down a hill "hell-bent for
leather."

Late in the afternoon we were riding a mountain ridge and came to a group
of four houses right on the roadway. The lead truck signaled for a stop, but
Captain Chui waved us on, then signaled for a stop about a hundred yards
down the road. He pointed to the houses and said, "Bu hao!"

Then the other truck's lights failed. We remained in our truck while the
Chinese worked on the lights. The captain wanted to drive another sixty miles
to a friendly village for the night. Suddenly, as if a curtain had been raised, fifteen rough, ugly, and fierce-looking bandits stood there in the road, nearly
surrounding us on both banks. Their guns were pointed at us; my M1 was
already pointed at their chief; I inched as much as I could behind the drum of
alcohol. I began to think of our chief bosun, who was sitting with his back
against our truck cab, holding his tommy gun over several of our heads. I was
still afraid he might really mess up our group if he wasn't careful. Captain
Chui began a fast and loud exchange of words with the leader of the bandits.
We were ready to fire and so were they. I heard the captain shout the name of
Tai Li several times. He was standing up in the truck and gesturing for all he
was worth.

Finally the bandit leader remained silent a minute, then gave a sharp command, and the bandits disappeared as suddenly as they had appeared. It was as
though the ground opened up and swallowed them. We were all alone again.

The truck without lights fell in behind us, so we had to proceed slowly for the next three hours. At a bend in the road we came upon, of all things, a teahouse with seven other houses nearby. We were glad to depart the truck and have some tea and steamed bread. The captain explained as best he could in English that this village was called Solachi and an Englishman lived in a big house about a mile away.

"Do you wish to spend the night with him?" he asked us.

Anything would be better than the trucks, so we pulled off the road and left armed drivers to care for the vehicles. With a local Chinese as escort, we proceeded in single file on a path leading through farmland until we came to a ravine. It was about thirty feet deep and twenty feet wide. A large log spanned the ravine as a bridge. All but one of our men walked the twenty-five-foot-long log to the other side. A Jewish boy who had joined us in Kunming was afraid to walk the log. The others had gone ahead, so I was left to bolster his courage. First, I carried his seabag across along with mine, then I showed him how to straddle the trunk and persuaded him to follow me in this way, haunching ourselves carefully across. We made it. We soon saw lights in the distance and knew we had found the Englishman's house. Our shipmates were already there.

To our surprise, the house was called The American Mission for Lepers and was operated by a Mr. Baker, a member of the Friends group back in Kutsing. He welcomed us to the newly built house, which had three bedrooms and a laboratory on the second floor, which contained an old hand-cranked centrifuge unit. It was now 10:00 P.M. and we had not eaten a meal since the tea and steamed bread that morning but, of course, Mr. Baker did not know that, and it was getting very late. So we put our bedrolls on the second-floor porch and slept outside. The next morning, Mr. Baker apologized for not having any food to offer us.

"We do not have money to buy food in the village," he explained. We all chipped in 100 CN, and immediately Baker left with his cook and a servant, all carrying baskets.

While he was gone we observed the lepers from the porch of the house and the walls of the compound. There were separate partitions for the men and women. We counted fifteen men and six women who were outside their quarters. Their slightly abnormal features differed from person to person. Several of the men had a line of wartlike "beads" across their faces and foreheads, and the women's faces had white splotches resembling freshly made dough. The

skin on their cheeks and necks sagged piteously. Two of the women tried to
give a ghastly smile, revealing no teeth. Their arms and legs were covered with
white blotches, too. None of them had warm clothing for the cold weather, and
they looked as if they were starving, for their bones were very prominent. All
their movements were slow and deliberate.

When Mr. Baker returned, he gave us a little of the mission's history.
Several Lutheran sisters from Germany and one from Switzerland had supervised the mission for many years, but when Germany became an enemy of
China, the sisters were interned in the China Innerland Mission located in
Pichieh (Bijie). This was a village on our route and one we would probably
reach by evening. He said the sisters, headed by Sister Margaret, would be
happy to have us spend a night at their mission. When the sisters were forced
to leave the leper mission, he had volunteered to come from the Friends
group.

"We had a sad occurrence here just a week ago," he said. When the villagers
had discovered a mother and her two small daughters had leprosy, they burned
their house and all three died.

"Is leprosy contagious?" I asked Mr. Baker. He replied "No," but actually
there are some contagious types of leprosy, one of which is called Hansen's
disease. He explained the Chinese folk belief that leprosy was passed from
man to chicken and back to man again. This was accomplished by a leper spitting and a chicken eating the spittle. The eggs then caused people to contract
the dread disease.

"You're a frontline soldier, Mr. Baker," said one of our men. He certainly
had our admiration.

We ate a delicious breakfast of biscuits, honey, fried eggs, pancakes, and
tea. We collected another 500 CN and left it with Baker when we left.

We arrived at the small village of Pichieh in the afternoon and drove to the
Innerland Mission. Sister Margaret bid us welcome and assigned rooms in the
two-story building to all our men. She spoke German, French, and Chinese
fluently, so I recalled some of the German my grandmother had taught me as a
youngster and conversed fairly well with her. I was surprised at how it came
back to me after all the years. Sister Margaret said we would find places to
shop in the village, so we left the trucks in the mission compound and walked
to the stores.

Most of the men bought skins taken from wild animals killed in the nearby
mountains. Some were quite beautiful, especially the tiger skin. I did not buy
any of them. We watched a barber shaving the head of a small boy. He shaved

it bald except for a hairy cross left on top. The next boy's head was also shaved bare except for two funny little tufts of hair sticking up on top. I was unable to get anyone to explain whether the strange patterns were the whim of the barber or the boy or perhaps indicated a family code.

When we returned to the mission we received the surprise of our lives. After the blessing, Chinese servants brought in large platters of wonderful-smelling sauerkraut, pork, mashed potatoes, and whole wheat bread and butter. There was plenty of food here, so we stuffed ourselves and complimented the hostesses and cooks. After dinner the sisters held a church service and we all sang hymns, then went to bed for a good night's sleep.

After a good hot breakfast the next morning, we packed to leave, but we had a problem getting our drivers underway. The Chinese captain gave them a severe lecture, and it was nearly 9:00 A.M. before we finally left the mission. Sister Margaret gave each of us a small parcel (wrapped in yellow boardy paper and tied with a string), the contents of which were to be eaten as a snack, she explained. We bought a few handmade articles from the mission and left 100 CN to each of the sisters. One hundred Chinese dollars in this out-of-the-way place where there was no inflation was worth 500 CN in the larger Chinese cities. Later, when we unwrapped the parcels, we each found about a dozen freshly made cookies. They were so good that we ate most of them during the noon stop.

The ride in the beautiful mountains this day was precarious and spectacular. As we ascended the mountains we were treated to a different vista at each turn. One view took my breath away! It was like looking into the Grand Canyon, with depths of smoky blue tapering down to a valley sliced by the silver thread of a river. We descended into the valley via hundreds of hairpin curves maneuvered by our driver with the truck in low gear. Even the brakes had to be applied. Fortunately, we did not meet any other vehicles on this long, harrowing road. A single-width wooden bridge, which was frequently washed out, judging by the stubby posts sticking up here and there, barely cleared the shallow river. We decided to walk across, and the truck followed, very slowly. A short distance up a slight grade from the river we stopped for tea. We were about halfway through our Chinese vegetable dinner when the second truck arrived. We ate the last of our mission cookies with our tea, and when we were about finished, the host served us about twenty salted peanuts in a small bowl. The large, red-skinned roasted peanuts were doubly good because they were still hot, and I hastily asked the cook to sell me a catty (about one and one-third pounds) to go.

We climbed out of the canyon by negotiating another series of countless hairpin turns, eventually reaching an escarpment where the cliffs dropped away in rugged falls of thousands of feet. We finally reached the good-sized town of Shin, important to those who traveled the highway. There was a choice of several places to dine, but there was no evidence of many people traveling either north or south.

The hostel seemed clean, the rooms were large, and the food was good. We remained two nights because both trucks needed repairs. I suffered both nights from pain in my back; it was so hard getting in and out of my sleeping bag. And then the fleas or bedbugs, or both, kept me irritated and scratching at night. I think the bites all over my body were making me giddy, because when I got up I felt dizzy and would almost fall over. It was a strange feeling. Each morning I counted more than forty insect bites on my right arm.

Shin was famous for making water pipes. The metal used in them resembled pewter. We all bought a water pipe, and later wondered why. The tobacco bowl was so small it could hold only a pinch of tobacco, and with two puffs, the smoking was over. Later I saw many Chinese boatmen using the water pipe stripped down to its basic purpose of smoking and without the older tobacco storage part. The price of the pipe varied according to the engravings on the unit.

Our next day of travel brought one tense moment. We were descending a mountain road when a whizzing sound zipped past my head and hit the stone bank to my left. Then I heard the sound of a rifle. Immediately the truck stopped and we all jumped out with our carbines ready. We watched and waited for a full five minutes, speaking in whispers. As we were about to get back in the truck, a lone man rounded a turn in the road. Two of our men covered him with their carbines and allowed him to walk toward us. Our Chinese captain questioned him and searched him. He had no gun, so the captain let him go. We got back in the trucks and did not stop until we reached a hostel in the next valley.

Toward evening we arrived at Luhsien, a town on the mystical Yangtze (Chang Jiang) River, about which I had read and heard so many stories. It was like a dream, walking along its banks. The longest river in China, the Yangtze flows 3,500 miles to the East China Sea. Two of our companion Navy radiomen had been assigned to this town, completing a team of two Navy and the two Army radiomen already there. The Chinese Army also had an outpost here, headed by General Chow, who was somewhat of a legendary character.

We were quartered in Hostel #2, a Navy-designated hotel. Andy and Holly, two storekeepers in our group, returned to the hostel from a walk through town to find that 10,000 CN had been stolen from Holly's clothes. The captain was very upset and began an intense investigation. In about three hours he returned with the money, explaining that the truck driver and his assistant on the other truck were being punished. We never saw them again.

Those of us still traveling north had to wait several days for a boat to take us down the Yangtze to Chungking. I had traveled by carrier ship, trains, planes, and trucks; now I was to go via one of the quaint powered riverboats about thirty feet long. We would have to wait for the boat's arrival. On our second night General Chow gave us a lavish dinner. The hot wine went down easily and we all had too much. Chinese hot wine is a powerful drink without seeming so.

To pass the time during the days we played poker, and I was on a lucky roll. I won 6,000 CN the first day, 1,500 the second, and 2,200 the third. We were learning to *think* in Chinese, money and all.

A German Jewish refugee came up the river one day to visit us. She was a laboratory technician and her husband was a doctor of pathology. They lived some ten miles south of Luhsien.

"My husband could not come," she explained, "because he cannot walk so far, but I come occasionally to visit and catch up on any news I can." She said a German ship named *The Gripsholm*, which went around the world dropping off German Jews in ports that would accept them, had left them at Shanghai a few years previously. During our visit, which lasted the afternoon, she laughed about their plan for coping in a strange land.

"My husband and I decided to set a two-year goal of understanding the Chinese way of life," she said, but at the end of two years they extended it to five years, realizing they had not approached an understanding of Chinese philosophy "to any reasonable degree." Since the couple had already been in China five years, they were extending their plan for another five.

"The Chinese do not hesitate to seek my husband's services, however," she noted. She bought medical and food supplies while in Luhsien and left before night for her home in the mountains.

The boat for which we waited arrived sometime in the night of February 20, 1944. Captain Chui supervised the loading of all our gear and equipment and we started moving down the Yangtze, called "the long river" by the Chinese, early the next morning. The boat was very sturdy with a built-in engine, an enclosed cargo cabin, and a very busy captain.

Two men, one on each side of the boat, thrust long poles into the water at intervals to determine the water's depth. After each pole thrust at the bow, they walked toward the rear to call out the depths to the captain: "Chee sah, ba sah, loo sah" (seven feet, eight feet, nine feet). Numerous times the boat scraped the bottom of the river, but it never got hung up. The captain would always put on a wide grin when we hit deeper water. The river was at its lowest point of the year, I was told, but these master boatmen knew what they were doing and what to expect every minute of the day.

At the end of the first day downriver, we tied up to a small wharf for the night, but we did not disembark. Our only food was some C rations, which we had gotten from the Army radiomen in Luhsien. The next day we sat on the freight boxes piled inside the cabin and played poker. We started with an ante of 100 CN and jacks or better for openers. But no one could open, so we anted again with queens or better. Again no openers. We anted once more with kings or better for openers. Again no openers, so we anted with aces or better. Still no openers. The pot kept growing. We dropped the ante back to queens or better, and I drew a pair of queens. I opened weakly for 800 CN. I had no raisers, but only one man dropped out. I drew three cards. One was a queen and the other two were sixes. I bet 2,000 CN, and only one man decided to see me. He had drawn a third ten to a pair. It was a wild game. After one hand, I had an astounding 11,600 CN, but no one wanted to play poker after that.

We watched a few large boats, about the size of ours, making their way slowly upstream. Each one was pulled against the current by more than forty men who strained in single file along a path running parallel to the river. A rope looped around each man's shoulders was attached to a heavy rope from the boat. When they reached some of the stronger currents, they seemed to "pull their hearts out," and I thought of Russia's Volga boatmen of story and song who pulled until they died. These Chinese were burned almost black from the sun and weather. I did not see any slack in the individual ropes, so I knew every man was pulling his fair share of the boat's weight. They called out in cadence as they strained to put one foot in front of the other.

Toward evening we pulled into a small village and tied up for the night. Our boat was taking us closer to Chungking, one of the most heavily bombed cities of China. It was the current capital of Nationalist China and the home of Chiang Kai-shek.

# CHAPTER 6

# Chungking and Happy Valley

*April 1944—Truk's usefulness as a major Japanese military bastion and operational base is ended.*

**A**t 6:00 A.M. we were on our way downstream to SACO headquarters, finally! After more than four hours, we emerged from a canyon and saw the severely bombed city of Chungking sitting high up on a hill to our left. As we neared the foot of the steep hill, we turned into the Chialing (Jiang Jiang) River, which joined the Yangtze, then stopped on a flat, sandy island in the middle of the river. Small boats sailed in every direction, some overcrowded and others with only a solitary poling boatman. There was activity everywhere.

We saw that all our gear was ready to be unloaded and then we waited for the customs official. The Chinese captain had a conversation with the inspector and we were all cleared automatically.

One of the guys who had bought furs back in Pichieh decided to unroll his for a look.

"Son of a bitch!" he yelled.

The hide was full of stinking worms and was well into rotting apart. The others began inspecting theirs and found them to be in the same deplorable condition. With our cool weather, the skins should have endured if they had been properly tanned. The guys were so disgusted they threw all the furs into the river.

We watched a Chinese National Airlines Corporation passenger plane come in and land on the flat island in the middle of the river.

"He's going for the water," someone yelled.

But the plane stopped right on the button, right at the edge of the sand. China's national war capital was getting more interesting by the minute.

We lifted anchor and moved farther upstream to another small, sandy island near the foot of a steep, stone stairway that led to Chungking. The river was so shallow here that we walked over planks and rocks to the bank.

Now began the climb up the countless steps. We had to carry our seabags, carbines, ammunition, .45s, footlockers, and knapsacks. I thought about my aching back and hired three coolies to carry the seabag and the footlocker. When we reached the top of the hill, we were all bushed, but our journey had not yet ended. We were on the south edge of the city, which was teeming with traffic. We waited four hours for a navy truck to drive us the ten miles to the U.S. Navy Command Headquarters in Happy Valley. It wasn't really in a valley; it was halfway up the side of a mountain, but that was what SACO had named its China headquarters. From the place where the truck left us off at the end of the road it was haul your own gear (no coolies). We walked forever, taking frequent rest stops, before we arrived at camp level.

"Nothing got me into condition for this," puffed Griff, one of our store-keepers.

We all laughed and continued slowly up the path, which was punctuated here and there with a series of crude steps. Two more steps, and there was Happy Valley! We would have known it anywhere. The SACO "What the Hell" pennant was up, as was a large American flag. The "What the Hell" pennant originated one day when Captain Miles was skipper of the USS *Wickes*. He needed a signal that he could use as a "snapping of the whip" to maneuver ships that did not precisely follow orders. It was with this in mind that he asked his wife, Wilma (Billie) that evening how she would say "What the Hell" on a pennant. She suggested that when some writers or cartoonists want to avoid curse words, they substitute with question marks, exclamation points, and asterisks. So the next day the skipper had a special pennant made that became the trademark of our outfit. It was white with red markings and was inscribed with lots of punctuation.

The SACO camp at Happy Valley was made up of about ten permanent buildings, the largest of which was the mess hall. There was a medical building, a post office, the commodore's house, several small quarters for the permanent personnel, and a number of tents, all set apart from the central area.

In the central area were a communications center for SACO, a warehouse where all kinds of equipment and supplies were stored and received, and the mess hall. Happy Valley's permanent staff comprised about sixty navy men. Some twenty transients, coming and going from SACO stations throughout China and from other military posts, were there most of the time.

Sleeping accommodations were better than the truck, the roadside, or a dirt floor. We had cots. There were four men to a tent, and only room for the four cots, which had thin, interlaced ropes as mattresses.

For the first time in almost four months, we had mail call, and I had forty-four pieces of mail waiting for me! Hurray! After a wonderful dinner, I read and reread my letters until midnight. Tentmate Charlie K. learned for the first time of the death of his mother. He cried until he fell asleep. The Jewish fellow I had helped across the ravine received a U.S. Navy letter advising him that he had been selected for Officers' Training School and was to report back to the States upon receipt of the letter—a real navy SNAFU!

One of my packages contained a holiday fruitcake, which, sadly, was moldy and had to be thrown away. A hard salami fared better on the long trip, so my buddies and I enjoyed treats of thick salami sandwiches for several days. Included with the package from my wife, Audrey, was a large can of baked beans, which I conservatively stashed in my knapsack for a time when I might get real hungry.

February 23, 1944, the first morning in camp, I checked in with the personnel officer, visited with other SACO men, and had a breakfast of fried eggs with coarse white bread, toasted on a hot stove lid, and honey (honey was on the table every morning in Happy Valley). Later I wrote letters and saw the group doctor for my back and bites. I was still taped from neck to buttocks and still in pain. He gave me something for my misery and a powder to dust in my sleeping bag, blankets, clothes, and shoes. This stopped the bug problem immediately. That night we all went to see a movie in the mess hall.

In the cold of the next morning, I tried to pull myself out of my sleeping bag and experienced excruciating pain. Finally I made it up and swallowed a pain pill with water from my canteen, but then it was painful all over again crawling back into the bag until the sun appeared to help warm the tent.

"It's too cold to get up," I complained to Charlie one morning. "I'm going to do something about it."

I bought a large wok-type pan. I punched a few holes in the bottom, set it on several stones, and opened the top of the tent to allow smoke and gas to escape. Then I built a small charcoal fire in the pan. It did help, but what helped most was a Chinese houseboy assigned to us a day or two later. Thereafter Chan made the early morning fire and generally kept the tent and cots in order.

I returned to the doctor's office a few days later. The sixteen-day trip and hard riding in the truck had aggravated my back problem so much that I continually complained and began feeling sorry for myself. It was a surprise and consoling to find my friend, Warren Higby, attached to the doctor's staff.

Among Saturday nights' inspired entertainments were animated horse races in the mess hall, in which players moved their imaginary horses according to points made by throwing dice. China was my lucky place. The first Saturday night, when some fifty men were playing, I took in over 5,000 CN, winning five of eight races.

The first Sunday four of our men decided to attend church. We might have thought ourselves real Christians, as we did it the hard way. We traveled down our side of the mountain for three miles, crossed over a stream on a small arched bridge where public letter writers were set up for business, and walked up another mountain for some two miles to a little suburban settlement that boasted a mission and a girls' school. This Sunday there was a guest minister from Minneapolis. After church we visited the mission school where the Chinese girls sold their needlework, the most exquisite I ever saw. I bought several items, most notably a crib coverlet; I was thinking of my baby son back home. At the moment I didn't realize that when I returned to the States little Craig would be almost too big for his crib. The piece was beautifully appliquéd with laughing pigtailed Chinese people in colorful costumes tumbling through space. I found myself so fascinated by the artistry of these girls that I hated to leave.

In returning, we decided to take the quick way down the hill to the river crossing; we hired rickshaws. The road down was more gradual and longer than the little path we had come up. When my rickshaw coolie started down, he held back, but soon he gained momentum. He was running and taking seven-league strides as our weights were almost counterbalanced by his position in the shafts. Faster and faster we traveled! He kept hollering for people to get out of his way, never once slacking his pace. We nearly sideswiped a bulging busload of people coming up the road. I wanted to close my eyes every time we nearly collided with other people or rickshaws. To say that I was glad to get down safely would be putting it mildly. Our four rickshaw men all gathered at the bottom of the hill and enjoyed good laughs and comments, presumably about their scared passengers. It took some time to find out the minimal cost of our perilous ride. The coolies seemed happy with the money, and we learned later that it would cost four times the price we paid for a rickshaw to pull us up that hill.

Chinese fleas took a special liking to me. They were voracious, but didn't seem to bother the other guys. Either my skin was more delicate or I was more attractive to them. I thoroughly enjoyed the clean showers in Happy Valley, for we had gone more than two weeks without a real bath en route from Kunming to Chungking. With my body now cleaner, the fleas had a field day. I wrote home for flea powder.

I could write a whole book about Chinese insects. One day we watched something totally beyond our imagination. I wouldn't have believed it if I had not seen it with my own eyes. I heard a lot of yelling behind the camp. Charlie ran into the tent and said, "Mish, come look at what's coming down the mountain!"

A moving "belt" of ants about twelve inches wide was making its way down the mountain. The seething, undulating army of ants crossed the path not far from our navy post office and continued down the hill as far as we could see. We watched the phenomenon for over four hours, on and off. The whole camp's complement turned out to observe and comment on this migration. The ants did not stray from the main path; none got out of line.

"I didn't know there were this many ants in the whole world," I told Charlie.

After a while, we stepped over them and went about our duties, and the next morning we saw a clean, clear path going up and down the mountainside that had been made by the traveling ants. Yet there was nary an ant in sight. Still, I imagined for days that I had ants crawling all over me and scratched myself without reason.

As a storekeeper I was assigned the task of opening several boxes of Colt automatic .45s, checking their serial numbers and issuing them to newcomers. When I unpacked one box I found two beautiful blue-steel Colts mixed with the mass-produced gray ones. I exchanged my gray for a blue and did the same for a friend of mine. They were the envy of Happy Valley's men. I also unpacked several large crates of food from the United States.

"Hey, guess what we got from the States? Rice and tea!"

Because of my back trouble my next assignment was as a supervisor in the kitchen. I observed the cooking, boiling of water, and washing of dishes; and if I saw a deviation from camp policy, I was responsible for correcting the problem (with a Chinese major at my call for enforcement, if necessary). It was never necessary, as the twelve-member kitchen crew and I got along just fine. I sat on a tall stool and taught them English, and they worked at their various jobs and taught me Chinese.

I pointed to my eyes and asked, "Summat?" One of them would answer with the Chinese word. Then I pointed again to my eyes and repeated "megwa" (eyes). I learned that hot water was "kash ssway," cold water was "ling ssway," tea was "cha," shoes were "hi," and my ankle-top shoes were "pee hi." Kitchen duty was a worthwhile detail. Mandarin was the national language and also the most modern of the Chinese languages. In spite of all the dialects represented in the kitchen, Mandarin was the basic tongue, and I concentrated on learning it.

Our kitchen had a very interesting storage device for flour and rice. They were stored on the kitchen floor in straw, wraparound belt contrivances about four feet in diameter. When a new supply arrived, the belt was spiraled upward in a wraparound curling fashion. As the flour or rice was used, the wraparound was unwrapped so that the user could always get into the supply with minimum effort.

Holly and Minnie Perril left one day for Camp Three accompanied by two Chinese soldiers, a Chinese lieutenant, and a truck driver with his assistant. Holly was from upper New York State, a tall rangy guy who was easy to know. His best buddy was Andy, who was the other one who came down with malaria in Madras, India. Holly and Andy were always together, but this assignment was their first breakup. The truck was loaded with guns and ammunition and, like all trucks in China, was a vintage Dodge from the early 1930s. It was a marvelous thing that they could run variously on gasoline, alcohol, charcoal-generated gas, or by sheer manpower.

March brought early spring flowers, and nearly everyone felt revitalized. Red, white, and pink roses bordered a number of the camp paths and encircled the mess hall and quarters of Captain Miles. I looked closely at the rosebushes one day and added another Chinese mystique to my collection: these rosebushes had no thorns! Since my back began to feel better, I told the executive officer I thought I could continue to my assignment, but he said that I was under the doctor's care and would remain in Happy Valley until the doctor discharged me.

"When that happens I will send you on your way," he said.

My back had to improve because I had a temporary daily assignment that required me to descend and reclimb the 217 steps each day. After the first week the going became easier. As a general rule the men at Happy Valley were not permitted to go to Chungking. To do so required official permission and a special pass. Inflation was as rampant in Chungking as in Kunming, and shopping and eating were very expensive. I understood that our commander, Captain Miles, went into Chungking almost every day, and sometimes more than once. In addition to keeping in constant contact and cooperation with Gen. Tai Li's Chinese forces headquartered there, the captain supervised bringing in and taking out naval personnel from the sandbar airfield in the river below Chungking. There was constant rebuilding in the Chinese capital, for the bombings had devastated the city. People lived and worked in all kinds of makeshift dwellings.

One Sunday I walked to a nearby village named Sha-Pin-Pa to buy some of their beautiful table linens to send home. Through the open doors of household workrooms, right on the street, I could see the old foot-treadled Singer sewing machines. Now I knew where all those trade-ins went! Scratching around in the dirt of the road everywhere were pretty, pastel-colored baby chicks—yellow, pink, robin's egg blue, and white. I asked a shopkeeper what the colors meant, and he explained that owners picked different colors and dyed their chicks to keep up with them. The little birds certainly added a bit of color to the otherwise drab surroundings. The chicks wanted to follow, so I had to be careful where I placed my feet when walking.

Soon I was assigned to teach my first class of Chinese storekeepers. I taught them how to strip, clean, and reassemble the M1 .30-caliber carbine. They were good students and learned quickly. It was a long walk up to and back down from the firing range. There my assistant and I explained all necessary details for handling, carrying, and posturing guns. We lined up the novices and had them squeeze off five shots at a target from standing, kneeling, and prone positions.

When they had finished they insisted that I fire a round. Fortunately, I scored fifteen straight bull's-eyes. I felt good about my rise to the occasion, and my students mumbled "Ding hao" all the way back to camp. Payne and I continued working with them. Some were natural marksmen, others needed additional time and help.

"You know, Payne," I said one day, "sometime one of these Chinese soldiers may save an American life."

Most Chinese have small hands, making it difficult for the soldiers to get their hands around the .45 Colts to squeeze the trigger. So my next class featured handling the .38-caliber Smith and Wesson revolvers. This was some-

what better, but I think the best handgun for the Chinese soldier would have
been a .32 revolver, which, unfortunately, we didn't have.

After one of the classes on the shooting range, I dismissed the students and
remained to shoot a few rounds. Before I could get started, appearing out of
nowhere was a horde of small children. Some ran for the brass shells lying on
the firing line; others darted toward the back of the targets for the spent lead. I
tried to wave them away, yelling "Ting-yi-ting" (Stop). It was useless; they
paid no attention. I gave up and started walking away.

An old Chinese man had been watching from the sidelines. He suddenly
came forward and shouted a few words to the children, who took off as fast as
their legs could carry them.

"Shih-shih ni" (Thank you), I told him.

The old man, who was dressed in typical farmer's faded blue cloth shirt and
pants, replied in perfect English, "You are quite welcome. I speak English,
French, and German."

As I found during my entire tour in China, the people never ceased to
amaze me in the most surprising ways and at the strangest times. We talked
awhile and I learned that he had worked in England for seven years as a young
man, then spent another five years in Germany. He accompanied me back to
camp where he excused himself; I never saw him again, but I treasured
moments like these. Who could have expected to find such a well-educated
person in the countryside of China?

One of the men in camp was missing a pair of reading glasses. He had read
at night on his cot, placed them on his musette bag, and found them gone the
next morning. Since he couldn't locate them, he reported the loss to our executive officer. The next day they were returned. When we saw Chinese punishment being administered the next morning, we learned the story. The
American's houseboy, also a soldier, had taken them. The Chinese secret
police had ways of finding their culprits. Gen. Tai Li, also known as the
Mystery Man of Asia, whose request brought SACO to China, was chief of the
Chinese secret police or Bureau of Investigation and Statistics (BIS), and
nothing escaped his surveillance.

For punishment, the soldier was made to hold out his hands while standing
in front of his company, and his hands were switched one hundred times each
morning for two weeks. I got a close look at the man's hands on the fourth day.
He took them out of a jar of saltwater brine to show me. They had cuts almost
to the bone, and his wrists and arms were swollen. The man who owned the

glasses made a plea in the soldier's behalf, but to no avail. In fact, we were informed by our officers not to interfere with Chinese military punishment. At the end of two weeks the poor soldier's hands were nothing but bones; hardly a piece of skin remained. There was no stealing at our camp after this incident.

Chan was transferred and a new houseboy came into our tent. Anxious to please, he hung all the bedding and towels outside to air. Suddenly there was a "ching pao" (air raid alert), and we scattered into the hillside, away from all buildings and tents. Our bed linens were conspicuously waving in the breeze. The Japanese apparently were not looking for bombing sites that were launderers, so they passed over us without incident.

I conducted a class in compass reading, including map locations and preparedness for night direction-finding. At the conclusion of the course, we held a night exercise, beginning at midnight. All the men appeared at the designated rendezvous point at 2:00 A.M. except for one group of two. We learned the next morning that they had fallen into what the navy men euphemistically called a "night soil" gathering pit. Night soil gathering pits were the collecting points of outhouse toilets and cesspools. The two-man group of Chinese soldiers would have lost face if they had appeared after falling into such a thing. Working at the pits was the most menial of jobs. It included collecting the thin green water at the pits and pouring it on growing vegetable plants as fertilizer. This was why the navy insisted that all vegetables be properly washed and cooked.

While I conducted my classes, the rest of the men were teaching and learning radio and weather skills, rough-and-tumble fighting with knives, sharpshooting, demolition techniques, and tommy gun procedures. I wasn't very good with a tommy gun, perhaps because they were heavy and hard to carry.

By now the cold weather had gone and spring was almost over. The rains came—days and days of rain. When it finally stopped, the sun came out very hot and stayed hot. In a week's time our bamboo water pipes, which brought the water from a spring on the mountain, dried out and began leaking. Our water supply was drastically reduced; showers were prohibited on some days. Chinese and U.S. personnel took turns going up the mountainside every day to bind, replace, and rejoin the bamboo pipes. This was an ongoing battle.

April 3, 1944, was payday, and a very happy day, since we had not been paid since we left the States in November 1943! I sent most of mine home in a money order. We considered cigars a type of pay; we were allotted one every two weeks. I did not smoke cigars but loved the smell, so I made a deal with a friend: I would give him mine if he would smoke it sitting beside me at the movies. That way I received some satisfaction from my portion.

My back started hurting terribly again, so the doctor gave me more pills and I was assigned to the kitchen water watch again. It was a friendly reunion with the cooks and helpers. I sat on my stool and watched the kettles boil for more than a week. During this time, I cussed my continuing trouble with the fleas. One of the Chinese cooks told me to put a small amount of chloroform on the bites. I couldn't get chloroform, but I took note of all suggested remedies because the fleas were a real problem.

Colonel Shaw, the Chinese officer who had screened me and other SACO prospects in Washington, D.C., spent a number of weeks at camp; and when he was to leave, we threw a big party for him. Hot Chinese wine again!

At lunch one day a newly arrived navy officer, appearing in the mess hall wearing his lieutenant bars and a couple of ribbons, was introduced to the SACO men (about eighty of us) by Captain Miles. The word spread that all men were to wear their insignias, ribbons, and medals that evening for dinner. At dinner Captain Miles explained that in the future no one in the group would wear anything to designate his rank or rating. In this way the new officer learned our policy without being personally embarrassed.

We heard that Gen. Tai Li down in Chungking had wanted to assign a girl to each tent or building occupied by our men so that she could see to our well-being. Some of the men were all for this "dish of candy," but Captain Miles politely declined. So one evening when we heard some strong language coming from the captain's quarters, we thought it might have something to do with the prospect of the girls.

It was hard for anything to happen in Happy Valley without all the men knowing the gossip. For one thing, it helped pass the time in an interesting manner. This time we learned Captain Miles had given a commander hell for coming to the camp from Kunming for a visit without specific orders. It seemed one of the captain's drivers, Bill Sharrard (a storekeeper from my draft), had been sent to pick up the commander at Chungking's riverbed airfield. Bill offered to carry the officer's bulging brief bag up the steps.

He was indignant and said, "If I had wanted you to carry it, I would have ordered you to do it!" So Bill pointed out the hundreds of steps up the mountain.

"I'll wait for you at the top with a jeep, sir."

Of course, Bill was used to these extended steps and took off. He waited a long time at the top for the commander, who did not realize what a distance he had to climb. Bill drove him to the jeep-truck station at the bottom of the next mountain, parked the jeep, and began the climb upward. The commander followed, but the upward path with hundreds of steps really bushed him. On top of that, Captain Miles forced the man to cool his heels in the outer office for more than an hour, then asked him why he had come to Chungking without orders. After listening to some kind of lame excuse, he called Bill and ordered him to drive the commander back to Chungking, find him overnight accommodations, and see that he was on the first plane back to Kunming. We had all heard that this particular commander, Marcus Goodrich, was married to a gorgeous movie star and had written a book entitled *Delilah*, which was about a small U.S. Navy vessel. I had read the book.

"Well," said one of the men, "he got his comeuppance when he tangled with our captain!"

Finally, I got my traveling orders and left Chungking in the back of one of two trucks headed to Loyang, on the Yellow River in north central China. Each truck carried an American, two Chinese soldiers, a Chinese truck driver, and a helper. The trucks were also loaded with carbines, ammunition, explosives, and aerological gear. I felt that *now* I was getting down to serious business. With the truck and its cargo under my personal command, I began to feel a heavy responsibility.

I said my goodbyes to my buddies, walked down all those mountain steps I probably wouldn't be climbing for a long time, and couldn't help but wonder if I would ever see Happy Valley again.

CHAPTER 7

# The Road to Baoji

*May 1944 — The U.S. lands 12,000 men on Biak, New Guinea.*

Our truck was to carry R. B. Prescott, captain USMC; me; two Chinese soldiers; a truck driver and helper; plus a cargo of guns and ammunition. We waited at the truck station below our camp from 11:00 A.M. until 4:50 P.M., but the truck only took us 500 yards before it broke down. We started once more at about 10:00 P.M., drove upward for three hours, and stopped for the night in a tiny village where the only accommodations were in a true "fleabag" inn.

I could not sleep because of little screechy sounds that seemed to float overhead. Finally, I turned on my flashlight and saw rats on an overhead beam, their eyes flashing like mirrors when the light hit them. I reached for the .45 under my pillow, took careful aim, with my left hand holding the flashlight, and fired. It sounded like the place blew up! It caused quite a hullabaloo. I couldn't hear much of the yelling going on because my ears were still ringing, but shooting the rat was a big mistake; its blood fell over several of the sleepers. Of course, everyone was awakened and very annoyed. I gathered my gear and went out to sleep in the truck.

Our next stop was 120 miles to the northwest, where we waited for the other truck to catch up at a beautiful little village named Tsai Jung, a popular honeymoon and vacation spot for the Chinese of the area. We were served

60

good food at a pleasant hostel, which even had white bread on the menu. Late in the evening a U.S. Army soldier drove into town; his new six-by-six truck was almost out of gas.

"Ride with us to Chengdu," I offered. "You can get some gas there." I knew there was an air base there.

So when the second truck arrived, we drove to Chengdu before bedtime. This big city had wide, clean streets and now accommodated the prestigious University of Peking (Beijing), which had moved inland when the Japanese occupied that city. The U.S. Army had an air base in the Chengdu Valley, the largest level area I had seen since arriving in China. Since, of course, one of our trucks needed repairs, we stayed at the army's hostel where we had wonderful warm showers, good food, and barbers. Many planes were stashed in outlying buildings at the base, as well as in revetments around the city. I saw several P-38s, which I had never seen before. We also met our first Russian soldiers, who supposedly were military advisors. I never found out for whom.

We were up and gone early the next morning, but after a few hours our truck fell behind the other because of overheating. We stopped, and a Chinese soldier crossed a field to a stream and brought back a bucket of water. When it was poured into the radiator, we saw the leak. The driver and his helper decided to take the radiator to the next town to be fixed; but since it was almost dark, they decided to wait until morning. There was very little traffic on the road, so they had only a slight chance of hitching a ride; they'd have to walk the fifty kilometers. We all slept in the truck.

When I awoke just before daybreak it was very foggy. Suddenly one of the soldiers sounded a warning, and we grabbed our weapons and strained our ears. What followed was straight out of *Hamlet*. When the soldier hurled a challenge into the fog, an old lady carrying a baby on her back emerged like a ghost. She was followed by a girl of about nine or ten years carrying a pack on her back. The soldier called out to her; she slowly advanced toward us and he started asking her questions. Then he turned to me with a big smile.

"Ding hao!" he said. Somehow we were in luck.

What happened next could only happen in China. The little girl lowered the pack to the ground and opened it. She set up a small clay firepot and started a fire. After the charcoal began burning, she placed another little clay pot over the hot embers and fanned them. Meanwhile, the old lady lifted the child from her back, opened the buttons of her jacket, and began nursing him. The truck driver carried the radiator to where she sat and pointed out the leak.

"Ai, ai," she said, nodding her head.

The fog had now lifted and the sun was shining. While we waited for the solder (or whatever the base metal was) to melt in the pot, a red, gaily decorated wedding sedan chair passed by, carried by four men.

Soon the soldering iron was hot and the old lady busily worked on the radiator. The two Chinese soldiers in our party went for water again. When the lady finished her work, the radiator's bottom valve was closed and the water was poured into it. We all watched for several minutes; there was no leaking water. The radiator was installed, hooked up, and filled with water. We looked again; there were no leaks. The driver paid the old lady and she bowed her thanks repeatedly. Then the strange pair loaded up: the young girl helped to hoist the baby, papoose fashion, on the old lady's back, and then she shouldered the pack of equipment. They proceeded down the road, leaving as mysteriously as they had come.

The people we saw on the mountain road to Baoji (Paochi) were typical of most of China. Now and again we would see a lone man or a group of several trudging along carrying heavy-hewn stones in a harness on their backs. Each man carried a well-worn, polished staff in his right hand. When a man wanted to rest he looked for a resting bank just the right height along the road. Then he would back up to the bank, and let the resting bank support the load he carried. To get up, the man used his staff as a fulcrum, placing the bottom end on the ground between his legs and pulling up by holding the top of the staff. Then he could continue his demanding journey. It was a mystery to me as to what the stones were for. It was many miles to the nearest town. These men always wore a heavy cloth belt, about four or five inches wide, around their waists. Their belief was that as long as their belly buttons were kept warm, they would not catch a cold or suffer stomach cramps. I had no doubt that the Great Wall of China was built by men such as these.

We stopped in a large village named Kwunyuan for lunch, while our driver had the truck's engine checked at a local garage. The other truck had been waiting for us and immediately took off. All afternoon we traveled on a fairly level road. Late in the day we saw in the distance what appeared to be a sheer rock wall thousands of feet high. The nearer we drove, the more majestic and impenetrable it seemed. When we arrived at its base, we found an angle split in the wall large enough to drive through. We continued until we entered a beautiful, green valley without trees.

We approached a wide, fordable stream, and a pretty little Chinese girl of about ten years was standing near the ford. She was wearing a white blouse with a black flowing tie and a black skirt.

"Do you want a ride across the river?" I asked her in the best Chinese I could muster. She eagerly climbed into the truck and sat beside me. Her bobbed hair and bangs reminded me of the Colleen Moore hairstyle popular back in the States years before. When we had crossed the stream she wanted to go on with us. The truck driver looked at me.

"She wants you to adopt her," he explained.

The rest of the crew laughed when they saw I was seriously thinking about it. She explained that her mother and father had been killed by Nippon bombs and she lived with an uncle in the village. We let her out near a group of houses.

Although we were still in the mountains, all the land was barren and desolate. There were no trees or grass and no farmland. The winding road north led us toward another mountain. For a couple of hours we had not seen anything that looked like a house or building. I was surprised when we rounded a curve and saw a tiny roadside tea stand. We were hoping for a meal, but there was no food available at this tea hut, which consisted of a couple of poles topped by a thatched roof. I noticed six English walnuts on the makeshift counter. The Chinese man sold me one, and I peeled and tasted it. It was good, so I bought all he had, five, without quibbling about the price. I wondered if the English walnut might not have originated in China.

On our fifth morning out, we stopped for a breakfast of fried eggs and rice at a roadside restaurant. Normally these eating places were near or in a village. Now and then, however, they were isolated and one wondered how they could function with such little business. They were independently owned and operated. Generally I could see what might be a place to sleep in the restaurant.

A fierce-looking, swarthy man, tall for a Chinese (about 5 feet 10 inches), entered the restaurant. He wore two partially filled bandoliers crisscrossed on his chest and carried an ancient rifle. When he saw my carbine with its beautiful well-polished stock, he was eager to examine it. His rough manner and unpleasant voice made me reluctant to let him handle my gun. Finally, after some sign language between us and a little interpretation from the truck crew, I removed the clip and bullet and handed him the M1. He shouldered the gun, sighting with it several times. He then indicated he wanted a bullet. I refused and reached for my gun. The man grunted and stepped back, and our two Chinese soldiers put their carbines at the half-ready. I reached again, and grudgingly he gave me the weapon; but not before he asked, through the crew translators, if I would trade it for his rifle and two bandoliers. I was glad to leave the place and get on the road again.

We slept on the truck beside the road that night. At least two in our party were assigned guard duty every night, whether we slept outdoors or in a hostel. The next day we came to a swiftly moving river where there was a tea stand and four flimsy buildings. The "ferry" for the trucks and for us was a contrivance of inflated animal bladders, which we rented from the Chinese man at the dock. We loaded the truck and ourselves, and the burdened ferry slowly moved away from the dock. The Chinese ferrymen manuevered the thing with poles. We stood on the logs and the current swooshed under them. In the middle of the river, the ferry began moving faster downstream. There were some anxious moments until somehow we were swept over to the other shore, about 200 yards downstream from where we had begun. We drove the truck and gear off the ferry and left it for the next passengers. On this bank was another tea stand.

The roads were still rough and dusty, the terrain rugged and mountainous. We talked little. Toward evening, the driver spoke up and said, "We're coming to the Sacred Shrine (a wall of over 4,000 shrines). It is very special to all Chinese. Look over there!"

I estimated we were about a half mile from a solid wall that rose high into the sky. I could see figures carved all over the wall. The closer we got, the more figures in hollowed-out niches of the sheer rock could be seen. Some of the shrines were very large, others small. The niches and figures must have been carved by someone suspended by ropes or vines from the top of the cliff. They were hollowed out at random, as there was no set design or spacing. This was an old religious shrine that held deep meaning for all Chinese soldiers and truck drivers. Some of the strange figures, perhaps deities, were so old that their features had been eroded, and they were no longer sharply defined. I wondered how many years and men it had taken to complete the entire shrine. The road paralleled the wall of shrines for almost a mile. I wished I had a camera. It seemed strange that there wasn't a village nearby.

The narrow road in the canyon forced our truck to travel dangerously close to the edge. A river ran below us. Eventually I got out and walked behind the truck because I was afraid of what might happen if we met another truck head-on.

The farther north we traveled the less we saw of rice paddy farming, but some areas lent themselves to rice growing, with water runoffs. The cultivation of the hillsides was a wondrous thing. Each hillside and each level area were planted with different things. They formed a beautiful pattern of colors. Water buffalo were few and far between; but when we did see them, they were belly deep in the water and pulling plows. I could hear the farmer with the plow talking to his buffalo as though it were a person. It was a slow process, one step at a time until the cultivation was finished. I wondered how the thin legs of the farmers could stand the cold water and mud in which they and their families planted and cultivated rice seedlings. When we left Chungking the soy beans were in blossom, beautifying the hillsides and filling the air with their perfume. But we had traveled far north, and spring had not yet come to this area.

Much of the time I walked beside and to the rear of the truck, which traveled slowly up the rugged mountain roads. My back always ached when I sat in one position too long. Sometimes as I walked I heard tinkling bells that became louder and louder until I met six or seven little ponies plodding along in single file, carrying heavy packs. Each pony would have a small bell tied with a small line around its neck. When the ponies walked, their bells would jingle, playing the most enchanting music one could hope to hear. The ponies were generally followed by two or three men carrying switches. Although I greeted several of these packtrain groups with a "Hao bu hao?" they gave me no sign of recognition. "Hao bu hao?" is a common Chinese greeting—similar to "How are you?"—and it means "Is it good or not good?" The usual reply is "hao," meaning that things or conditions are good. In the cities there always seemed to be some response, but the mountain people were reluctant to engage in conversation with a stranger.

The other truck traveled ahead of us. One night we caught up with it in the village of Pao Gen (Paocheng), where its lights were being repaired. We found clean beds and passable chow in a little hostel. Both drivers determined that the trucks needed to have their main bearings changed, so it was early afternoon of the next day before we got underway.

I was riding on the roof of the cab and suddenly spied about ten ring-necked pheasants off to my left. I thumped the top of the cab as a signal for the driver to stop. I got down and walked slowly to within ten feet of the beautifully plumed birds. They must have never been hunted before, because they were almost tame. I aimed at the largest bird, squeezed off a shot and blew his head off. The others flew a short way; I walked toward them again and again got another bird. After a third kill, I went back to the truck. The bag was worth a few "Ding haos." They must have weighed three to four pounds apiece.

It was just at last light when we arrived at Mao Tai Tsu, a religious settlement named for a prime minister of the Han dynasty. Several monks met us at the entrance to the compound and eagerly welcomed us as overnight guests. None spoke English.

The temple was over 2,000 years old, and the entire compound of a few buildings and a courtyard was fascinating. Inside the temple were a number of shrines. We each were assigned a cubicle containing a bed and washstand. I put my gear down and went back to ask the monks if they could cook the pheasants and join us for dinner. They were willing. When I returned to my cubicle I found hot water in a bowl, a washcloth, and a towel. I washed and shaved as best I could by candlelight. I felt we were fortunate to have such a good place to stay for the night.

Within the hour I heard a heavy gong, whereupon a monk appeared at my door and said he would lead the way to "shio-fon." The dining room, large and drab, could have served as background for a Fu Man Chu movie with Charlie Chan. We sat at a long table set for twelve people. The main dish was already on the table: dumplings stuffed with shredded pheasant, which was delicious. The monks called it Lion's Tongue; and since there was plenty, we ate our fill. We also had cooked vegetables and tea. During the night, every so often I heard a soft gong echo and reecho throughout the monastery, letting sleepers know that someone was up and about. It may have been a temple watchman.

The monks were up at the first sign of daylight, bringing us hot water and tea. Our breakfast consisted of hot white biscuits and scrambled eggs. In addition, we were served chicken (or perhaps it was pheasant) soup. We toured the ancient temple and found ourselves in an unbelievable place. Some of the gods were carved of stone. They were all sizes and shapes, but most were four or five times the size of a normal human being. Only a few gods had smiles on round faces; most were grotesque and awesome. When we departed, I gave the monks a donation, and then we all bowed to each other.

Later in the morning we passed through a village of several hundred fierce-looking, dark-complexioned people who had mere slits for eyes and enlarged goiters. The women's goiters, about the size of an orange, were three times the size of the men's, and made their necks look short. One of my men explained that the men of this primitive village considered goiters a sex symbol; the larger the goiter the more beautiful the girl.

I had anticipated an interesting trip in this part of China, but even my expectations were topped at times. Once we rounded a bend in the road and came upon a caravan of camels. I counted about seventy-five of the hump-backed creatures carrying bags and bundles. They kept to the right side of the roadway most of the time, but once or twice our driver slammed the brakes to keep from hitting a camel that drifted out of line. Only a few men rode the camels, which, with their great strides, really covered the ground. It was a long

time before we could finally pass them, and as soon as we did we came to a
hostel where we spent the night.

The hostel was in a tiny village named Schwan-Shaap, and I was surprised
to even find it on my map. It was the only town within a hundred miles in any
direction. Not long after leaving Schwan-Shaap the next morning, we passed
the camel caravan's campground. They were preparing to travel, and some of
the people dragged long bags around picking up loose strands of camel hair
that had rubbed off during the night. The thriftiness of the Chinese! They
were going to make cloth out of the strands.

Two hours later our truck broke down, and we had no place to go for help.
Our driver reached into the birdcage in the cab and sent out one of our three
homing pigeons with a message. The pigeon rose into the sky and headed for
Baoji. While we sat at the roadside, the camels passed us. I could imagine the
old American expression, "Why don't you get a horse?" only now in far-off
China it would be "Why don't you get a camel?" The driver kept tinkering with
the truck, and in about two hours it was running again. Soon the road climbed,
cutting through a mountain that was made of shale, which periodically slid off
the road into the abyss. I decided to walk again.

We caught up with one of the camel drivers, who was pulling handfuls of
hair from his camel that had just died. Dozens of vultures were waiting for
him to complete his job so they could do theirs. When we overtook the main
caravan, it was just leaving the roadway. It was heading northwest on the Old
Silk Trail. This trail was thousands of years old, and I couldn't believe I was
really traveling on such a storybook route.

At this junction, where the Old Silk Trail went into a mystical land, our
road took us north on a route toward the more populated and modern city of
Sian (Xi'an) via the interesting town of Baoji.

There was a teahouse, several inns, and a dozen houses at the junction. As
usual, I called for "kaswei" (hot water) and washed my chopsticks before eating. The round tables and high chairs, without backs or arms, were typical furnishings of inland teahouses. Not so typical were the newly varnished surfaces
of the furniture, which immediately caused the arms of all of our crew to break
out in a rash. The soldiers raised hell with the owner, who apologized and
brought warm water and towels to wash off the sticky varnish. Along the next
strip of roadway we observed many caves with people living in them.

When we pulled into a compound in Baoji, we found our other truck already
there. I could not figure out where it had passed us. The other driver laughed
and told me it was magic. The carrier pigeon had carried his message in good

order and was cooing in his cote. He had advised Chinese intelligence in Baoji of our breakdown and when we could be expected to arrive.

Baoji, which means "precious chicken" or "pheasant," is located in a fertile valley near the western end of the Lung Hi Railroad, a narrow-gauge railway of Belgian manufacture. A bustling, mushrooming town, it was filled with thousands of Chinese fleeing from the Japanese in Peking and Shanghai. The name was the only thing pretty about this city. There were great and dirty flea markets everywhere, and people were selling anything they had or could obtain in order to buy food. Small bazaars, stands, and thatch-roofed places bustled with trade.

There was a wide expanse of railway yards. We watched trains softly puff to a halt with people hanging all over them, even riding on the tops. Men, women, and children were riding, clinging, and sitting on coaches, boxcars, and flatcars. Near the entrance to the freight yard I saw a small boy's body, without a head. Apparently he had been shaken off in a shunting action and a wheel had run over his neck.

On top of one boxcar several women were standing in a circle. I watched, and in a few minutes I heard a newborn baby's cry. The baby had just been born on top of the boxcar. When a train pulled into the yards, the people wedged between the cars started to untangle themselves in order to get off. When the boxcar doors opened, the people spilled out by the hundreds. How could so many people have been jammed into one car? Just beyond the end of the railroad yards the town had grown in waves. Small bazaars, stands, and thatched roofs were held up only by their poles. There was trade of every description.

White potatoes were a rarity in China, but in Baoji we found a restaurant that cooked french fries (young yee), so we went there often. Later, when I was stationed at Sian to the east of Baoji and had to make runs back there, I always stopped at the restaurant for the french fries. Mostly I returned for mail. There was a small airfield on a mesa just northwest of the city; the roadway was steep and it was a good hike to the top, but I was to make it many times. I learned that a Chinese National Air Corps plane was scheduled to fly in every other day, bringing mail from SACO headquarters in Chungking.

Most of us were lucky to find hotel quarters, and lodging costs were high. A number of transient missionaries also stopped at the hotel. They moved on as soon as transportation was available.

There were two other Chinese trucks waiting for our two trucks when we arrived in Baoji. Our naval group now numbered seven, but Paglia, a Marine

Corps radioman, and Henderson, a Navy radioman, received a directive to establish a radio station at Su-li-pu, ten li (about three miles) east of Baoji. They left us the next day.

The next leg of our journey was aboard a train bound for Sian. There seemed to be adequate space available for our trucks on flat cars. At 12:30 P.M. we entered the small passenger coaches of the Lung Hi Railway. The air was stifling. Tiny cinders from the old locomotive's smokestack filtered into the cars and clung to our sweating faces. The trainmaster signaled for the engineer to start by blowing a single long toot on some sort of mouth whistle. The train made so many stops along the farmland country that I thought we would never get to Sian, an important stop for me.

# CHAPTER 8

# Sian and the Jao da Sol

*June 6, 1944—Gen. Dwight D. Eisenhower lands his Allied forces in the Normandy area, France. The Battle of the Philippine Sea proves a decisive victory for the Allies in the Pacific.*
*July 1944—Our forces take Saipan.*
*August 1944—Guam is taken.*

It was twelve hours before we reached Sian, the capital of Shensi (Shaanxi) Province, which had a population of well over a million. At one time it was called Changan and was the capital of China during the Tang dynasty (A.D. 618–907). Sian was important throughout Chinese history as a crossroads of the nation. From 200 B.C. to A.D. 200 it was the center of the Han dynasty.

We were quickly passed through military inspection at the railroad station when we showed the round blue badge with silver Chinese characters that Gen. Tai Li had issued to all SACO men. This was the first time I had used the special badge, but it was to come in very handy in several military emergencies in days to come.

The Jao da Sol was the largest and best hotel in the city, and it became our temporary quarters. It had an elegant appearance from the street, fronted by a semicircular driveway where rickshaws waited for customers. The Number One Houseboy, a big fellow who spoke good English and was always helpful, led us to our rooms. Each room had a bath but only cold water. Water was heated in the hotel kitchen and carried to rooms as requested by patrons. We slept two or three men to a room. My room was on the second floor and had two windows, which provided good cross ventilation. I was pleased that mattresses bore the label Simmons.

We were joined by an American, Major Misely, at our first dinner in the hotel's round dining room. I never did find out who he was. The dining area was encircled with white columns that supported a domed ceiling. We were pleasantly surprised to find the food was so good.

I awoke the first morning to music and softly banged on my ear for a moment because I couldn't believe what I was hearing: *Marching Through Georgia*! I peered out the window and saw a band leading a funeral procession past the hotel. The body was in a coffin carried on a four-wheeled flat wagon. The mourners were dressed in white, and a few were crying very loudly. I learned later they were professional mourners, wailing being important to the success of the funeral and to the well-being of the bereaved family. Long after the funeral procession was out of sight I could still hear *Marching Through Georgia*.

Bad news! We received a message through the Chinese radio network that Loyang had been overrun by the Japanese. It also informed us that I, with Shorty Lee, would remain in Sian. The gear from our four trucks was unloaded and then reloaded onto three trucks. Five men and the three trucks would proceed south and try to join up with Camp Three personnel, who had evacuated Loyang and were traveling south and then west. Since Loyang had been overrun, there were no more trains scheduled for the east, except to the roundhouse about ten li east of Sian.

Sian was a walled city with massive gateways leading off to the east, west, south, and north. Within the city was another walled area, once the city of the Manchus, which was now occupied by the Chinese military. The main streets were very wide, perhaps eighty feet, with curbing and brick sidewalks. Every shopkeeper dutifully and carefully swept the street in front of his establishment daily. In the early evening, the streets were filled with thousands of people out for an evening stroll or shopping. At each major cross street was a platform from which a policeman directed traffic. Although automobiles and trucks were rare, there were plenty of rickshaws and horse-drawn wagons, as well as countless bicycles.

The Japanese had observed the vast migration of people into Sian, and they also knew that Chinese military personnel were there, so they sometimes flew over the city, occasionally dropping bombs. Sian developed its own system of air raid alerts called "Ching Pao." On the top of the wall surrounding the city were a number of large wooden structures in the shape of a "T" that could be seen by nearly all inhabitants. When an air raid was believed likely, a single large ball would be hung on one wing of the "T" pole; when a raid was imminent, a ball would be hung on both wings, and that was when people disappeared. I was informed that our hotel had an underground cave for its guests and staff.

My second day in Sian we came under enemy fire. Since the walls of our hotel were at least thirty inches thick, I decided to watch from my window. Suddenly the second "Ching Pao" ball went up. Three Japanese planes approached from the southeast, the first of which flew over the wall headed in my direction. It followed the street and dropped eight bombs in a row. Then it zoomed upward and out of earshot for awhile. One of the other planes circled and headed back straight for the hotel. I was right in his line of fire, so I dropped to the floor. I could hear the machine gun clatter above the roar of the engine, and the window beside me flew into bits. When I opened my eyes I could see dirt, glass, and dust all over the room; I stayed on the floor until I could no longer hear any engine sounds. The three bullets that smashed the windows were embedded in the wall behind me. Within minutes the manager and Number One Houseboy were in the room to survey the damage.

"What! You here!" they said in surprise. In the street in front of the hotel were six small and two large bomb craters about six feet deep. People began emerging from their shelters; the two balls were already down from their yardarms. I had witnessed my first enemy fire in China, a "Ching Pao" to remember.

Almost every day I met American or English missionaries fleeing the Japanese advance. They traveled in rickshaws and carts, on ponies, bicycles, and foot. I met one older American missionary who was lugging her few luxuries wearily down a street. She had carried them over the high mountains and harsh roads.

"May I help you?" I asked and took some of her bundles. She looked so tired. We began talking, and she told how she was almost captured in Loyang. Her cook helped her to escape. She and her cook waited for nightfall and then walked south on the main road overnight. The cook then left her, saying he had to go back and look after his family. She had to abandon half her possessions on the roadway. The next several nights were a nightmare as she slept along the road.

"Come on over to my hotel," I offered. She slept on the bed, and I took the floor. In the morning, the poor woman was somewhat rested; and when she left, she insisted I accept a quart of homemade strawberry preserves, two glasses of jelly, and a jar of apricots, all of which she had carted over the long road from Loyang. She could have been anyone's grandmother. If I remember correctly, her name was Mrs. Wilson. I walked with her to the railroad station where she was to catch the train to Baoji, and maybe later a plane to the United States.

"Take care of yourself," I said as I kissed her on the cheek. The train, bulging as always, pulled out, and Mrs. Wilson was gone.

General Hu, who was in charge of the Chinese SACO operation in Sian, gave a dinner for us at the hotel, including Shorty and me, three male missionaries, and two Chinese officers. I was sure the purpose of the dinner was to gather information from the missionaries. We all slurped our soup as loudly as the general and his staff, showing our appreciation for the fine flavor and quality. I lost some face by not drinking as much hot wine as the rest of the party, but I felt the best of the group the next morning.

Soon I received an assignment from Chungking via General Hu's messenger. I was to remain at Sian and be the camp courier. My assigned assistants were Shorty Lee, a navy storekeeper from east Los Angeles, California; and Hu Kung Lu, an interpreter we called Raymond, from the Chinese Army. Shorty was not a member of my draft; I had met him when I arrived at the hotel. He was about 5 feet 4 inches tall and a genial companion. Always grinning, Shorty told one joke after another and found humor in most situations.

Orders came for the two of us to take our one remaining truck, loaded with M1s and ammunition, and head south until we found the group I was supposed to have joined in Loyang. We took Raymond with us.

We started early in the morning and headed south to a village called Hochiatsum, then through a lush valley abundant with farms. The road was filled with potholes; and when we began climbing into the mountains, it turned and twisted continuously. Coming down into one canyon we saw that the wall on one side of the road was pockmarked with caves. Stone steps and wooden pegs embedded in small holes and cracks provided handholds and footholds for people with the nerve to climb the sheer walls up to the larger caves. We didn't see anyone climbing, but we did see a few people in the cave openings, watching us as we went by. Sometimes a little smoke drifted out of the mouth of the caves.

The road we took south was the main escape route for the thousands of people who were going north, most traveling in groups of ten to twenty. Now and then as many as a hundred walked together, and once we drove through a large body of Chinese soldiers marching north. Along the route were worn-out sandals (the weather in May was still cold in the mountains), many with broken thongs, and most with large holes in the straw soles.

I developed a great respect for the Chinese foot soldiers. They moved great distances by marching almost twenty-four hours a day on two thin meals of gruel, which I would not have considered equal to one good bowl of oatmeal. When I said "thin" gruel, I was laying it on a bit thick; and, of course, there was no milk or sugar, ever.

The first evening we slept in a one-room school in the small, walled town of Shanyang. The truck crew and I pushed several desks together for a bed. As we were about ready to pull out the next morning, I was approached by a khaki-clad American who asked me questions like who was I and where was I going. I hedged, remembering words of caution back at the Potomac training camp regarding SACO and its operation. After a little word sparring, something was said to further identify ourselves and, in a most surprising revelation, he said he was the SACO commanding officer of the Loyang unit I was to have joined. Major Young said he was a day or two ahead of his camp's movement.

"Six hundred Chinese guerrillas, almost fully trained, are with our camp's complement," he told me; he was overjoyed to learn what I had brought on the truck.

"I have picked out this town for a temporary camp," he explained. He waited anxiously for his men to arrive, while I set about finding better quarters for the incoming SACO men. Raymond and Shorty went to look for a suitable place and returned in an hour. They had found another school with several buildings and a large courtyard where we could keep trucks and the jeep. From somewhere they got whitewash for the interior walls and about twenty cots for the navy personnel that we estimated would arrive within the next day or two. Raymond, who served as our interpreter, made a deal with the mayor of Shanyang for space outside the walls where the 600 Chinese guerrillas could camp. With the acquisition of a cook and the construction of washstands and a kitchen, we thought we had a special place for our men.

As it turned out we had one problem. Scorpions! We woke up the first morning in the new quarters to see scorpions on the top of the mosquito netting suspended over our bunks. Taking great care, we crawled out of our bunks and used our carbines to knock the horrible insects onto the floor, where we killed them by stomping on them.

Our daily baths were taken in a sparkling stream about fifteen feet wide located just outside the city wall. One day just as we passed the north gate, we saw the inert body of a newly born girl. To our horror two dogs were gnawing at the tiny body.

In the marketplace old women sat by their colored silk cocoons spread out on straw mats; and since there was a critical shortage of food in this area, many things were for sale, including young girls.

"This is good," explained Raymond, "because it shows the great love of the parents for their child." It seemed that the parents figured that anyone having the money to buy a girl would have the money to feed her. If she remained with her parents she would likely starve because male children always had priority for any available food. Food was very scarce and the people were eating budding leaves from the trees.

On May 14 we heard a bugle sound outside our compound. Upon investigating we saw a swarthy Chinese man with his hands tied behind his back being escorted through the streets by six Chinese soldiers and an officer. Sticking down in back of the prisoner's head and into his shirt was a piece of wood shaped like the broad end of an oar. The wood was painted white and had six or eight bright red characters on it.

"He is a bandit ready to be executed," said Raymond.

The prisoner, I was quite sure, had never had such attention paid to him in all his life, so he walked erect and smiled at the people watching. Once outside the walls, the officer gave a command and the squad turned the man around. A second command was given and the squad walked back ten steps. A final command, and the soldiers took aim. "Fire!" The prisoner's smile faded and he fell to the ground. As was the custom, the officer pulled his Luger from its holster, walked to the man and shot him in the back of the head. The Chinese execution squad marched back to the city, leaving the body where it was. The next morning it was gone.

Shanyang, the county seat, was full of hustle and bustle as people, mostly refugees, filled the streets. They were fleeing the Japanese army. Rumors abounded, and the air was full of fear.

We met an English missionary at a small food store on our second day in Shanyang who said he had lived there for twenty years.

"I will not be driven out," he insisted, but he planned to send his wife and two children to Sian and then westward to safety.

The family invited our officer, Shorty, and me to dinner that evening. The wife clearly was worried. The nine-year-old son, who had been born in the village, did not speak any English and, obviously, had been raised as any Chinese child. The missionary told me the family spoke only Chinese except when they had English guests, which had not been often during the past two decades.

The twelve SACO men arrived late on the third afternoon, bringing our total unit number to fifteen. With them were a number of missionaries. They said Japanese planes had strafed them on the road, killing two oxen and damaging many possessions. Carts, bicycles, and luggage had been left on the road when the people scattered for shelter.

In briefing us on our overall operations at this camp, Major Young outlined two plans that we might execute if our situation deteriorated. Plan One was to hightail it westward across the country and through the mountains. With no roadway to follow, we would move in two groups and use our compasses for direction. The two groups would try to rendezvous every night. Plan Two involved heading north to Sian and then west, as most evacuees were doing. Our unit had several radiomen and we had several contacts a day with Chungking.

The Loyang unit brought with them the three trucks previously sent on ahead and a jeep with very poor tires. Since I was the camp's courier and my duty station was Sian, Major Young said I should take the jeep and return to Sian. The jeep needed repairs, and I needed to get back on schedule with a mail run to Baoji. The jeep gave me trouble all the way back to Sian, especially tire trouble. I had so many inserts put into the tire casings it felt like I was always driving over a bumpy road.

My duties in Sian were never boring. There was always something of interest to see, and fascinating travelers and military personnel came and went. Many shops from the eastern Chinese cities had set up temporary quarters in Sian and they were filled with enchanting art objects.

Every few days I visited the small supporting airfield the U.S. Army had built a few miles southwest of Sian. I usually walked to the airfield and then took a rickshaw back to the Jao da Sol hotel. There were usually six P-40s sitting on the airstrip, with caricatures of the mouth of a smiling shark painted on their noses. The main purpose of the field was to supply fuel for Allied planes.

About once a week a P-38, stripped to bare essentials, would stop to take on all the fuel it could hold. The pilot, Major Red Varner, who usually joined me for dinner, took aerial photographs of all areas occupied by the Japanese. Armed with only a .38 revolver, he flew the fastest plane the United States had at that time. It was a good thing, he said, because only his greater speed enabled him to escape the Japanese Zeros. His normal routine was to fly over Tokyo and back to the Sian base for refueling, then continue on to his home base of Chengdu. If he had any minor engine problems, a mechanic at the airfield worked on them, but if they were major, he tried to make it to Chengdu. Major Varner told me numerous stories of the scary adventures he'd had while taking aerial photographs. Only his plane's superior speed enabled him to outfly the Japanese Zeros and evade ground fire.

A U.S. Army intelligence team, consisting of a lieutenant and two radio specialists, showed up at the hotel one evening. The lieutenant was Chinese, but had been born in America, and so spoke only a little Chinese. The team had been observing Japanese movements in a certain area and sending their findings daily to Chengdu by radio. They had recently been spotted by a Japanese patrol and nearly captured. They had literally run for their lives, lugging sections of the hand-powered transmitter with them. They had been shot at several times, although no one was hit, and had hidden in a wheat field for an hour. When the sun went down, one man stood up, only to have a fusillade of shots ring out and bullets whiz by him. He dropped to the ground and they all crawled to a safer place. Later, in the darkness, they walked thirty miles to Sian.

Number One Houseboy informed me that forty newspaper reporters from the United States and several other countries would be arriving at our hotel, en route to the Chinese Red Army headquarters to the north of the Huang He (Yellow) River. The Reds were allied with the Chinese Nationalists at the time to present a united front against the Japanese. I was out of the city when the contingent arrived, but was in Sian when they returned from the north. They reported being well treated by the Reds, and marveled at the Communists' expert horsemanship and their accuracy in mortar firing. Mao Tse-tung had been the group's hospitable host.

Among the interesting people I met in Sian was a young girl who was a distant relative of Raymond's, her girlfriend, and her brother, who was a soldier. They all spoke remarkably good English. The brother, a former student at Peking University, was assigned to our camp as an interpreter. The unusual thing about him was his height; he was over 6 feet tall. Never before had I seen such a tall Chinese man. He was also very strong.

On one trip to Baoji, I brought back three bags of mail, a truck loaded with small arms and weather equipment, and a navy aerographer. The latter was to set up a weather station near Sian. I helped him find the spot and unload the equipment, then I set out for our camp with the truckload of supplies and the jeep. I knew the men would want their mail as soon as possible.

While climbing up the mountain road, however, the truck burned out a main bearing. We parked the jeep and truck under a large stone ledge that stuck out over the roadway. Having this shelter was fortunate because it soon began to rain. While the mechanic and driver worked on the truck I walked back down the road to a small house. It was raining harder and I was very wet. I knocked on the door and it opened slowly. I pushed the door wide open and stepped into the one, and only, large room. Sitting on a bench, I began trying to communicate by signs with the man and woman who lived there with three children.

It was normally cool in the mountains, even in late spring, so a fireplace at one end of the room heated the entire house, including a built-up clay mass. As best I could determine, it was a huge bed on which the entire family slept. It felt nice and warm.

"K'ang," laughed the man, and I guess "k'ang" meant oven-heated bed. This home, with its clay walls, clay floors, and clay bed, had central heat. I waited in the warm hut for several hours and eventually dried off. When I left, I bowed to the family several times and left two cigarettes with the man. The rain had changed to a mist. When I got back to the truck, the mechanic was still working on it.

After six and a half hours of work on the bearings, we proceeded along the muddy road to Shong, where we stopped again for tea. Here we met Major Young, now the commanding officer of our new camp. He had come up from Camp Three to investigate a report that a Chinese pilot had made a forced landing in the area. I accompanied him down the main road and soon, as luck would have it, we met the pilot, who took us to his wrecked plane a short distance away in a creek bed. Two Chinese soldiers were already guarding the wreckage. I wondered where they came from but never learned. The pilot spoke excellent English. He said he would return with us to camp, then asked if he could go with me to Sian.

We reached camp before nightfall. Mail brought the good news that my fellow storekeepers and I had been promoted to storekeeper 2nd class.

We met Bishop Megan, originally from Chicago, who would be around camp for a while. He did not resemble a clergyman at all. He dressed in Chinese clothing and spoke the language fluently. His first evening with us turned out to be a jovial event, because he conjured up a gallon glass container filled with white lightning (Bi Ju).

"This is more like stateside whiskey than any other liquor found in China," he explained.

We sampled it to see if he was telling the truth; and because we could not decide for sure, we took another drink. And another. That's the way it went and that was the way the jug went. Bishop Megan said the brew, which had no specific taste, but did have a hell of a smell, was made from guilang (maize, or corn). He added that he artificially colored it. While we were sampling the guilang, the bishop posted us on the locations of Japanese in the area and practically all of China. It seems this man of the cloth had a widespread network of informants who fed him the latest war information. Because of this activity, he was on the Japanese "wanted" list and had several times narrowly escaped capture. Once when he was trapped, he played the part of a Chinese with a contagious disease. The Japanese stayed away from him.

The Japanese had located our camp, and twice the next day we had air alerts. One plane flew over our location several times, but there was no strafing or bombing. We were eating eggs three times a day. Our cooks scouted farms for poultry and eggs daily. All food was expensive. Once I even shot four doves for dinner.

The weather was very hot and dry, and the creek where we got our water slowed to a small trickle. The Chinese commanding general (war lord) for the southern half of the province was now crowding his army of about 1,000 men into our small town.

Each morning a Chinese bugler awakened us at 3:30 A.M. By gentle persuasion we tried to get him to stop blowing the horn so early in the mornings. We had at camp a Lieutenant de Montgomery, formerly of the French Free Army, who somehow had become a freelance SACO member. One morning he got up and seized the bugle. It was quiet for two mornings, so the lieutenant returned the bugle and told the man not to blow it anymore. The next morning at 3:30 A.M., it sounded loud and clear!

The following morning, even before we had been awakened by the bugle, we heard a tremendous explosion. I got out of my sack in a moment, slipped on my pants, and grabbed my .45. It was barely light in the east. I climbed to the top of the wall surrounding the town and peered over, looking for any sign of movement. Other men joined me. Finally, at a distance of about 1,000 yards, we spied smoke coming out of a small ravine. "What the hell are you doing on the wall," yelled Lieutenant de Montgomery from behind us.

"Didn't you hear the explosion?" I replied. "And look at that smoke down there."

He began laughing. Then he explained that he had risen before the bugler and set off four units of Composition C close to where the bugler usually blew the horn.

"I just can't take that damned bugling!" he said.

We all returned to our cots for another hour's sleep and found out later that the smoke we saw came from a farmhouse.

On June 10 I returned to Sian, accompanied by the Chinese pilot and Raymond. Raymond warned us that bandits were active on the road, so we had our weapons ready at all times. On this trip, however, we saw no one.

On June 14 I rode the Belgian train to Baoji to take out mail and pick up a sack. When I got there I found out that our mail plane would not arrive for two days.

The first thing I did was get a room at the small hotel where last I had stayed. Then I went directly to the restaurant that served french fries. I saw two U.S. Navy men sitting at a table.

"May I join you?" I asked.

They identified themselves as Bo and Pag, both radiomen, who had set up a station at Su-li-pu, a tiny settlement ten li east of Baoji. Pag, a cocky marine, and Bo, a heavyset navy man, rode two small Chinese horses. These little horses were very durable and would run until they died if given the chance.

"What is going on at Su-li-pu?" I asked.

"Nothing much," answered Bo. "We get so bored we come to Baoji a lot."

At my hotel I met a Mr. Wang, who said he was a contractor and had built the big stadium in Shanghai. Like so many of the people in Baoji, he was a refugee.

"What do you miss most in the way of United States food?" he asked me one day, as we sat in the lobby.

"A good cup of coffee," was my instant reply.

The next day he appeared at the hotel with a vacuum-packed can of S&W coffee, which was delicious! Bo and Pag were there and shared my first coffee brew, which I supervised in the kitchen. Later, back in Sian, I saw two cans of S&W coffee in a shop window. I went in and asked the price, "Hao do chen?" It was 6,500 CN per can, or about 50 dollars American! I would have put such a purchase far from my mind. Mr. Wang might have bought it for a little less, but no matter; he had certainly given me a generous gift. I never saw Mr. Wang again.

I picked up four and a half bags of mail for Camp Three. I had twenty precious letters and two packages, one from Audrey and one from the Red Cross. The latter was a Christmas package; since it was June I wondered if it were for last Christmas or the upcoming one. Audrey's package contained many welcome items, including flea powder. Glory, glory for the flea powder, my remedy and aid in getting to sleep.

Even though Baoji was overcrowded, smelly, dirty, and ugly, it always held some highlight for me on my trips. Shorty Lee made the trip with me only occasionally. One time I attended an opera performed by a troupe of traveling Koreans. I ate roasted sunflower and melon seeds during the performance, placing the seeds on a little shelf built on the back of the chair in front of me. Hucksters moving up and down the aisles measured out the seeds in little cups about the size of a coffee scoop.

The packed audience seemed to pay little attention to the performance; instead, they talked and visited with each other while they cracked the sunflower and melon seeds, spitting out the hulls. Surprisingly, the Korean troupe presented their opera amid beautiful lighting effects and interesting sets. I could hear it raining outside. Then came the tea vendors up and down the aisles, passing the hot cups over people's laps and trying to brush aside the seeds on the little trays in order to put the cups there. This resulted in numerous arguments.

In the meantime, the rain storm heightened outside, and the woven mats above our heads began to bulge from the weight of the water. Up on the stage the play called for cannon fire and gunshots. The thunder outside and the arguments inside resulted in total bedlam. I left the opera before it ended and got thoroughly soaked on the walk back to my hotel.

The next night I stopped on the street to listen to a public storyteller. He depended on contributions from listeners for his livelihood, a profession probably as old as China. First he read a news item from a recent newspaper, then he enlarged upon it, usually going into Chinese folklore or history. Sometimes he commented on the war. The storyteller was always surrounded by twenty to twenty-five people who sat or squatted around him. I understood very little of what he said, although now and then I caught an expression or several words.

One diversion for the Chinese men in Baoji was playing a version of mahjongg. I did not know if this type of gambling was against the law, but it was always played on a side street. I usually got a hostile look when I stopped to watch the dice throwing, but when I exclaimed "Bu hao" at someone's poor luck or "Ding hao" at a person's good luck, they accepted me, and even offered me the dice. I never played; for one reason, I couldn't entirely catch on to their system of play, although sevens and elevens won on the first pass, and twos, threes, and twelves lost on the come.

By now I was able to eat the tasteless white bread available in Baoji, Sian, and villages in the area. It was made of millet flour rolled into very thin sheets, piled one on top of the other until they were about a half-inch thick, cut with a three-and-one-half-inch-round cutter, and baked (or half baked) with the edges pinched. Each baker gently stamped his trademark in a light purple or pink dye on the patty. The end product, which did not rise, was like Jewish matzo.

One day I met the wife of an English missionary in the marketplace. She had been in China four years and had hated every minute, but she cautioned me not to tell her husband because he was very disappointed that they were returning to England. They had come from their mission in Nanking en route home.

"I am so happy to be going home," she said. "The war is doing me a great favor."

One time when I was at the airfield outside of Baoji I accepted the invitation of the CNAC pilot to fly with him to Lanchow (Lanzhou). This city, which was the capital of Kansu (Gansu) Province in northwest China, was populated by over half a million people. We dropped off freight and stayed overnight at a small hotel. Lanchow was famous for its melons and fruits, so all of us (pilot, copilot, crew chief, and myself) bought bags of melons. Back in Baoji I shared some of them with our Baoji men, who praised them highly.

On this trip I had picked up five new jeep tires and tubes and two large bags of mail. With the new tires and tubes mounted on the jeep, I proceeded on to Camp Three with Shorty and arrived at night. Someone was loudly beating a drum. I lugged in the two bags of mail and asked for something to eat.

"Notice anything unusual when you parked the jeep?" Shorty asked me.

"No," I replied. "But what are they beating the drums for?"

"Go look," someone called out.

When I did, I saw a severed head hanging by one ear on a wall near the parked jeep. I went back into the building.

"What's that all about?" I inquired.

The story was told. It seems that the town had been without water for two weeks. The stream where we once bathed was now dry. The Chinese Army, our 600 guerrillas in training, and our camp men, made the utmost demands on what little food was available. The native population was starving. There was so little to eat that the people were eating fresh buds and leaves from the trees and bushes.

The military had been executing one to three men each day after marching the prisoners through the west gate. A Chinese seer or prophet said the reason for the famine was that shooting the prisoners was wrong. Instead of shooting them, they should behead them and beat the drums. This was the cause of the famine and lack of water. Beheading the prisoners and beating the drums was being done to bring on the rain.

The next day I saw two heads roll. These were a Chinese sergeant and corporal whose duty was to roam the countryside for eligible youths for the army. One farmer, who had a thirteen-year-old son, begged them not to take him because the farmer had only one arm and needed the son to help him earn a living. The two soldiers suggested they would overlook the boy if they were paid enough. The poor farmer scraped together all the money he had plus some he borrowed from neighbors, whereupon the soldiers lived it up for a few days.

When they returned to the farmer for more money, he begged for just a few days to try to get it. The father had been bled dry and could not borrow any more, so he went to the Chinese general and told him what had happened. The general exempted the boy from conscription for one year and had the two soldiers beheaded.

The heavy sword swung downward twice, and each time a head rolled onto the ground. Blood gushed at first, then slowed to a trickle. When I talked with the missionary about this, he said that the soldiers were executed not because they collected money from the poor farmer but because they did not share it with the general.

On my return trip to Sian, my road intersected a route being taken by retreating Chinese forces that had been badly shot up. Some of the wounded were strong enough to walk, but thousands of bearers struggled up the trail carrying litters of pitiful casualties. I stopped the jeep. Some litter bearers lowered their charges and rested. Many wounded were also walking with the never-ending line. Their wounds were not bandaged or covered.

There was little I could do, but I had two cartons of cigarettes in my seabag, so I tore them open and broke each cigarette into two pieces, giving half to the bearers and half to the wounded. It was a task lighting all the halves, so I indicated to the Chinese that I would light one, give it to a bearer and he would light the next, and so on.

I was running out of cigarettes when four Chinese officers drove up in a jeep and told me to stop the handouts. However, they each eagerly accepted a whole cigarette when I offered. I pointed to my blue-and-silver identification badge from Gen. Tai Li, and their manner changed immediately. They said they had suffered 3,000 casualties in a battle with the Japanese just two days ago. They wanted to be friendly, but I grew reserved, and a few minutes later I drove on to Sian.

Soon after I arrived at my Sian hotel early in the evening, Japanese bombers came over the city in droves. Raymond, Shorty, and I sought shelter in the cave below the hotel. We could feel the reverberations from the planes' engines even in the cave, but we couldn't see them because of a low cloud formation. When I sensed they were nearly over the cave, I would fire my carbine from the entrance, hoping to hit something.

The next morning we took stock of the city. A few buildings still burned, but the primary target had been our small airfield, where everything was leveled. Fortunately, our planes had taken off prior to the attack. A number of casualties occurred during the morning, long after the planes had left, because people began picking up small incendiary bombs that had failed to ignite upon impact with the ground. When anyone grasped them and twisted the fin, they exploded, and both Chinese soldiers and civilians were horribly burned. Sections of the great wall around the city were also damaged; the imposing seventy-five-foot west gate, through which I passed frequently, had been hit but not severely.

Sian's weather was hot! One day Shorty, Raymond, and I went to a bathhouse. The bathtubs were similar to those in the States but were filled manually with water. A bath cost about fifty cents U.S. money, but bathers always tipped. When a customer left the bathhouse, there were always men at the exit talking loudly and laughing. It seemed that the larger the tip the louder they yelled and laughed, and the amount of the tip was always mentioned in the yelling.

On July 3 I was browsing in a curio shop in Sian when a poor-looking farmer entered and politely asked the owner if he would buy the object in his hand. It was about six inches long and five inches tall and was covered with dried mud. I could not tell exactly what it was. The owner spoke a few words to the farmer, waved his arms, and made the man leave. I followed and caught up with him when he was about to enter another shop. "May I see?" I asked in Chinese. The object was heavy for its size. It appeared to be a carved animal.

"Hao do chen?" (How much money?)

He answered that he would sell it for 800 CN (about six U.S. dollars). I suggested he go with me to the Jao da Sol, where I asked Raymond to query the farmer. The farmer said he was plowing his field when his foot hit this object, and he knew it was not just a sharp stone. He did not know if it had value but decided to come to town to see. No one wanted to buy it.

I offered him a cigarette, which I lit, and he exclaimed it was a good smoke. Then I offered him 600 CN for his object, and he accepted. It was one of my luckiest days in China. I did not know exactly what I had bought, but it appeared to be a solid metal figure of considerable antiquity. After soaking it overnight in water, I used my "ki yi" brush to clean it, revealing a thin, tiger-like bronze figurine with a long neck and round head. The tail nearly reached the ground and was coiled at the end. The cat, as I called it, was in a walking position, with leg and feet joints and ribs distinctly marked.

I continued to try to clean and shine my bronze cat, and later learned that doing so was a big mistake. I had removed much of the valuable green patina from this rare art piece. I wrapped the cat in a handsome, handmade rug and shipped it home. Years later I showed it to the curator of the Detroit Art Institute who insisted I take it to Dr. Lee at the Cleveland Museum of Art. Dr. Lee identified it as a tiger of the early Han to late Han dynasty period (200 B.C. to A.D. 200) and wanted to know all the circumstances under which I obtained the tiger. I loaned it to the museum for two years, then finally sold it to a patron of the museum who made it a part of the museum's permanent collection.

Another purchase I was proud of was a gold-embroidered, silk robe that I found in a Sian shop. The shopkeeper said it was about seven hundred years old and had been found in a ravaged tomb. He thought it must have belonged to some high-ranking scribe or perhaps a secretary because there was plain black silk sewn over each elbow. The colors were predominantly blue and gold. We haggled over the price for two days before I bought it for the equivalent of eight U.S. dollars. I sent it home, along with a woman's robe embroidered with many beautiful Chinese characters. I was told that the characters showed one hundred different ways to wish the wearer a long life.

One of the days when I was at the airfield near Sian, seven Japanese Zeros flew over. Our six P-40s took off and chased after them. However, no dogfights ensued; both the Zeros and our planes, manned by Chinese pilots, flew round and round the Sian area. Those of us on the ground just stood and watched the "play." Finally the Zeros headed for home, and our planes came back to the field. Not a shot was fired.

During the sky watching, one of the four young Chinese officers who stood near me suddenly tried to remove my .45 from its holster. I came down hard with my right hand and struck his wrist sharply, crying "bu hao!" (no good!). Immediately the other officers came to his defense, explaining that he meant no harm and that he just wanted to see the blue Colt. They also informed me

that he was Chiang Wai Kuo, son of Generalissimo Chiang Kai-shek. I apologized, unloaded my .45, and handed it to him to examine. He showed no ill
feelings, and I explained to him that it was wrong for him not to ask to see it.

Soon I was on my way back to Baoji again for mail, supplies, and messages
from SACO headquarters. One of our radiomen and I rode out about thirty li
east of the city in a horse-drawn cart to tour a large spinning and textile mill
located in a cave. The company, which also made high-quality paper, had
moved the extensive operation inland 400 miles to escape falling into Japanese
hands. Both owners of the plant had graduated from English universities, one
from Oxford, so they spoke excellent English.

Rows and rows of looms filled two man-made caves, which were each about
a mile long. Many very young girls were moving about tying broken threads
and replacing shuttles and bobbins. The cave openings were covered with
camouflage nettings. The nettings also were spread over a power plant and
office buildings just outside the caves. The whole operation was a wonder to
see. I was particularly impressed with the plant's toilet system, which was the
best I had seen in China outside of our Sian hotel. The system consisted of a
U-shaped trench lined with white tile. Water was constantly sluicing down the
trench and carrying away the feces. Most other toilets I had seen in buildings,
homes, and other places were mere enclosures, which bred maggots by the
tens of thousands.

When we returned to Baoji I met two navy lieutenants: one named
Daniels and the other named Lon Connor, a storekeeper from Texas. They
had arrived with a truckload of equipment and were to accompany me to
Sian. Meanwhile I had a message that some mail was due to arrive in a day
or two.

When we reached Sian I wasted little time in getting them on the road to
Camp Three. Shorty and I were in the jeep, and in the truck were Lieutenant
de Montgomery, who needed a ride to camp, along with Lieutenants Daniels
and Connor. The trip was uneventful and I returned to Sian in two days. I was
mighty happy to have the new tires on the jeep.

On July 22, 1944, I received an invitation from Mr. Drumright, the U.S.
consul in Sian, whom I had met at the army airport, for ice cream and cake at
his home on July 24. He invited all the Americans he could find, plus a scatter-
ing of Norwegians, Danes, and Britishers. He set off a couple of fireworks after
dark, celebrating a late U.S. Independence Day. That night the city suffered a
heavy bombing. Although there were no casualties, the streets were left with
large bomb holes, some as deep as eight feet.

General Huang in Sian invited all available Americans for tea. Tall, slender glasses were filled with hot water and a lid was placed on top of each glass. When the tea leaves settled to the bottom, the tea was ready to drink. It smelled wonderful, but tasted only passable; I drank tea that tasted much better at other places in China. My favorite tea, which incidentally was one of the cheapest, was a brand called Victory Tea, the leaves of which were almost black. Tea merchants blended the leaves to a person's taste, and they always measured the tea very precisely on a special weight balance. As a gesture of honesty and generosity, however, merchants always added an extra pinch of tea to the measure.

It was after midnight before the gathering at the general's headquarters was concluded, and I decided, since it was such a beautiful night, to walk back instead of going with the others in rickshaws. I tipped the rickshaw man who had waited for me and started walking back to the Jao da Sol hotel. The streets were deserted. I passed the house and courtyard where General Chiang Kai-shek had once been held prisoner by the Chinese communists. As one of just several Americans in this huge city, I walked alone surrounded by a million Chinese. My holster was open and I walked tensely with my hand over the butt of my .45. My hearing was acute, and once when I heard a noise or voice, I backed up against a wall so I could see in all directions and waited for a few minutes. Japanese spies were known to be about the city, and a few informers were being arrested almost every day. It took me about forty minutes to get back to the hotel. Raymond was still up waiting for me.

It was getting hotter by the day. We had heavy and frequent rains, followed by insufferable humidity. Mid-July afternoon temperatures were reaching 104 to 115 degrees Fahrenheit. One time it remained at 115 degrees for four straight days. The nights never turned cool enough for comfortable sleeping. Food prices escalated every week, and the rate for my room at the hotel went up 50 percent.

One afternoon I was walking down the main street when I came upon a crowd of people gathered in front of a butcher shop. A police sergeant and two policemen were trying to arrest the butcher. The shop was about ten feet wide by twenty feet deep. I could see the butcher was not about to go peacefully and was putting up a good fight. The police went into the shop, but almost immediately the sergeant came flying out the door, followed by his two men. Behind them came the angry 6-foot-tall butcher with a big cleaver clutched in his hand. The bystanders backed away in a huge semicircle that extended into the street. The butcher, hollering loudly, swung the cleaver menacingly in the direction of the police and then the onlookers. They fell back.

Suddenly, I found myself standing alone on the sidewalk, and then he saw me. He fixed his eyes on me and took steps in my direction, raising his cleaver. I unfastened my holster and drew the .45, pointing it in his direction. He challenged me by taking another step and lifting the cleaver higher. I fired a shot at his feet, and the bullet ricocheted off the sidewalk with a whine. The butcher stared at me for another few seconds. It was very quiet. Suddenly, he dropped the cleaver to his side, laughed heartily, and then turned around and walked back into his shop.

The next day two plainclothes policemen and a supervisor visited me at the hotel to get my version of the altercation. They told me the butcher had been accused of short-weighting meat for his customers. They indicated that they were glad I had not wounded the man and asked me to refer any future problems I had in the city to the police department.

That same day I met Ellwood Rice, the new provincial representative from the U.S. State Department, who became a good friend to us in Sian. He told us a story about two Englishmen and another American who, with him, became known as the "Rice and Price and Rouse and Krouse Team." They had all met before the war in Shanghai and had become good friends. A year and a half later I met Mr. Rouse, an Englishman, in Changchow, Fukien Province, when our unit was getting ready to move to Amoy. Mr. Rice hosted dinner for Shorty, Raymond, and me, after which we listened to the world news on his excellent radio. Unfortunately, the battery went dead before the program was completed.

U.S. personnel came and went, and most stayed at the Jao da Sol hotel because it was the best in the city. A special military plane came to take Bishop Megan, Major Metcalf, and Major Crombey to U.S. Army headquarters in Chungking. They were all army observers.

Ensign Wildman and CSF Shelley, who were down from SACO's Camp Four in the Gobi Desert, slept on the floor in my room, as there were no other accommodations available. Wildman was a physical fitness nut and spent most of his time doing pushups, knee bends, and jumping exercises long into the night, even during the hottest days. Shelley was a chief steamfitter for the navy and had lugged with him a heavy trunk of wrenches, pipe fittings, a vise, pipe threader, and some metal-filing saws.

"Shelley, do you use all those tools?" I asked him.

"Hell no," he answered. He said he just didn't feel right without the tools of his rating.

Along with the navy gear I originally delivered to Camp Three, I had a special stateside leather saddle for Dr. Goodwin, one of the officers at the Gobi Desert camp. Each man in the Gobi camp rode a small but sturdy Manchurian horse, and each became an excellent horseman. A movie entitled *Destination Gobi*, starring Richard Widmark, featured the SACO camp in the Gobi Desert. Several times, while I had possession of that saddle, I noticed Chinese horsemen looking at it in my truck; several asked to buy it. I was concerned with the responsibility of keeping it and was glad when I forwarded it with two SACO replacement men on their way to Camp Four.

Sian was rapidly becoming the hub of our naval group in north central China. I helped to set up, then later expand, the aerological station a short distance from Sian. Our man Chase supervised it with the help of one navy assistant, a Chinese trainee, and an interpreter. Lieutenant Daniels was now using the jeep more than I was for trips between Camp Three and Sian.

Major Young and Dr. Gang, from Camp Three, arrived in Sian on August 24, and I rode with them in the jeep southwestward to find a new campsite. The major drove and I rode on the hard back seat over the rough terrain. My back and butt were constantly jolted, and the pain became almost unbearable. We visited two Chinese Army camps occupied by only token forces, and we decided to use one of these for Camp Three. We returned to Sian; I was in agony and went to bed immediately. Dr. Gang took my temperature, which was 102 degrees, and gave me pain pills. I stayed in bed for more than two days. Thank goodness for my full-time doctor. Much pain, little sleep, and the squeaky fiddle someone in the hotel played at night combined to make my days and nights miserable.

Case, one of the SACO men, accompanied Major Young, Dr. Gang, and General Hu to the proposed campsite; and when Case returned, he said it was the roughest ride he had ever experienced. And he didn't even have a bad back. Case said the water supply was assured as there was a large concrete irrigation ditch close to the campsite, and the water was clear-flowing about one-third of the way up the bank.

I don't know where Dr. Gang found the raspberry jam, but he shared it with me when I got up for my first breakfast in three days. Out of gratitude I took him with me for a visit to Mr. Rice's house. I had become a regular visitor there and was always asked to stay for dinner. He kept his work very private and only employed two Chinese men, a cook and a general servant. Mr. Rice was his own radioman and quite professional in its operation.

On August 28, 1944, about twelve Japanese bombers hit the southeast section of Sian, where General Huang's military headquarters was located. Many civilians were killed. Looking out the window from the hotel, I could barely make out the bombers in the light of a quarter moon. The next day Shorty, Raymond, and I looked over the bombed area. Later I went out to the airfield. All the planes had been flown out before the Japanese bombers arrived. I hung around a while until several P-40s returned from Chengdu.

When it got dark I hired my favorite rickshaw man, whom we called "Joe," and he set off at a gait that ate up the distance quickly. Since it was raining, he had tied a piece of oilcloth across the front of my seat so that I could just see over the top. Houses of the poor lined the road; I could see people in the dimly lit doorways.

Suddenly a five-year-old child ran out from a doorway straight into the side of the rickshaw. I heard a thump as he fell under the left wheel. Joe immediately set down the shaft on the wet street; I climbed out of the vehicle. In a moment loud cries were heard from several people who came running out of a doorway, and soon there was a group of people around the child, the driver, and me. A few of the people began yelling and hitting Joe with their fists. I held up my arms and hollered loudly, which caused everyone to calm down. I picked up the boy and carried him to the closest doorway. He was conscious and did not appear seriously hurt. Since I could talk to Joe better than to the man and woman hovering around who seemed to be the parents, I told him to tell them I would report the accident to the police and pay 500 CN for any needed doctor's fee. The father accepted the money, smiled, and bowed. The woman continued to be hostile. I gave Joe an extra tip that night.

"Ding hao" (very good), he said.

The next day I went to the police station and related the incident to the supervisor. He told me I had done enough and should not concern myself further.

After dinner one evening I walked down the main street of Sian alone, joining the crowds of evening strollers. I stopped now and then to look in a store window or just gaze at the scene around me. After walking about ten blocks I had the strangest feeling that something was not right; I thought I caught sight of someone seeming to do exactly what I did. So, I abruptly crossed the street and stopped to look in a store window. I watched out of the corner of my eye to see if someone would cross over after me. A man in a Western suit followed me. I began walking casually, stopping here and there. Each time I stopped, he did too, looking at something just a few windows away. I crossed back to the other side of the street, and he was still tailing me. I felt I was not mistaken now; I knew the man was after me. I was very uneasy, but tried to show no anxiety or difference in my manner.

I watched my chance and took it when I reached a busy intersection where a policeman directed traffic. I crossed over and watched my man begin to cross; as he did, I turned quickly and retraced my steps, meeting him half way in the busy street. We were in front of the policeman. I grabbed the man by the arm and asked the policeman to arrest him as I believed him to be a spy. The policeman was quite taken back and uncertain until I showed him my badge from Gen. Tai Li. I could not speak fluently enough for the policeman to understand my meaning, but a crowd closed in, and a Chinese man who spoke excellent English suddenly stepped from the crowd and helped me convince the policeman to arrest the man. This surprise interpreter was also well dressed in a Western suit and looked like the typical modern Chinese merchant. The policeman blew a whistle and two more policeman arrived. My newly found friend explained the situation to the other policemen. In a few minutes they roughly led the man away.

Early the next morning two police detectives came to see me at the hotel. They briefly recounted the circumstances of my adventure the previous evening. One cleared his throat.

"Mister Mishler, the man who followed you, was one of Gen. Tai Li's men."

"What," I exclaimed. "But why?"

"The man was to see that you came to no harm in Sian. He is here to help you if you need it. We have released him under the circumstances." And that just goes to show how very wrong one can be sometimes.

One afternoon Number One Houseboy met me as I walked into the hotel.

"Two American soldiers are in the barbershop looking for anyone who can help them," he said excitedly.

A colonel and a major of the U.S. Army Air Force, as noted by their insignias, were getting haircuts and shaves. I identified myself, and they both said at the same time, "What in the hell is the Navy doing here?"

I joked and shrugged it off at the moment and learned their story. One engine of their B-29 had been shot up, causing a forced landing. First they almost landed on a hard-surface runway north of the Yalu River, but then they recalled from a briefing that there were no hard-surface runways north of the Yalu in Chinese military possession. They managed to continue a short distance south and landed along a railroad track between Loyang and Sian.

"We left the crew with the plane," said the colonel, "and made our way to Sian on foot. We were guided here to the hotel by several Chinese."

"Are you hungry?" I asked. What a question! We figured later that they had walked forty miles to Sian.

After dinner, I took them first to Mr. Rice's house to get a message off to Chengdu. Then we went to our support airfield where another radio message was sent to the Chengdu air base. There was a great need for speed in getting the B-29 engine repaired and the plane and its crew out of the way of Japanese planes, which might have already spotted it. It was very vulnerable.

The commander at Chengdu sent a succession of P-40s to the site to circle the downed bomber from daybreak to dark. One plane would fly in circles until relieved by another; and this continued until the bomber could take off again.

A new engine and twenty drums of gasoline, together with three U.S. Army mechanics, were flown from Chengdu to Sian, then taken by special train to the closest point to the disabled plane. The equipment was then transported by horse-drawn wagons to the giant B-29. I advised General Huang of the plane's value and its problem. He immediately sent 1,000 soldiers to the site. About 500 soldiers surrounded the plane to discourage any Japanese ground force that might wish to take it from the ground. The other half ripped up railroad ties from a nearby spur of the main railroad line and made two paths of runway, one for each wheel of the plane. In two days the new engine was installed, the undercarriage of the plane repaired, and the runway completed. I drove the two pilots over to the plane in the jeep.

When all was ready, a horde of Chinese soldiers and civilians pulled on ropes and pushed the plane onto the makeshift runway made of railroad ties and dirt. Twenty drums of gasoline were poured into the tank, the crew waved to everyone, and the big plane sped down the runway . . . and up. Shorty told me later when I returned to Sian that the pilot had circled Sian twice at a very low altitude. Almost half a million people were looking skyward and cheering. They had followed the process closely via front-page stories in the local newspaper every day and via word-of-mouth in the streets. He saw the U.S. plane head southwest toward Chengdu.

To me this situation symbolized what the Sino-American Cooperative Organization was all about more than any other single venture I witnessed. With all those Chinese people in Sian showing their concern and then their happiness for the American plane's rehabilitation, the SACO code of friendship held dramatic meaning. All that shouting and cheering made me feel awfully good.

The two pilots had stayed at the hotel while their plane was being repaired, and one night I decided we should have watermelon to eat. Raymond and I took off in the jeep and found a farmer entering the south gate of the city wall with a two-wheeled cart full of huge melons. He didn't want to sell to us; he told Raymond they were already sold. But while Raymond negotiated I picked the biggest, which I could hardly lift, and put it in the jeep. We gave him a good price, 200 CN, and drove back to the hotel, where I asked Number One Houseboy to bring it into the dining room.

"That's a watermelon!" the colonel both asked and exclaimed.

"They grow 'em big in China," commented the major.

I asked Raymond and Number One Houseboy to eat also, and the five of us could only stuff down half of the largest watermelon I have ever seen. It was crisp and sweet to boot.

"Spit the seeds on the floor," I instructed the colonel and major. "That's the Chinese custom." They looked at the beautiful, highly shined brass spittoons in the hotel dining room. I shook my head.

"They are never used."

I must admit that I put a number of the seeds in my pocket on the chance that one day I could amaze everyone in the States by growing the largest watermelons in the country. I kept the dozen or more seeds for about twenty years and then threw them away.

Watermelons were cut up in slices or wedges and sold on the streets of Sian. Their meat varied in color: white, red, pink, or yellow; or sometimes a combination of colors such as yellow and white, red and white, pink and white. The watermelons looked like they had been painted in pastels by an artist's brush.

Ices, too, were sold on the main streets. In view of the fact that ice was always scarce in the city, I was surprised that on any summer day I could find these finely ground ices ready for sale. The vendors had five or six bottles holding various colored flavoring syrups, so a customer could have his pick of colors and flavors.

Folk traditions blossomed everywhere in Sian. Youngsters played games that could have been centuries old. Both girls and boys were experts in getting spinning spools on a string to go up or down continuously depending on the way the string was tightened or loosened.

I would always stop and watch the little girls. The girls played a game all their own where they kept little round papier-mâché balls in the air by bouncing them off the insides of their feet, similar to bouncing a tennis ball on a racquet. The girls seldom missed, and they would continue for four, five, or six minutes at a time. Sometimes I would see a half-dozen of these girls all bouncing at the same time.

The most unusual contest was among boys of about ten or twelve years. The object, it seemed, was to be the one who could "pee" to the highest mark on a tall wall. Each contestant stood a certain distance from the wall, and each boy got one try only. There were no warm-ups or false starts. Usually several dozen onlookers cheered their favorites among the contestants. Two judges measured the heights attained and called out the measurements. If two boys peed over the wall, they both won. Raymond explained that when a boy reaches manhood he loses a great deal of bladder elasticity and can no longer compete with the younger boys.

Shorty Lee was back from Camp Three for a while, and one day he suggested we take a walk. We went into places I had never seen before.

Sian had had an early morning rain; but when it cleared, the whole city looked like someone had just kicked over an ant hill. Streams of carts, bicycles, and wheelbarrows filled the streets. Everyone was in a hurry. Chinese bicyclists pedaled backwards to stop their bikes because few of them had brakes. Most bicycles cost around 30,000 CN (200 American dollars).

All the carts and wheelbarrows had squeaky wheels. Raymond told me one time that it meant either the owner cannot afford grease or he does not grease the wheel on purpose so that the squeaks will alert spirits and people to get out of the way.

Pavements gave way to unpaved areas on our walk. The streets were covered with slippery mud, but there seemed to be a slightly higher and drier place in the middle of the roads, so everyone wanted to use that. A little elbowing and we made it, laughingly.

Dirty, bare-bottomed boys played in mud puddles and made mud pies— "just like at home," I thought. Women with uncovered breasts nursed their babies. Small children anxiously waited for discarded watermelon rinds thrown away by those with enough money to buy melons. The children also collected the seeds spit on the sidewalks. These were taken home where they were boiled in salt water, dried, and eaten.

Farther on appeared shops selling pottery, electrical supplies, silks and cottons, tobaccos, baskets, and salt. We passed jewelry stores with expensive clocks; soap stores where homemade bars were piled several feet high on the sidewalks. Many places sold the Orient's magic medicine, ginseng, a root used for numerous things, even as a material for carving figurines. We passed a druggist's window with real seahorses displayed in little containers, and we passed a bathhouse where we viewed ourselves in a huge outside mirror. We stopped to watch a big construction job on a site where a few big bombs had hit a few days before. As usual, several Chinese had stopped to watch also and were already arguing about it.

Several fairly good-looking girls and their "business managers" met us head on. Commonly known as Temple Girls, they giggled as we passed. At each street's intersection were big earthenware jars about four feet high, which held water. The water was used to settle dust, fight fires, wash hands, and give children something to play with. There was always at least one "shao heitza" (small child) dabbling his hands in the water and swishing it on a play-mate. No one ever drank this water.

We observed a special machine that was busily making long thin strips of fresh noodles. This food was the main source of sustenance in northern China, while rice predominated in the south.

"These noodles will probably end up in a bowl of soup before the day is over," said Shorty.

Down one street we passed an open-air noodle restaurant that catered to the lower-class workers. Most of the customers seemed to be coolies, who were as brown as roasted coffee beans. Continuing on, we saw a hospital supply store where some wild-looking equipment was on display. Shorty and I differed as to what each of these strange "tools" could possibly be. Next door to this was a store window displaying a distillation still. It was for sale.

"So that's what Bishop Megan uses to make his guilang," I laughed.

"We ought to buy it and set up competition," said Shorty.

Many dogs roamed the streets, seemingly unowned and definitely uncared for since most had terrible skin diseases and were always skinny. Had I been the mayor of Sian I would have ordered 80 percent of the poor dogs killed and put out of their misery. They frequently ate the excrement of other dogs.

Shorty and I had heard about a good eating place called the Russian Restaurant. When we reached it, we wondered how it had gotten its name because there wasn't a Russian to be seen. The Chinese owner led us to the best table. The food was good, and the dessert was cocoa-flavored ice cream. A large, old, hanging mat fan was used for cooling. Suspended from the ceiling, the fan was pulled back and forth over us by a young boy, and it felt nice and cool. It was a simple and efficient air-moving device with no working parts to get out of order. It pleased several waiters to try out their few English words on us. We liked this restaurant and returned a number of times.

A melon merchant cried out in Chinese as we passed, "Americans!"

I stopped and called back, "You are Chinese!" Everyone around laughed.

Bags of Chinese mail were piled high on carts, and heavy fiber bags of millet flour were stacked on wheelbarrows. The latter were deftly handled by sturdy men wearing shoulder harnesses fastened to the handles of the wheelbarrow so that they could lift and better balance the heavy load.

A child played with a whistle that blew a paper wheel in a spinning motion. Musicians, much better than ordinary, marched down the street, and I was reminded of the Pied Piper as kids by the score followed them. The little girls wore dresses, but many of the little boys were as naked as jaybirds sitting on a fence in Kansas. Some of the children carried tiny cages containing crickets and grasshoppers that made a music all their own.

Numerous fortune tellers and public storytellers were popular with the people and always drew crowds. There were all kinds of beggars. We saw one woman beggar who cried continuously, making the tears run down her cheeks at will. A blind man with a deep-toned bell in his hand walked slowly down a sidewalk filled with people. He hit the bell with a small metal bar to warn people he could not see. He was quite tall and wore a kind of cloth saddlepack on his shoulders.

Shorty and I went back to our hotel after spending a memorable day in these unusual parts of one of China's great inland cities. We found that the group of musicians we thought so talented had also played for a military wedding at the hotel. We knew the day was a good luck day because weddings are only held on days that are proclaimed by a prophet or wise man to be fortuitous for a couple getting married. Hosts for the wedding reception invited us to join them. We did, of course, because not to accept a wedding invitation would show poor manners and be discourteous. Although the bride's dress was strictly Chinese, the groom's attire was European.

On August 7, "the Double Seven," autumn began in China, but hard rains continued and the weather remained hot and humid. One evening I was invited to dine at Mr. Rice's again. It was delicious, with excellent beef, waffles, and apple pie. Another dinner guest was Mr. Hensley, a civilian friend and perhaps a member of the Office of Strategic Services (OSS), who told of his experience when the merchant ship on which he was traveling was sunk by a Japanese warship. The crew and a few passengers were set adrift in lifeboats and a raft, and they were picked up ten days later, suffering from severe sunburn. They had been without food for five days, and only a pint or so of water remained.

On the first day of September, 1944, I received orders to report to Chungking. I knew that when I left Sian, I might never see the city again. It took fourteen and a half hours for me to get to Baoji on the Belgian train, the longest time I ever spent on that route. There I boarded a plane for Chungking, and among my traveling companions were Bo, Pag, Perril, and Coombs, who were also reporting to Chungking, presumably for further assignment. Coombs, a SACO man, had arrived in China only the previous week.

We left ground in a drizzle, and the visibility remained at zero for the entire trip. I was apprehensive about the landing strip in Chungking, which was in a narrow valley with very limited landing space. We all stopped talking as we started the descent and held our breaths. But our CNAC pilots landed right on the edge of the sandbar runway; they could not be praised enough for their skill and daring. When we turned to taxi back, I noticed the river was dry.

As I climbed the steps up to Chungking, I wondered what my next assignment would be. I was sure it would not be the plush duty of "Sian Courier."

## CHAPTER 9

# Loose Teeth
# On to Kanchow and
# Changchow

*September 1944—U.S. forces make an early raid on Iwo Jima, and Wake Island is raided.*
*October 1944—U.S. carrier strikes against Okinawa begin. Allied troops land at the mouth of Leyte Gulf.*

The climb up the familiar steep path took the starch out of me. My life in Sian had put me out of good climbing condition. A navy truck awaited to take us to Ti-li-ko, our base camp truck terminal, and transported us to the next upward climb. We had been in a constant drizzle since we landed, but I hardly noticed that I was dripping wet as I lugged all my gear, which seemed to weigh a ton, on the long walk up to Happy Valley.

It was good to get back to our primary base, where we had luxuries not available at other SACO camps or duty stations. For the first time in four months I could take American dollars and spend them in the Ship's Store. I bought a couple cartons of cigarettes, two pocket combs, three packages of razor blades, shaving cream, toothpaste, and, happily, flea powder. The cigarettes were the most important. Although a nonsmoker, I found that in China cigarettes were usually better than money for getting things.

I saw movies at the camp, and the chow was definitely better than what we had been eating lately. Once again we had stateside dinners weekly where we could eat with knives and forks instead of chopsticks. Southern fried chicken, pork chops, sweet and sour pork, and rice with scrambled eggs were welcome fare.

I was glad to see old friends again, like Bill Sharrard. Bill was a tall, good-looking, lanky fellow from Michigan; he looked like a sailor ought to look. A member of my draft of storekeepers, he was the fellow who found the Australian pound note in Melbourne and went to the horse races, winning six races in a row. As the commodore's driver and scrounger, he had a good assignment. He drove a jeep into Chungking daily, and sometimes more often. Some ten years after the war, Bill drowned in a storm on a small Michigan lake. Warren Higby, who was now a chief pharmacist, was still on duty as camp pharmacist. He was a good egg.

Happy Valley was the only camp that had a regular navy postmaster, Ens. Edward O'Toole. He was a fine person and hard worker, and he had his share of problems with wartime mail in China's interior. Once a truck carrying mail from Kunming went over a hill and landed in a stream of water. All the mail was soaked and barely readable, but O'Toole, using his experienced eye and powers of deduction, got about 95 percent of the letters and packages to where they belonged.

The second day at Happy Valley, I reported to the executive officer, who surprised me by asking, "Where would you like to be assigned next?" It stymied me.

"Let me know tomorrow," he said.

I was assigned a vacant room in one of the permanent buildings. The walls and floor had been whitewashed and sprayed with DDT. There were no bugs to be seen! When I returned to the exec's office the next day, I told him how pleased I was with my quarters.

"And, sir, I would like to be assigned to a camp that has a lot of activity."

The officer considered a moment, then advised me that a new camp was being set up and as soon as the organization table was firm, he would get in touch with me. In the meantime, I worked for three days with supply inventory paperwork, after which I was detailed once more to the "water watch." Some of the older kitchen help were still working there, so we greeted each other like old friends, and they shared such things as delicious sliced pineapple desserts with me.

The Chinese had a rock quarry operation on the mountain above us, so from early morning until late in the night, we could hear the ring of steel on stone. It was a plaintive pinging sound, followed by the quarryman's "Hayoo'o" or "Hay ho'oh." The soft rain did not slow the pinging cadence of the workmen or the call of the quarryman. I fell asleep to these sounds and their echoes every night as they rolled softly down the slopes to Happy Valley.

The area was blessed with heavy showers every day, and the streams, creeks, and rivers were filled again and flowing rapidly, which made everybody happy. When I first arrived in camp we saw many deeply dug holes in dried-up creek beds where people had gathered bowls of muddy water as it seeped into a pocket.

One afternoon the exec called me to his office. The word had finally come. The new camp was to be set up in southeast China not far from the coast.

"The Japanese are to the east of the campsite along the coast," he explained, and pointed to the map behind his desk. Far to the west of the campsite an inland railway paralleled the coast and supplied the Japanese forces in north and south Asia.

"You will be assigned to a coastwatcher's headquarters either in or near Changchow in Fukien Province. Be ready to leave in a week or ten days," he told me.

"The assignment suits me just fine," I smiled, and the executive officer shook my hand, wishing me luck.

On September 17, I bid Happy Valley and all my friends goodbye once again and boarded a C-47 plane for Kunming. There were only eight passengers and very little cargo, as the plane was on a return flight. Our seats were known as bucket seats, which ran lengthwise on either side of the cabin. Passengers in these seats sat with their backs to the windows.

The runway of Chungking's water-surrounded airfield was quite a bit shorter than normal because the river was high. There were sheer mountain walls on cither side of the plane, so the pilot had to swerve from the Chialing River to the left and follow the Yangtze River for a couple of miles while we gained altitude. Suddenly we were above the rivers and had a panoramic view of beautifully terraced rice paddies, vivid green trees, and foliage beginning to turn brown for autumn.

Before we reached Kunming, we ran into high winds and pelting rain, which presented a landing problem for our pilot. He touched ground, then at the very end of the runway, he turned the plane quickly. It tilted sharply to one side, and I was thrown against a reinforcing rib, smacking my face against the fuselage. My nose and mouth began bleeding, and several teeth were knocked loose. I was lucky that the navy had a dentist in Kunming, and that he proved to be one grand guy. He took me to the U.S. Army Air Force base nearby, where he appropriated their good dental facilities. He removed one tooth and a bridge and repaired another tooth.

"Don't eat any solid foods for several days," he told me, assuring me that the other teeth would tighten up by themselves.

During my first night in Kunming, a rat chewed his way through my musette bag and took my piece of tropical chocolate. I guess he knew I couldn't eat it anyway. The next morning, the dentist checked my mouth and gave me some sedatives for relief from the pain.

That night I began by killing a spider that measured five inches across. A second one climbed up into the rafters and made me nervous. I don't know which was worse, the rat or the spiders, but it was a long time before I dozed off.

In the morning I received my new mailing address and a notice to be ready to leave the next day. The executive officer informed me that I would have a storekeeper third class accompany me and that I would carry five million Chinese dollars, along with some ammunition and miscellaneous gear. These items were to be delivered to the commanding officer at Chienyang in northern Fukien Province, and then I would continue to my new station in southern Fukien. When I reported to the plane next day, they were loading 144 carbines that no one had mentioned to me. The navy man loading the gear explained that I could tell the difference between the ammunition and money boxes by their heft. For the next several days, I thought a lot about the responsibility I had.

We left Kunming at 6:00 A.M. under a cloud that could hardly have been more than 4,000 feet off the ground. In a little under three hours, we landed at Liuchow (Liuzhou), then took off again under the cloud cover. I saw a wrecked plane below us on a hillside and told the pilot. He flew back and over it, but we saw no signs of life, so we continued. Shortly after that we spotted a small plane in the distance and immediately climbed into the clouds. The ride became very bumpy and my traveling mate, Verdi, and the two other military passengers became airsick. I lay face down with my stomach draped across the strapped-down cargo where I could look out the window. There was nothing but foggy whiteness. When we landed at Kanchow (Ganzhou) after another two and a half hours, the other three continued to heave their guts.

We were at a supporting U.S. Army airfield located in a pretty area surrounded by small pine trees. The first thing asked of me when I reported to the mess hall for a good meal was the usual question: "What the hell is the navy doing around here?" We had a real banquet that evening in celebration of the evacuation of the entire field. Already 90 percent of the air force personnel and equipment had been shipped out, and the balance was scheduled to leave in a few days.

I had scarcely crawled into my sack for a good night's sleep when the air raid siren sounded, so I got back into my shirt and pants, shoes, ammo belt, .45 and carbine, and out to the closest slit trench. Seven of us were there, waiting, when we heard the sound of a plane's characteristic "Vroom, vroom, vroom." An enemy plane dropped a brilliant flare that swung gently to one side and then to the other, lighting up the whole airfield and landing at one end of the runway. A few minutes later we heard the muffled roar of heavier aircraft in bomber formation. Another flare was dropped, and we could see tracer bullets near the end of the runway flying skyward.

"What in the hell is that?" asked someone.

To which another replied, "That's that crazy medical doctor firing. He's not supposed to do that!"

Then a machine gun opened up, and we could see his tracers reach into the sky again. The doctor was shooting back at the Japanese planes with a machine gun!

Suddenly the air was filled with the heavy engine sound, and "kaboom!" The airfield was being hit with exploding bombs. We had a good view of the action from our trench on a slight hill, pointed in the direction of the field. I saw a string of bombs exploding and heading in our direction. We all started counting, "one, two, three, four." When the fifth one hit very close, we hunched down as deep as we could. We heard number six, then someone yelled, "no, no." The ground vibration was terrific, and we breathlessly waited for the next one, which we expected to fall right on top of us. We waited, and waited.

Finally someone shouted, "The son of a bitch ran out of shit!"

A moment later one of the fellows piped up, "He might have, but I sure as hell didn't!" That broke us up in laughter, relieving the tension.

A second wave of bombers came about five minutes later. They had another soft flare to guide them. This time we didn't experience the severe moments of tension we had earlier. The field got plastered again, but this time the doctor's machine gun was silent. There were no major explosions from a hit on any ammunition or fuel cache. In about twenty minutes the all-clear siren sounded.

We went back to our quarters and had just settled ourselves into our sacks when the damned alert sounded shrilly again. We entrenched ourselves for the second time. This time two small planes dropped flares and flew away. We waited until we heard the all-clear sound again. This time we slept the remainder of the night.

The few airmen who were left and Verdi and I were up early for a good breakfast of thick smoked ham and eggs. The best part was the white bread, butter, and coffee! I had not had a good cup of coffee for over a month. The cook announced at breakfast that there would be only two more meals served at the base. The cook, of course, would leave with the forty men who planned to pull out on this day or the next. There was a sense of urgency in the air.

A plane landed on the least damaged part of the runway in late morning, and who should walk out but Sinks, the aerographer that I had last seen in Chungking! The plane took off as soon as its cargo was unloaded. Sinks, who was escorting a large and heavy Raytheon weather machine, and two other passengers would continue their journey by truck. The truck would be there before noon, assured my Chinese contact. Sure enough, Sinks left by midday for Chienyang. This left only fifteen airmen on the base, along with Verdi and me.

We sat around in the shade of the pine trees, talked, and lied to pass the time. An air force sergeant recounted the story of a navy commander who passed through the airfield several weeks previously. He had about fifty enlisted men who seemed to get themselves into constant trouble. Every time a complaint was lodged against one of the enlisted men, the navy commander ordered his entire complement to run up and down a nearby steep hill twice a day. It was supposed to be training as well as punishment. This was the commander married to the motion picture star and the author of the book *Delilah*.

"But we all felt sorry for those navy guys," said the sergeant. I gazed over at the hill.

"Think I'll go look at that hill," I said.

I took it easy, but it still was a good climb to the top. Once there, the view was panoramic. The hill stood in the midst of a pine forest. On the way down I found a flashlight, two clips of tommy gun ammo, six tubes of toothpaste, and four packages of razor blades. Evidently, the navy men had to run up the hill with full packs. Around the camp, I gathered up other abandoned army air force supplies, which I intended to take with me. I found enough tubes of shaving cream in the wash house to last me a long time.

"What we can't take with us, Verdi," I said, "will go to either the Chinese or Japanese, whoever arrives first."

After the last meal in the mess hall, with good coffee again, the cook gave me two jars of Nescafé, a few cans of Spam, and some yellow mustard, for which I thanked him profusely. There was a Chinese boy who washed dishes and set the table. I wondered where he would go after the camp's total evacuation.

By evening only three officers, two radiomen, a sergeant, and the cook remained in camp. I heard that the doctor who had fired the machine gun at the planes had been slightly injured and had been flown out for medical treatment.

We were now entirely dependent on Chinese air raid warnings for our safety. Two Chinese Army men manned a signal tower with the yardarm balls. I learned that only one plane in a revetment had been hit the night before. Before the sergeant and other airmen left they blew up the plane and runways. One officer told me the camp had been bombed for eight straight nights! Chinese coolies were kept busy repairing the holes in the runways.

We had no alert the second night, although I did hear a plane fly over before I went to sleep. The next morning two army airplanes came in, loaded up some gear, and took off. Radio equipment was the last to go. The last air force officer expressed concern about our safety.

"We estimate there'll be 400 Japanese troops arriving here in forty-eight to sixty hours; you can't remain here," he told us anxiously.

"Our Chinese friends will take care of us," I replied as he and the last radioman boarded the plane that had just landed. They waved to us as they cleared the field. Verdi and I were the last Americans at the site. We had the evacuated airfield to ourselves. There were only a few Chinese to be seen. The last thing I thought before I fell asleep was that our Chinese truck had better be there in the morning.

At daybreak on September 21, our driver arrived in a 1934 Dodge truck, which was not in the best condition. It had seen hard wear, but he assured us it would get us to our destination. A mechanic worked on the motor while several coolies loaded our gear. Like any military installation it was near a Chinese village of sorts, and there were always a few Chinese around. We filled the truck tanks with gasoline and also loaded two drums of aviation fuel that had been left at the field. We were overloaded and had only about two feet of space on the top of the load under the raised cloth cover over the truck bed. I didn't want to leave anything behind, so Verdi and I realized that we would have to ride in spread-eagle fashion under the cloth top.

The mechanic, who was still working on the truck, brought an elderly, well-mannered, nicely dressed Chinese man to see me that evening. He indicated he wanted to talk to me in private.

"Will you walk with me?" he asked. I nodded. He spoke very good English. We walked slowly around the quiet campsite.

He said he knew of the fifty-six drums of gasoline remaining in one of the hangars, which we could not take with us.

"Are you under orders to destroy these drums?"

"No," I replied.

"Would you be willing to sell them to me?" he asked.

"No. The gasoline belongs to the U.S. Army Air Force and it is not mine to sell."

"I will pay you 56,000 American dollars," he offered, talking slowly and almost in a whisper. He looked at me anxiously.

I hesitated.

"If you do not sell me the gasoline, the Nippons will take it in a day or two."

He held out an attaché case to me, but I would not take it. Then he opened it. It was filled with crisp green hundred-dollar and fifty-dollar American bills arranged neatly in packets. Here was the opportunity of a lifetime. Who would ever know?

"Please accept," he continued trying to persuade. "The gasoline will be removed quickly, and the Nippons will not get it."

His argument and logic were going through my conscience. I certainly did not want the Japanese to have our gasoline, so valuable in this war. My mind was working like a trip hammer. I had never seen that much money at one time before in my life. I asked myself what would happen if I took the money and somehow was found out. It would mean a court-martial and prison, to say nothing of the disgrace. Was it worth the risk? I reached into his attaché case and picked up one of the packets of the large-denomination bills.

Suddenly I made myself say, "No. I can't do it." Once I had decided, it was easy to put my crazy idea aside. The Chinese gentleman closed the attaché case, and we parted politely.

The next morning the first thing I did was to destroy as much of that gasoline as I could. I set a charge of Composition C on one of the drums in the hangar, opened several other drums, and placed two #8 caps in the plastic comp. I lit a fuse of five minutes' duration. Then I ran. About four minutes later there was a big explosion. At first it looked like there would not be the fire I had wanted, but suddenly it took hold and the drums and hangar were a mass of flames. Still, the fire did not have the intensity I had hoped it would, and I knew that all the drums had not been destroyed. But it was the best I could do. I wondered if the elderly one would claim these after we left.

I went back to the truck to find the mechanic having trouble getting the engine started. A little later another truck rumbled up; the coolies transferred everything to it, and we were on our way by early afternoon. We had only Spam to eat all day and were anxious to find someplace where we could get a bite to eat. This second truck operated principally on charcoal gas, using gasoline only as auxiliary fuel on steep hills. The charcoal, which was fired in the bottom of an old hot water tank, was mounted vertically on the truck's running board to the rear of the driver's seat. It gave off a gas that was fed into the engine, where it functioned as a source of weak fuel, just powerful enough to move us along a level road. The tank resembled the old-fashioned gas hot water heaters that once sat in American kitchens on a cast-iron pedestal and reminded me of the power-propulsion devices we had seen in Australia.

Once we got started, we didn't stop until almost midnight and made about 120 miles. We were in a small village that had one primitive Jao da Sol, composed of two mud rooms with thatched roof. Our pillows were of ancient style: four inches wide and twelve inches long and solid as any rock. Actually, I could use them only if I slept on my side. They smelled from many coats of varnish-like tung oil, which the Chinese applied to such pillows. I was tired enough to sleep.

SACO men could sleep anywhere, I thought. Many times Admiral Miles's description of SACO men was to pass through my mind. "My men are flexible in any area or situation," he said, close-mouthed, "able to get along with people of any race or rank, extremely tough with inexhaustible endurance, and they have to be slightly crazy."

We had a big breakfast of fried rice and fried eggs with a hard biscuitlike bread. We made excellent time, traveling in mostly level country in a north-easterly direction. Several times the overloaded truck would not make it over a moderate hill. So the mechanic would hop out and place a chock under a back wheel. Then he would add charcoal to the fire and turn the crank that operated as a bellows. When he thought sufficient gas had been generated, he started up the truck, and away we would go up the hill. The mechanic's job was to grab the chock, run to catch up, and hop into his cab seat.

On the few long steep hills, the driver would listen until the engine failed to turn, then he would turn on a petcock valve located on a tank over his head. This allowed gasoline to flow into the engine on a gravity-feed basis. Then the truck would really get pep and would take the hill with zip to spare! Needless to say, the driver was quite stingy with his gasoline, using it only when absolutely necessary.

Verdi and I had no choice but to ride in our spread-eagle fashion, which was very tiring. Our next night's lodging was in a Catholic mission presided over by a Father Degman, formerly of Chicago. He shared a meal of rice and pork, soup, and a rice pudding with us and gave us sleeping accommodations in the mission: a cubicle room with a bare cot and a washstand. Verdi and I left a contribution with him, for which he was very grateful.

Another full day of travel, and we arrived at a village called Lichwan, where we were welcomed at a mission by Father Byrne. He had a hot shower ready for us, a good dinner, the usual accommodations, and a fine breakfast. It was almost noon before we left, because the truck needed repairs. Whenever we stopped we inquired about our man Sinks, who had left the air force base before us, but no one had seen or heard of him. We finally caught up with him at Chienyang, a SACO field operation.

Our next night's stop was at a beautiful and picturesque German Catholic mission where Bishop Dermody was a gracious host. The large mission was surrounded by gardens lush with flowers, plants, shrubbery, and many small pools. It was like a park within the compound. Our austere sleeping rooms had solid wooden beds, a chair, a washstand, and a pitcher of water with a basin. There were no pictures on the walls, no floor coverings, no lights, no chair cushions, no closet. A few pegs driven into the wall served as hooks for our clothing.

The food served by Bishop Dermody and the other four priests was adequate. They were amused when I attempted to use my limited German. The bishop was concerned about Japanese movement in the area, and he was afraid he would be forced to evacuate the mission. He and his staff had already been told by the Chinese government that they were restricted to the mission and the nearby village of Kuanno, where a Chinese Army base was located.

I went into Kuanno and spoke with the Chinese general on behalf of the German missionary, who wanted to remain in the mission. Through an interpreter, the general told me that if the priests left their compound, his troops would take over the mission for his headquarters. I never learned whether I had helped the German priest or not.

While in the village, I examined a pillbox that had been constructed by Chinese soldiers at the main intersection of Kuanno. Eighty percent of this defense construction was below ground; it faced the four different directions, and I knew it would be hard to capture if properly manned. The soldiers appeared to be well disciplined and alert. We spent one night at the mission, then left after a breakfast of bread fried in egg batter and served with honey.

When we arrived at the SACO compound in Chienyang at 4:00 P.M., I immediately turned in the money and supplies to Lieutenant Morgan. I was glad to be rid of the banknotes and the responsibility.

Chienyang was in a precarious military position because the Japanese army was less than fifty miles away. Chienyang was teeming with Chinese generals and their troops. Verdi and I were assigned quarters at the small U.S. Navy disbursing point, and welcomed the opportunity to take a hot bath, shave, and change clothing. Our meals consisted of pancakes and honey for breakfast and for supper. I got a haircut and secured medicine for my athlete's foot, which had been bugging me for a couple of weeks. At this small, busy post there were six radiomen, and at least two were on duty around-the-clock.

My new assignment was Changchow (Zhanzhou) located up the river from the strategic coastal island of Amoy (Xiamen) in southern Fukien Province. Verdi was to head off in another direction. My new traveling companion was Cosgrove, a radioman who was to be a coastwatcher assigned to our Changchow unit. We waited five days for the truck that would take us, with pieces of various equipment, weapons, ammunition, and medical supplies to Camp Six. In addition, Lieutenant Morgan entrusted me with two million of the five million CN to be used for expenses at the new camp where I was going. Sinks was told to wait in Chienyang for a week or two and then follow me to the new Camp Four with his bulky Raytheon aerological equipment.

On October 1 at 8:00 A.M., Cosgrove and I climbed on top of the cargo in the back of the open, bumpy truck and watched Sinks fade into a dusty Chinese sunset.

# CHAPTER 10

# Riding the River to Hua'an

*October 1944—U.S. carrier strikes begin against Okinawa. Allied troops land at the mouth of Leyte Gulf. Battle for Leyte Gulf is a Japanese attempt to stop American occupation of the Philippines. The Japanese begin their desperate kamikaze attacks on U.S. aircraft carriers.*

One reason we were glad to leave Chienyang was to get away from the pancakes and honey, which had been stepped up to three times a day! This was in spite of the fact that when traveling, sometimes Cosgrove and I didn't eat at all. Cosgrove was a good radioman, but he was terrified of water buffalo.

We had a good driver and a good truck. Rain followed us most of the way to Nanping, a fair-sized city with an excellent hotel. We were soaked to the skin by the time we arrived. A Chinese officer appeared with men to guard the truck and its contents during the night, but nevertheless, I lugged the two million CN into my sleeping room.

While getting the truck ready for departure the next morning, we saw about eighty Chinese prisoners being marched down the main street of Nanping in the custody of soldiers. The prisoners had chains fastened to rings encircling their ankles, with connecting chains strung up and fastened to large rings around their necks. They wore ragged clothes and were the most pitiful bunch of humanity I ever saw. Sores, wounds, scabs, and dirt covered their skinny bodies.

"They're army deserters and robbers," the truck driver told me.

In the afternoon our truck broke down, so we walked back to a small village we had just passed and found an inn for the night. I slept with my clothes on.

A replacement truck didn't arrive until nearly sundown the next day. Things like this were very mysterious, and I never found out how our Chinese compadres knew when we needed help. They appeared almost out of nowhere; whatever their system of communication was, it was working. Another puzzlement was that the broken-down truck was not carrying the homing pigeons normally used to send for help.

Unloading and reloading the trucks took considerable time because we could not obtain additional help. We depended a great deal on local Chinese or military help when we were in villages and towns, but neither were here on this lonely road. The driver, helper, Cosgrove, and I did the unloading and reloading.

We slept a second night in our clothes on the truck along the roadside, and started again at daybreak. We were in mountainous country where the roads were narrow, steep, dusty, and full of hairpin curves. Still taking a southeasterly route toward the coast, we made it up the steeper mountains fairly well because this truck did not have charcoal-generated fuel. Once a Ford truck came up swiftly behind us, then passed with such speed we thought we were standing still. That truck flew up the hill with what appeared to be a full load.

Our next night's stop was at a tiny settlement called Yungan (Yong'an), where an American army officer with the War Information Department was quartered. Lieutenant Hopkins arranged quarters for us in a four-room hotel. He indicated that he knew we were from the Office of Naval Intelligence, and he was definitely seeking information. I remembered the briefing during which we were told what to say and what not to say at just such a chance encounter. So we did very little talking while eating dinner with the lieutenant that evening and left the next morning at 8:45.

Our lunch stop was at Ta T'ao, where I was pleasantly surprised to find "pei tong" (white sugar). This was the whitest and cleanest of any sugar I had seen in China, so I promptly bought five catties. A catty was one and one-third pounds. Normally we depended on "tonga," a basic sugarcane sweetener that had hundreds of fine slivers mixed in it, giving it a brownish appearance. When I stirred a spoonful of this sugar in a cup of tea the thin slivers would float to the top, and I could then remove them before drinking the tea. If you had a good mustache, you could remove most of the slivers by drinking through your whiskers, a skill I developed later on when I grew a mustache and goatee.

By evening we rumbled into the jumping-off town of Lungyen (Longyan), the farthest point the truck could take us. Here we were met by two navy junior lieutenants, Lovell and Jantzen, and two enlisted men, all of whom had been waiting for us. They needed our supplies to help set up the new Camp Six downriver from Lungyen. Malcolm Lovell was to be one of my closest SACO associates during the remainder of my tour in China, which was more than a year. We also would visit after the war when we returned to the States. He went on to become the Assistant Secretary of Labor in the Department of Labor in Washington, D.C., and took me to lunch when I retired from the Veterans Administration in 1971.

Lovell was about 5 feet 10 inches, with light hair; but when he grew a beard in China, it was reddish bronze. He was a graduate of Brown University and had been sent by the navy to Harvard to take a business course. Using this training, he set up files and office procedures for Camp Six, so the first thing he did when we were settling in was to order several desks, chairs, filing cabinets, and the largest cash box I ever saw. We could have kept a 400-pound hog in it. Lovell, who presented an air of boyishness, had the habit of pacing the floor, musing and not speaking, when he had a problem to solve.

"Where is your assignment?" Lovell asked me.

"Changchow," I answered.

He said he was going to set up a supply and disbursing operation for the southern half of Fukien Province in Hua'an.

"I sure would like for you to be assigned to my office."

"My orders, sir, say Changchow, and that is where I must report," I explained. "I understand that is the base of the Coastwatcher's Unit, where I am set up for duty."

Lovell, Jantzen, and the enlisted men left on the first leg of their journey to the Camp Six site on two sampans loaded with supplies. Cosgrove and I waited two days for the return of these sampans for our own trip down the river. In the meantime we found rooms in Lungyen's only hotel in the center of the town and directly across from a market, which opened very early in the morning. Vendors sold bamboo shoots, various vegetables, which were in good supply, and tobacco leaves. The tobacco leaves were low-quality and were placed around plants to keep bugs from eating the new shoots that emerged from the ground. Cosgrove and I ate a lot of bananas, which looked green but tasted ripe, and pomelos, a new kind of fruit to us. Pomelos were about the size of a grapefruit, but had very thick skins which made them hard to peel. The edible meat of the pomelos came in segments, like an orange. Although they were not as juicy as oranges, their taste was excellent, their odor slightly piquant.

Early the second morning, we were awakened by the babble of the vendors. It was the biggest market day of the week. It was pleasant getting up at 5:00

A.M. to enjoy the early morning freshness. The tobacco man explained that some part of the tobacco plant was steeped in water and the juice or dilution sprayed on cotton plants. This was the China where they squeezed everything to the limit for possible use. Nothing was wasted.

On the third morning, we were told that our sampans were at the dock. Cosgrove and I boarded one sampan with two boatmen and part of the gear, and the remainder of the gear and two boatmen followed in the other sampan. Both boats were heavily loaded and sat low in the water. At 11:15 the boatmen steered the sampans toward a small landing and tied up. Many porters were waiting. They unloaded the boats and placed the gear, supplies, and other goods in slings and on yo-yo poles to carry them up the mountain path that loomed in front of us. We started climbing the mountain, the second step in our journey to Hua'an.

The path was good, but I was amazed at the ability of a 120-pound man to carry nearly 150 pounds up the steep path. Each porter carried a box of ammunition on one end of the yo-yo pole and other gear on the other end. Some carried two boxes of ammo. We were getting nearer Japanese-occupied territory. The boxes of carbines were carried between two carriers. I carried my musette bag, ammunition belt, .45, and carbine, and found my own load heavy.

When we reached the short level stretches, the carriers would fall into a certain timed gait that caused the shoulder poles or yo-yos to bounce up and down a few inches in exact cadence with their steps. At the top of the mountain, we all stopped for a rest. The air was cool, and the magnificent view extended for miles and miles in every direction. Cosgrove and I gave each of the carriers half of an American cigarette, which made them happy.

That night we were shown to the second floor of an unoccupied round wood blockhouse, built like a fort or tower, in the village of Gansee, located on the other side of the mountain we had climbed. Just as things were getting settled for the night a middle-aged Chinese man climbed the stairs, poked his head into our large room and said in English, "What can I do for you?"

After talking to us for some time, he revealed that he was a schoolteacher who had never had an English lesson. He said he taught himself as best he could by reading English books and pronouncing words using a hit-or-miss approach. He was a remarkable man with a wonderful memory, and worthy of the highest respect. He said he made it a point to talk to every American or English-speaking person that came through his small village, so that he could exercise his pronunciation of words. We invited him to be our guest for dinner. He was overjoyed and accepted. He said his name was Mr. Mao (Horse). He arranged to have two local soldiers stand guard at the door of the blockhouse while we ate.

The only restaurant in Gansee was an open-air affair. Its most reliable food was chicken, eggs, and pork with rice. I ordered "chee" (chicken) for three. The cook picked out a chicken, killed it right there, dressed it, and deftly halved it. He was about to slap each half with the broadside of his cleaver when I jumped up and stopped him. I showed him how I wanted it cut and separated at the joints. He began laughing and continued laughing all the time we were eating, but he followed my directions.

There was no enjoyment, at least by us "foreign devils," in eating Chinese-style fried chicken with its hundreds of small, splintered bones. I always had to dig out the bones from my mouth, somewhat like eating unboned fish. This time I wanted *our* kind of fried chicken. The cook deep-fried the chicken in a huge wok and served it with rice and tea, which was very tasty. The schoolteacher seemed to enjoy our style of fried chicken as much as we did. I should add that schoolteachers throughout China have a loyal following, and we saw people follow our new friend just to listen to him talk to us.

After supper, the teacher checked on our sampans and showed us where they would be waiting for us in the morning. He arranged for carriers and walked with us back to the roundhouse. There was a trapdoor at the top of the first floor's steps; so, for security's sake, we closed it and slept on it.

There was only one sampan available in the morning, but it was a large one with three boatmen. The teacher was up early, supervising prompt loading of our gear. We left him and the village of Gansee at 6:30 A.M., and within five minutes we shot our first rapids on the Nine Dragons River.

I saw the falls coming, and yelled to Cosgrove, "Look out, we're going over!" We went over the breast of a dam and down into the rapids created by the dam's overflow. At the bottom of the sluice the river was calm, and a brisk current carried us easily down the river.

The boatmen used their oars now and then, but for the most part we glided along smoothly. Each bend of the river was like a mountain road's curves: I wondered what was coming up. As we went around one bend bounded by high trees on both sides, Cosgrove suddenly grabbed his carbine, stood up, and took three shots before I knew what was happening. I had my own carbine in hand by this time. There was a monstrous bird sitting on the topmost branch of a very tall tree.

"I'll get him," I yelled to Cosgrove. Then I told the men to stop rowing. The bird just sat there about 100 yards away. As we glided slowly through the water,

I fired one shot, bringing the bird crashing earthward through the branches. He landed in the grass and one of the boatmen immediately dove overboard and began swimming toward the shore. The other two boatmen held up their thumbs in a gesture of "Ding hao," and Cosgrove said, "That was a damn good shot, Mish." The swimmer never came back, so we were minus one boatman, and nobody explained it. I would have liked to have seen the bird he went after.

The remainder of the day the river was beautiful and the air exhilarating. By nighttime we had tied up at Chen Ping, where coolies transferred all our gear to another sampan we were to use the next day. A Chinese lieutenant appeared from the village and assigned two soldiers to watch our shipment. He said one of the soldiers would accompany us on the next leg of our journey. We found a small hotel where we ate fried chicken (with the broken bones inside) and warm red wine.

At 6:00 A.M. the next day, we boarded our vessel and began gliding smoothly out into the river again. The river soon emptied into a large body of water, which could only be described as a lake. We watched a fisherman who had lashed two large bamboo tree trunks together for a raft and had, as his fishing helpers, several trained cormorants. It was fascinating to watch the birds as they dove off the raft into the water. When they came up, they had fish in their beaks and took them to the fisherman. He would remove them and put them in a basket. Sometimes, however, the cormorants would jump up on the bamboo raft with their catch, then quickly gulp down the fish. I realized that a pattern or procedure was in effect. For every three fish that a cormorant gave the fisherman, it could eat one. I later learned that a fisherman trained a young bird by tying a string around its neck so it could catch a fish but not swallow it. After the fisherman collected three fish, he removed the string so the cormorant could swallow the fourth. After enough training, a cormorant learned to bring three fish to the fisherman, after which he was allowed to eat the fourth one.

Our boatmen let us watch this fishing endeavor for a while and then continued down the Nine Dragons River. Soon the lake narrowed and the current became stronger, and stronger! The rapids were breathtaking. Only the expertise of the boatmen kept us from crashing into large rocks that stuck up in the middle of the stream or jutted out from the banks. The river was now no more than seventy feet wide. White water was everywhere! Like knights of old on their chargers, the boatmen used poles to fend off the perilous rocks.

By this time I had taken off my ammo belt, the .45, and my shoes, just in case I landed in the river; although, as I later recalled, it would have made no difference. If I went into the river, I knew everything would go. After about thirty minutes of this hell-bent-for-election ride, the river became smooth again. It was three o'clock in the afternoon when, to our relief, we pulled up to a small dock. We had arrived at Hua'an.

I had hardly stepped off the sampan when I saw Lieutenant Lovell walking down to the wharf. He began shaking my hand.

"I'm really glad to see you," he said. "I got your orders changed, and you are to remain with me in Hua'an."

It was apparent that I would now get a chance to do a little disbursing duty at Camp Six, which was to be the principal navy group in southeast China. Actually, the camp was to be finally located about three miles downriver from Hua'an; but while Chinese workmen built the camp, we operated out of the small village.

Our first quarters were in a building that formed a square around a court-yard. A porch with a railing ran along the entire length of the second floor with a protruding roof for shelter. We were all put up on the second floor, while several Chinese families lived on the first floor. We could see all village activities from our quarters.

Hua'an was located in a valley surrounded by mountains; there was very little flat land for farming, but there were many rice paddies, where water buffalo were as common as cattle on a midwest U.S. farm. The paddies also were breeding grounds for mosquitoes and leeches. The mosquitoes in our valley were legendary, reminding me of the story in Admiral Miles's book on SACO. The first men in SACO adopted the mosquito as their mascot and drew a big one on their first emblem, calling him "Saco." Said Admiral Miles:

> One day when several of us had gone to Chungking and were at work at Fairy Cave, we caught Webb Heagy standing on the terrace studying the unusual number of planes that were lined up beside the river airstrip far below our hilltop.
> "What's on your mind, Webb?" I asked.
> "Some of those planes," he began, "have army numbers. Some have CNAC (China National Airways Corporation) insignia. And some aren't marked at all. Now you may not believe it, but the ones without any numbers or insignia are mosquitoes that have managed to get into that formation."

General Lui was the Chinese commander for this region of the Fukien Province. A short, likable man, this general was directly under Gen. Tai Li.

When I arrived in Hua'an there were five naval personnel in the temporary camp in the village, including Warrant Officer Andrews, who was a radio and communications specialist. He was suffering from what turned out to be cerebral malaria and returned to the States about a month after I arrived.

General Lui assigned a cook to our camp, who began serving chicken meat that was black as well as white. It was not just dark meat; it was *black* meat. Since I had been put in charge of the cook, I told him that Americans did not like black chicken meat, that we wanted white meat or none at all. He patiently explained that the Chinese considered this black meat a delicacy because it cost more than white meat. Nevertheless, we had white chicken meat.

Then we noticed that our eggs had a strong taste. Upon investigating, I discovered that the cook was buying duck eggs, whose yolks had a stronger taste than chicken egg yolks. Again, I had my way and we switched to chicken eggs.

From then on I accompanied the cook when he bought chicken or pork. I was not above believing that he was getting a "cumshaw" (payoff) from the sellers in Hua'an in one form or another. Our cook became a big man in town because soon we were the biggest buyers in the market and the merchants were anxious for our cook's trade.

The meat business in the village began at daybreak when a freshly slaughtered pig would be brought into the market and hung on a tripod. The butcher would then slice or cut off what each customer wanted. I found it interesting to watch a person buy a narrow strip of pork, perhaps one inch by eight inches and one-half to one inch thick. The butcher would select and twist several strands of rice straw together to fashion a thin string that was twisted around the purchased meat. Then he fashioned a small loophole in one end of the straw strand so that a person could put a finger through the hole in order to carry the item. This was done very dexterously. Finally the butcher collected his money and slipped the loop over the buyer's forefinger. The customer walked proudly toward his home holding the piece of meat out in front so all could see that he and his family would be eating pork that day.

Once our cook baked a very good pineapple-banana pie and another time a sweet-potato pie. Sweet potatoes were quite common in our area, but white potatoes, "young yee," were very scarce. We felt lucky to be able to get some now and then, usually from places where the missionaries planted and harvested them. The white potatoes caught on a little bit, and a few Chinese decided they liked them and began to grow them.

Another item that I bought regularly in the village was candles. The village supply ran out after one week, and our lighting situation was so poor that I would have to journey to surrounding villages to buy the valuable candles. I had to wait, however, until the return of Lieutenant Lovell, who had gone downriver to Changchow.

The week after I arrived, two radiomen came through Hua'an and dropped off a ton of supplies and equipment before proceeding on to Changchow for assignments to a coastwatcher team. To make sure all the equipment stayed in our hands, we established three storage points, or "godowns": two in the hills near Hua'an and one in the center of Hua'an. They were referred to as #1, #2, and #3. It was my responsibility to maintain inventories of each godown, but it was the Chinese Army's duty to guard all units.

Battle activity increased around us. Our B-29s flew overhead in steady streams to bomb Formosa, and our navy radio reported a big naval battle off Formosa island. One day shortly after a B-29 return flight over Hua'an, we heard loud explosions in the mountains. Later we learned the crew of the plane had jettisoned bombs that, due to a malfunction, it had been unable to release over the Formosa targets.

A storekeeper and a pharmacist arrived from Chungking via Chienyang on their way to Changchow, dropping off nearly a ton of carbines and ammunition. I was amused when they told me about a great restaurant in Gansee where they were served fried chicken American style (cut up at the joints). They reported it as the best they had ever had in China.

I was awakened about one o'clock one morning by Dr. Coleman, who said that Andrews was seriously ill and who asked me to go to godown #3, break open the #7 box, and take from it a smaller box marked Unit 12. He put a sample bottle in my hand so I would be sure to get the right drug. While I dressed, "Pop" Cannon in the bunk next to me awakened.

"Want me to go with you, Mish?"

"Sure," I replied.

Pop walked behind me since I carried the flashlight. We went up a cobblestone path that wound through the rice paddies and continued into one of the small valleys where the godown was located. I knew there would be four soldiers on guard, as usual, so I planned to identify myself and Pop before approaching too suddenly. I did not want to get shot.

Our path hugged the edge of a bank on the right side; and as the path made a little bend, my flashlight beam picked up a huge snake gliding down off the bank and across our path. I stopped abruptly, and Pop bumped into me, saying, "What in the hell are you stopping for?"

I just held the light on the snake. "Oh, my God!" he said.

Moving very slowly and fluidly, the snake appeared to be about five inches in diameter and perhaps fifteen feet long. As yet, I had not seen its head. Its unusual orange markings were sharp and distinctive in the light, illuminating like a reflecting sign. I took aim with my .45 and shot the snake in the belly. The bullet hit a cobblestone and ricocheted upward, tearing a big hole in the snake's side. My second shot hit it directly, and the creature began whipping about, then tumbled down over the side of the path into a rice paddy.

"You're crazy," said Pop. "If I'd had the flashlight and saw that snake, I'd have run the other way."

We continued on the path for another five minutes or so until we were suddenly challenged.

"Naga!" (Halt!) We were near the godown.

"Mei Guo bien, Mei Guo bien!" I called out, meaning "We are American soldiers."

In a minute, out of the darkness came one of General Lui's officers, pistol drawn. He recognized me and called out an order that was repeated several times by lower-ranking men. I explained our task to the officer, who spoke a little English, whereupon he and four soldiers accompanied us to the godown. Again, we were challenged by guards as we approached the building entrance. The officer called back. Once inside the godown, I broke open Box #7 and took the smaller box inside, which I brought back with me to Dr. Coleman.

At breakfast, Pop enjoyed telling everyone never to volunteer to go out with Mishler at night.

"He's crazy; he shoots big snakes."

Our outside toilet in the Hua'an temporary camp consisted of a large, open rectangular pit about six by eight feet and six feet deep. Four pairs of bamboo poles were stretched across the narrow width, each set spaced about twelve inches apart. Then the next set was about two feet away. We had to shuffle in on a set of poles with short steps, turn around, drop our pants, and then stoop. When we finished we precariously stood up, buttoned our pants, and then shuffled again off the bamboo poles to firm ground. The pit was thatched on three sides for privacy and had a thatched roof. During slack-use hours, the Chinese farmers collected the greenish, watery excretion in buckets to fertilize their gardens. This was the night soil we had heard about and the navy's reason for the taboo on eating fresh vegetables.

One early morning as I entered the enclosure in the half-light of dawn, I noticed something balanced precariously on one of the big bamboo poles. It was a wallet that, evidently, had fallen from an earlier visitor's trousers and was miraculously balanced on the thin round surface. I edged myself ever so carefully to a position where I could reach it. I opened it and read the name of the owner as Wasinski, one of the new gunnery mates that had recently arrived. It contained over 200 American dollars plus some large denomination Chinese notes. When I returned to our quarters, Wasinski was just getting up.

"Wasinski, did you use the toilet during the night?" I asked.

"Yes, why?"

"Have you lost anything?"

He replied, "No, I don't think so."

I handed him the wallet. He was totally surprised, but grateful, and later tried to give me fifty dollars, which I refused. The thought occurred to me that if the wallet had fallen into the pit, he would always have thought that someone had stolen it. It also occurred to me that if a farmer had scooped it up without seeing it, he might have a "cash crop" that season, or possibly a money tree!

The following day we began moving to the permanent site for Camp Six three miles downriver from Hua'an. Andrews asked me to take down the radio mast for him because he was confined to bed most of the time with the malaria. The thirty-foot telescoping mast, secured in a vertical position by four guy wires, stood in the middle of a weeded plot of ground about 150 feet square.

I waded into the thick three-foot-high grass. I wiggled one of the stakes that held a guy wire, pulled on it, and removed it. Then I went to the second stake. When I was about to lift the wire from the stake, a snake that I had inadvertently stepped on wrapped itself around my leg. Perhaps this was the natural thing for it to do, but it scared me half to death. I tried and tried to kick it free as I began running out of the high grass and finally managed to kick it loose. It fell away and slithered off back into the high grass again.

When I got out on the road a small Chinese boy, about twelve years old I thought, was laughing as if he would burst wide open. He began imitating me, weaving and wiggling with his hands and arms and shaking his leg, still laughing. In a few seconds I managed to join in with the laughter. Now I tried to regain my composure and show this kid I was not afraid to go back into the field to complete my job. When I started back in he followed me in his bare feet and bare legs. He helped me unhitch the aluminum mast and lower it to the ground. We telescoped the mast's sections, tied the four stakes together, and rolled the guy wires into a circle and tied them together.

I then went to visit General Lui, whose office was on the second floor of godown #1. I explained my adventures in the field dismantling the radio equipment and asked if he could have someone carry all of it to the new campsite. When I mentioned the boy and his help, he inquired who the boy was. We stepped out on the porch overlooking the only street in Hua'an, and there I pointed to the boy.

"Oh, he is one of my soldiers. He is twelve years old, but small for his age. He will make you a good houseboy, so take him with you to the new location."

While in the process of listing supplies in godown #1, Sinks, who had arrived for duty at Camp Six, asked me to give him a few pointers on firing a .45. So I removed the clip and ejected the bullet from the chamber. With Sinks standing to my right, I brought the gun downward from a 45-degree angle, approached the level of the target, and squeezed the trigger until it clicked. I repeated this four or five times, then replaced the loaded clip and cocked it. We completed the inventory checklist, and Sinks said, "Mish, show me once more just when you begin squeezing the trigger." He again stood to my right.

I removed the clip; and while talking, I brought the .45 down to position and squeezed off the trigger. Wham! The bullet ploughed into the wall with one hell of a noise. Sinks jumped a mile, and in less than a minute General Lui and some officers had hurried down the steps. I did not want them to think I was stupid, so I did not explain that when I previously replaced the clip, I routinely cocked the .45. How easy it would have been to have had a serious accident! I covered myself by telling the general that my firing had been intentional because I had questioned whether a certain bullet was a good one or not.

When the second large shipment of mail came in, there seemed to be something for everyone and a big surprise for me. Eddie Black, son of my former employer in the States, wrote he was in New Delhi where his brother, Bernie, was flying supplies into China. He had made up a box of food for me containing, among other things, four pounds of coffee. Bernie dropped it off in Kunming at our naval group headquarters for delivery to me. How good that coffee was at breakfast time! I shared it with the early breakfast eaters.

On October 20, 1944, we finished moving everything to our new camp, including our personal gear. I shared a room with Sinks; Birr, a pharmacist mate; and Sergeant Rainey, a newly arrived marine who would be the permanent drill instructor for the Chinese guerrillas we were to train. My new houseboy took over maintenance of our large room. I wanted to give him a short English name and began mulling it over in my mind. When we received an All-Naval Communiqué that day, I decided to call him "Alnav."

Two days after we moved into our permanent quarters, our new camp commander, Birthright, arrived. For some reason he did not fit into the camp's structure. The first thing he did was irritate General Lui. He looked the part of an officer but just did not function as a commander.

On October 21, 1944, I had completed the first nine months of my China tour of duty. All of us had heard, through the scuttlebutt network within SACO, that when we had served eighteen months in China, we would be transferred back to the States for further assignments.

We had bath facilities in Camp Six. The river that ran past our camp was our bathtub, but our shower was better. The Chinese workmen had built a stall topped with a fifty-five-gallon steel drum and a contrivance that would permit the user to turn water on and off for showers. At certain times of the day the water was warmed by the sun and became just the right temperature for a pleasant shower. An outhouse, similar to stateside outhouses, had been built under my supervision on a nearby hillside. It could accommodate three men at a time.

When Lieutenant Lovell finally returned from Changchow, he and I began setting up a smooth-working office. In reconstructing payrolls and orders, I found my storekeeping training and experience in Toledo very helpful. This was the reason Lovell had been so eager to have me assigned to his operation. Our office was located off the dining room, which was formerly a Chinese library and the only building that predated our camp construction. It had a beautiful ancient tile roof, was stable and serviceable, and had gables and lines that were typically Old Chinese. The largest room of this lovely building became our dining hall. At one end stood a huge fireplace, at the other end was a built-on kitchen. The cook had supervised the building of the stove and then had proved that no one could get as much fire or energy out of a few pieces of wood as he could. The wood burns at one end only; as the pieces burn, they are pushed forward in a pie-cut formation so that the flame is concentrated at one point.

Another small room off the main one served as the doctor's office. Birr functioned as a member of the doctor's top team. Meanwhile, Dr. Coleman and an interpreter left to canvass the nearby coastal towns for a refrigerator, since certain medical supplies needed to be refrigerated. They returned a few days later with a used refrigerator that operated on alcohol. It had been carried over the mountain from the sampan dock by eight Chinese coolies. Hua'an was as far down the river as a sampan could travel, since waterfalls and rough rapids made the Nine Dragons River unnavigable between Hua'an and the next village toward the coast. Any supplies or people destined for farther down, such as Changchow, had to go up over a mountain. After some trial-and-error adjustments had been made to Dr. Coleman's refrigerator, it worked just fine and continued to work perfectly as long as we were at Camp Six.

Our camp had one of three direction finders (DFs) located in China under the U.S. Navy's supervision. It was located in a small building on a small knoblike hill about 100 yards south of our headquarters. The DF was carefully guarded and one expert was in charge. Even our regular complement of men were forbidden to visit the building. Walking up the steep hill to the DF shack was arduous, so I went up only when necessary. The small operational team became accustomed to the climb, but they, too, did not make the steep climb any more often than was required. This DF, in conjunction with the two others, could be used to triangulate the position of an unknown point.

Navy personnel from our area came through our camp often on their way in or out of China. I remember Lieutenant Davies, a disbursing supply officer in Changchow, who passed us on his way to Calcutta and then the United States for reassignment. He wore glasses and said he had brought four pair of prescription glasses to China. As luck would have it, he had broken all four left lenses without breaking a single right lens during his tour of duty.

On November 5, 1944, our first shipment of mail arrived at Camp Six. I received a few of the forms I had requested for the office, but not the most important ones. A new Hermes typewriter also arrived for me. It was not a very good machine, and I was to cuss it something terrible in the days to come. The letter type was merely pressed into the striking arms, so that after a few weeks of use, letters would fly off, and I would have a fine old time searching for them on our dirt floor. I had to then fasten them back on the striking bar by squeezing them on with pliers. It was a cheap portable typewriter and acted like one of the first made.

I was able to buy a fairly good grade of rice paper in Hua'an, which the shop proprietor cut to my specifications. He sold everything from buckets to pins but did not stock carbon paper. I needed carbon paper, and he offered to try to find some for me.

Meanwhile, I bought some black cloth and paid a tailor to make a suit for Alnav. I also bought him some sandals. Alnav understood Mandarin, the national language, as did most of the Chinese youngsters, but in Fukien

Province, the older Chinese people spoke a different dialect in each valley. This made it difficult to converse with the elders.

Alnav performed a fine job for me and for the other men in our room. My brass washbasin was kept shining all the time because he scoured it with sand every few days until it looked like "ginza" (gold). Alnav tied bamboo poles to each corner of our new beds and draped mosquito nets over the beds. During the day the sides of the nets could be lifted and thrown over the top until needed at night. The wooden frames, like all the wooden parts for the bed, had been bought in Changchow and carried up the river in sampans. The springs were made of thin, twisted rope; and even then they soon developed a hip hollow. They were far more comfortable, however, than sleeping on boards or the dirt floor.

Windows in our room were covered with shutters hanging on wood swivels. One night during a storm one shutter was torn off by the wind, and rain poured in on Sinks' bed. He had a soggy time of it the rest of the night. With the weather turning cooler, there were fewer mosquitoes, as well as fewer new malaria cases. I asked myself how I could have been so lucky. Bitten by just about every kind of insect in China, particularly mosquitoes and fleas, I never contracted malaria. Most of the men had malaria, and some suffered very badly. After days of heavy rain, the mountains around us stood out bold and sharp; greenery appeared in no time. Oranges and bananas became plentiful in the marketplaces, but the wonderful tangerines were the favorite fruit for all of us.

By mid-November, Lieutenant Lovell left for a walking trip to Lungyen, which was at our end of the truckline service, and for Chienyang, so I was on my own again in the office. Five new men arrived and brought with them mail and supplies. My package from Audrey contained flea powder, Nescafé, canned goods, candy, and bouillon cubes. I couldn't use the bouillon because it had molded during shipment. Among the navy supplies were four dozen cans of mosquito aerosol bombs, the first we had received since arriving in China. At long last we could spray around the inside of our mosquito nets before going to sleep.

It saddened us when Dr. Coleman told us he was sending Andrews to a navy hospital back in the States. He felt he did not have adequate facilities here at Camp Six to treat the cerebral malaria, and Andrews' condition was deteriorating. Normally Andrews was a slight person, but he now weighed less than a hundred pounds. Thus, it was not too difficult for coolies to carry him in a padded sedan chair on the three-day trip to Lungyen. There a truck took him to an emergency airfield, where he was picked up just before sundown and flown back to Kunming, and finally to the States. Two of our men accompanied him to the air pickup point.

General Lui gave a party for us in Hua'an. Since I was now a little experienced in Chinese drinking procedures, I left the party early, but some of the new men had a night they would long remember. The Chinese approached the party process like a game that could appropriately be entitled "Get the Americans Drunk." The way they worked was to concentrate on one American at a time. First, the general gave a toast to President Roosevelt. Everybody drank to that. Then our commander gave a toast to Chiang Kai-shek, and everybody drank to him. Then, one Chinese at a table drank to an American at his table; a second Chinese would drink to the same American. By this time the American had downed four drinks, while each of the two Chinese at the table had three drinks.

Then another Chinese at the table toasted the selected American (five drinks) while the Chinese at the table had just had three each. These "gom beis," or toasts, always called for turning the cup upside down each time to show that it was empty. Of course, we still called it "bottoms up." Drinking cups were always quickly refilled with the warm red wine by the host, and it went down very easily. The procedure continued until the American fell over when he tried to stand up. It was much worse when only one American was seated at a table with four or five Chinese officers or NCOs. In that situation, an American would have to drink four or five toasts to each one of the Chinese at his table.

I was awakened about 2:00 A.M. and asked to search for two missing American men who had left the party and never arrived at their quarters. We found them sitting in a rice paddy laughing like fools. Birr had not joined us in the search; but when I returned and told him about it, he started laughing and kept me up another thirty minutes with his guffawing.

The "luxuries" were pouring into Camp Six! We acquired a small generator that supplied power for four lights in the mess hall and better power for our radio transmitter. The generator could operate on either alcohol or gasoline. Lieutenant Lovell returned with three drums of alcohol and a hundred candles. In addition, we received two new radiomen and twelve new radio transmitters for the coastwatchers.

Alnav was a wonderful houseboy. I trusted him completely. The weather turned quite cold; I slept later each morning, and he always had warm water ready for me to wash and shave. I decided I must buy him a warm jacket and heavier shoes. Once Alnav gave me the dickens for leaving money out on a small stand beside my bed. I started shaving less and grew a goatee and mustache.

On Christmas Eve our camp gave a party for General Lui and his staff of officers and interpreters. Since our dining room was the setting, there was no problem getting our men home! It was a bang-up party! The Chinese game of getting Americans drunk was in full force. We sang several Christmas carols and "Old MacDonald Had a Farm." The Chinese seemed to like the latter number best. When the party broke up, the general gave several of us a photograph of himself with a Christmas greeting written on the back.

I began to lose my voice (which didn't come back for several days). I had waited too long to get up and away from the drinking table. When I did, and made it into my office, I decided the best thing to do was type a letter to Audrey. It was the most confused and erratic letter she ever received. Even the lines were not parallel! This time I couldn't blame it on my typewriter.

The next morning Dr. Coleman said he was glad he had returned in time for the Christmas party with the Chinese. "There is nothing I enjoy more than being 'gom beid'." I replied that I had enjoyed it also.

A couple of days later Doc told me where he had acquired the refrigerator. He said he found it in a deserted American mission in a small village that, at the moment he was there, was not occupied by either the Japanese or Chinese. The Japanese had held the village several times but had not bothered the contents of the mission. In addition to the refrigerator, Doc said he saw a nice piano in one of the mission rooms.

"I played the piano in a small band on a summer cruise ship that went up and down the China coast," he continued. "That's one way I earned money for college, and I think I will borrow that piano for our camp. What do you think?"

The more we talked, the more we seemed to have in common. Dr. Coleman mentioned that he had some Coleman relatives in Johnstown, Pennsylvania; and before long, we found that we were distantly related through my uncle, Ralph Coleman.

We began having ideal winter weather: cold at night and warm and sunny in the day, although the days seemed very short indeed. At least we were not plagued with mosquitoes, flies, or fleas. We fashioned a stove out of a thirty-gallon metal drum in which Alnav built a fire on cold mornings. It heated our room very well. On one really cold night, Alnav came in to build a fire; and after he had it going good, I said, "Ni tsola swey jow" (You go to sleep).

Alnav replied "sidi, sidi" (yes, yes) and curled up beside my cot and went to sleep.

On the very first day of 1945 a heavy mail arrived. I received twenty-three letters and five packages, most of which were to have been there for Christmas. It did not matter that they were late; they were much appreciated.

Chinese workers continued to build our camp compound. When finished, it was supposed to have four main buildings and four minor ones. All the walls were built with two wood forms facing each other, anchored in place, filled with wet dirt, and tamped down to form a solid mass or wall. Windows and door frames were positioned in advance, with the dirt tamped around them. Later they were plastered both inside and out, which in my opinion, made a pretty good building. All the new roofs were thatched.

The first training class of Chinese troops, consisting of 600 men, was organized and underway at Camp Six. It was to last eight weeks, and each recruit would be paid 300 CN every month, in addition to receiving a weapon, ammunition, shelter, and food. I conducted a small-arms class three days a week.

With all this, Lieutenant Lovell's and my work was increased to such an extent that we suggested to General Lui that he assign someone to assist with the paperwork, especially the Chinese payroll and issuance of weapons.

"I have just the man for you," he smiled.

So Mr. Yip entered our life in China. He was a Chinese gentleman who spoke English and had a good background in bookkeeping and accounting. Slightly built and about fifty years old, he also had three wives, numerous children, and a gold front tooth. Yip was a stickler for exactness, so I knew we were going to get along just fine. However, the office was now crowded. Lovell moved into a small room just off our office, and we all awaited the arrival of chairs, desks, and tables I had ordered from Changchow. Lieutenant Lovell's large chest, with a hinged lid and a hasp with a Chinese lock attached, went with him into the smaller office. This was where he kept our money and vital records.

My mind was diverted from time to time when I had the 8:00 P.M.-to-midnight or the midnight-to-4:00 A.M. watch. A Chinese corporal, with his four guards positioned in the four sentry boxes, would spend some time with me in my office between rounds. About twice each hour he would check each sentry to see that he was awake. If he found a sleeper, he would bash him in the face with the butt end of his carbine to awaken him. Now and then a guard would be found sleeping standing up and leaning against the sentry box. The corporals generally had some special talent. Two were exceptional artists and brush-painted their subjects in a matter of an hour or two between rounds. I saved a couple of these drawings.

I was also amused at another trait the Chinese corporals had. They gently picked up the hair on the back of my arms with their fingers while I was reading or writing. I wondered why until I learned that they did not have any hair on their arms. As a matter of fact, I don't remember seeing any mustaches or beards on any of our recruits. It seemed that only elderly men sometimes had wisps of hair on their chins.

I rotated on the night watch. I didn't mind the duty because it gave me peaceful moments away from the harried office day work. I looked beyond the six-foot privacy fence surrounding our compound and beyond the four sentry boxes facing the four directions, and even beyond the sparse pine trees reaching for the stars. Nothing indicated what might be ahead for me in the near future.

# CHAPTER 11

# A Journey to the Coast

*January 1945—U.S. Army troops land in Lingayen Gulf,
Luzon, northern Philippines.*

**W**ord arrived at Camp Six that several new coastwatcher operations needed
carbines and ammunition. They were all located up and down the coast across
from the militarily strategic island of Amoy, held by the Japanese. I was elected
to take twenty carbines and sixteen boxes of ammunition to Changchow. The
mayor of Hua'an rounded up twenty coolies (actually conscripted farmers) to
carry the load over the mountain, and General Lui provided three soldiers to
accompany us.

We had gone about three miles when one of the coolies fell over in exhaus-
tion. One of the soldiers then called to an old man working in a rice paddy,
ordering him to come and take the fallen man's place. The old man bowed
slightly in our direction, then took off his hat to show that his hair was white,
indicating he was very old. The soldier leveled his carbine at the old one who
stood there resignedly awaiting death. I did not know if the soldier actually
would have shot the old man, but I called out.

"Ting-yi-ting!" (Stop!).

The soldiers talked together a few minutes, then made other arrangements.
The fallen man's load was shifted around so that two men carried extra boxes
of ammunition the rest of the way. We left the exhausted man on the trail

where he lay. The old man in the rice paddy continued to stand there until I could no longer see him.

We walked over the mountain and descended the 500 steps. A short distance beyond was a small village where a sampan, partially loaded with tangerines, was awaiting my arrival. When my gear and all the equipment were loaded below deck, I parted with the soldiers and carriers, who immediately began making their way back to Hua'an. The sampan's crew consisted of a grandfather, a father in his prime, a small boy who couldn't have been more than five years old, and the boy's mother, who cooked on the deck with a small charcoal firepot perched on some flat stones.

The river was without other sampan traffic as we started floating downstream. I ate tangerines galore. They were about four times the size of those in the States, and my, they were sweet! The grandfather, father, and small son manned a single long oar. The boy was positioned next to the davit; the grandfather, who took a longer stride, was in the middle; and the man, who would take three steps to his father's two and the small boy's one, was at the oar's end. For each sweep of the oar, the boy took one step forward and one step backward; the grandfather took two steps forward and two back; and the man three steps forward and three back. The same timing was used by all three. Frequently the oar or sweep was used as a rudder, and the man would then be in sole control.

We passed a good-sized village with many sampans and boats tied up at the docks, where the river water appeared surprisingly clean. At times the river ran close to tangerine and pomelo groves—groves that would eventually be consumed as the river gradually eroded large chunks of the bank. Here and there the river was as wide as a half a mile and so shallow the boatman was forced to find channels to keep us moving. He always did, and we never got hung up on any of the numerous sandbars.

We had one exciting moment when, in order to get into a deeper channel, the boatmen pulled very hard to swing the sampan sharply to the left. The long oar snapped in two at the oarlock, and the grandfather, father, and son were all catapulted toward the rear of the sampan. They fell onto the deck. The small boy began crying and the grandfather picked him up. The father looked at me and laughed. In a moment we were all laughing, including the wife. A second but shorter oar was unlashed from the mast, and we all helped put it in the oarlock. Our sampan had slowly turned around and we were drifting downstream without guidance. By the time the new oar was in place we had completed a full circle. Soon everything was again under control.

It was nearly dark when we arrived at a small village. The boatman went ashore and returned with the news that I was to sleep in a small inn at the village. He added that the mayor would provide carriers in the morning.

"The supplies may stay on the sampan for the night," he explained.

I found the inn and asked for a place to "sway jow" (sleep) and was shown a small room with a board bed. I was surprised to hear a knock on the door; and when I opened it, the boatman was there.

"There is a change of plans," he said, explaining that it would be best to keep the carbines and ammunition in my room, as it would not be a good thing for a Japanese patrol to see his sampan anchored at this village in the morning, especially if the sampan was sitting low in the water. "I will move down the river a short distance." He told me that some Chinese soldiers would be on hand in the morning to see that carriers appeared to help me. "Be ready at daybreak, please." We thanked each other. He gave me a sack of tangerines and I gave him several cigarettes.

As I was eating rice with eggs for supper, five Chinese men came in to eat and spend the night. One of them spoke English and came to my table to tell me he had seen a Nippon patrol during the day. I had a difficult time understanding him, but he was patient and repeated the story several times. It was hard for me to go to sleep, and I had a restless night.

I got up and dressed at 4:30 A.M. and found five soldiers waiting for me, with sixteen carriers. We were off within a half hour. The land was level from the village to Changchow, and the carriers made excellent time. These men had better-developed leg muscles and were in much better physical shape than the men in the mountains. The carriers had a fast rhythmic gait, and I had a hard time keeping up with them. I was glad when we arrived at a tea stand so I could rest a while. I bought tea for everyone, and the men all put on their best smiles. In another two hours we took another break for tea. I halved a number of cigarettes and distributed them to the men. They seemed to enjoy the smoke, but were careful not to smoke the entire half, saving the butt for some special future moment.

I developed a heat rash in my groin. I could not keep my mind off the increasingly aggravated area; and, step by step, I was looking forward to the end of my trip. The route to Changchow was slightly above sea level and the soil was very rich. The crops looked good. There were no trees anywhere and very few people on the road. I doubt if we passed five people during the last hour of walking.

We made a brief stop a few miles before reaching Changchow, which we could see in the distance. The carriers adjusted their loads. Two or three switched loads and then one called out to the others. With that signal, they all loaded up and away they went with me doing my best to keep up. Some walkers, these little brown men! I learned one thing on this journey: these carriers could outwalk me even with their heavy loads.

I arrived at our Coast Watcher Unit Headquarters before noon and reported to the officer in charge. My gear was stored on the second floor of what had once been a foreign mission. It was surrounded by landscaped grounds and an eight-foot-high brick wall. Each of the five coastwatcher crews consisted of one or two Americans, one Chinese radioman, and sixteen Chinese soldiers. There were five such groups already located along the coast, and there were plans to establish several more. They were indispensable to our Pacific fleet and war maneuvers.

The coastwatchers' vantage points were situated to allow a broad view up and down the coastline. The men lived with binoculars hanging around their necks and reported via their radios to Changchow any shipping movements or plane sightings. Living conditions were frugal at coastwatchers' units; we lived off the land and received a per diem of six dollars a day. Where the land was poor and sparsely settled, the food was poor, too. It was a sad situation, for we had money but were unable to buy food. We were located between the Japanese lines to the west and the coast to our immediate east. Food in this area, when we found it, was much less expensive than in the larger cities. It cost about ten dollars a day to live in Kunming, Sian, or Chungking. When we lived in those areas and did not occupy government (Chinese or American) quarters, we received an additional three dollars a day allowance.

During this trip I took time to visit the nearby mission that Dr. Coleman had visited. As I entered the compound I heard a voice speaking English in a strong but gentle manner.

"The Japanese eat rice with chopsticks like the Chinese do."

A voice responded in slow and hesitating words. "The Japanezi."

"No! No!" the first voice said. "The Japanese."

The other said, "Japanese eat rice with choppa sticks!"

"No! No!" the first voice objected again. "Not choppa sticks; chopsticks. Try again."

The second voice tried again until the first voice said, "Yes, you are speaking better English now."

At this point I walked into the group—an instructor and two Chinese soldiers. It took me several moments to realize that the instructor was blind! He was reading Braille as he taught. The lesson was immediately suspended while I talked with the instructor in English. He said he had been blind since he was a child and that missionaries had reared him. The missionaries had fled to the mountains about six months previously. When Japanese patrols began coming nearer to the mission compound, he was led off to hide in a farmhouse, but always returned as soon as the patrol left. He was aware that an American had appropriated the mission's refrigerator. On touring the several rooms of the mission, I saw the piano that Dr. Coleman wished to appropriate one day, but I did not mention this to the Chinese instructor.

We talked about half an hour, and I was surprised at his knowledge, and at his ability to find his way around the grounds and house. He did his own cooking, but people also brought him things to eat. His command of English earned him his living by teaching. As I left, the two Nationalist Chinese soldiers in faded green uniforms resumed their English lessons. It was fine testimony to how well a handicapped person can adapt to circumstances and make a useful living.

Our coastwatchers received an urgent message from Chinese intelligence on December 19 that an American plane had been shot down near Tung'an. The pilot of the P-51, Colonel Rector of the 14th Air Force, had bailed out near Tung'an, and the plane had cracked up about ten miles away. Chief Newell and Bob Sinks had chartered a motor launch to search for him. They found Colonel Rector at Kakmei, suffering from minor injuries. He was brought to the network headquarters where he convalesced for several days. We learned that the colonel was the author of the book *God Is My Co-Pilot*, which later was made into a movie. When he was able to walk, a coastwatcher's interpreter and a soldier accompanied him to Lungyen. They traveled over a seldom-used trail to the south and west of Camp Six. It was a three-day trip to Lungyen and another day to the emergency airfield where he was picked up and flown to Kunming.

Cosgrove, the radioman who had come down the river with me from Lungyen, was with a coastwatchers' unit that was constantly on the alert because they had been spotted several times by Japanese patrols.

He told me, "When we know a patrol is near, we pack up quickly and head for the mountains. When the danger passes, we return to our watch." Cosgrove sent his sightings about twice a day unless something appeared unusual. His information went through the coastwatchers' unit to Camp Six, which then sent it to Chungking and, from there, to the U.S. fleet. Frequent radio contact was made with the USS *Barb*, a submarine that surfaced almost every night to receive the latest shipping information from Changchow.

One morning Cosgrove staggered into our Changchow unit covered with blood. It was streaming down his legs; he was not wearing a shirt or cap and was using his undershirt to stanch the blood flow.

Lying on a cot, he explained what had happened. At his lookout post there was a four-foot mud wall around a little shack where they slept. The top of the wall was embedded with broken glass, sharp stones, and sharp pieces of bamboo as a deterrent to anyone wanting to crawl over it.

About dusk one of the sixteen Chinese soldiers in his unit spotted a Japanese patrol not far away hurrying in their direction. He rushed into the hut and warned the others, who fled, leaving their personal gear and radio transmitter. Cosgrove attempted to jump over the four-foot wall, did not clear it, and ended up straddling the wall. The sharp objects cut him severely, tearing his testicles wide open and lacerating the inside of one leg. He managed to get over the wall, caught up with one of his companions, and walked eighteen miles to our compound in Changchow.

The pharmacist mate, upon examining him, reported to the officer-in-charge that a doctor was needed to operate and repair Cosgrove's leg and testicles. I had been out of the unit for a few hours, but was alerted immediately upon my return. Within the hour I left with Cosgrove, in a chair carried by four strong Chinese men. Camp Six had already been notified, and Dr. Coleman awaited us. We made the trip to the river in record time, and began sailing up the river before dusk.

Understandably, Cosgrove was in great pain and not very talkative. As we sailed up the river, I remembered his dread of water buffalo and how he would give them a wide berth when they approached. Yet a small boy could lead them around with a ring fastened through the buffalo's nose. Fortunately, we did not meet any on this trip, for it would have excited him. The trip up the river, of course, took much longer than the one coming down. We did have the advantage of a sail, however. Several times the boat's crew and and passengers, except Cosgrove, had to get out of the sampan and, using finely woven bamboo-fiber ropes slung over our shoulders, pull the sampan over the sandbars into deeper water. It was slow work, but we pulled for all we were worth and, inch by inch, we managed to get over the bars and into deeper channels.

We sailed into a village late at night and tied up. As soon as it was daylight, while we waited for the morning breeze, I had time to visit a very old temple in the village. It was still in good condition and contained many statues of gods, some very colorful. They were matched in pairs, such as a "Good God" and a "Bad God." There must have been about thirty, all larger than an average-sized person. I counted seventeen gods before I got to the "God of Hell," a very large, black image. I had an uneasy, eerie feeling standing there in the temple and the shadows. The rays of the early morning sun added to the feeling.

When I returned to the sampan a breeze was just starting to develop. I brought a mess of fried eggs mixed with rice and tea for Cosgrove's breakfast, and we got under way. Before long, we were moving smoothly up the river. Ahead were some ducks! When we were close enough, I shot one. The sampan owner's wife had that fat duck on the fire in fifteen minutes, and roasted in less than an hour.

I told Cosgrove, "I don't know how she cooked it so fast." He and I ate the legs and thighs, and the crew ate the rest. It was a beautiful day, and we made excellent progress. When we pulled into another small village for the night, I walked into the town to look around. A small jewelry store had a display of beautiful, mint-new silver dollars. One side of the coins was engraved with a junk or sampan with its sails set; on the other was the head of Sun Yat-sen. I bartered and exchanged CN banknotes for ten of these elegant silver coins, which were about the size of a U.S. silver dollar.

The next day our progress was slower until the wind freshened. By afternoon we reached the dock near the bottom of the 500 steps below Camp Six. It was good to be at the foot of the mountain again, especially because Cosgrove was really in severe pain. However, we knew we could not reach Camp Six before nightfall, so we decided to stay in the village until morning.

While in the teahouse that evening I met an old man who carried a great broadsword. I learned that at one time he had been an Imperial Guard at the Empress's Palace in Peking. He had been pensioned off and was living out his life in his family home. He showed me some of the basic swings of the very heavy sword, causing me to wonder how a man could swing it fast enough to defend himself. As usual, a small group of onlookers gathered to watch as the old man went through his exercises. I talked with the old one a number of times as I passed through the village on my numerous trips up and down the river.

The next morning, instead of a litter, the carriers brought a sedan chair for Cosgrove. They really earned their pay carrying him up those endless steps into the sky! After many rest stops along the way, we reached the top, where it was easier going for all of us. Dr. Coleman was waiting for Cosgrove and went to work on him soon after we arrived. He removed quite a few pieces of foreign material and did some cutting and stitching. Cosgrove recuperated, but it took him a long time.

While he recuperated, a SACO replacement was sent to his coastwatcher unit, where they continued to play hide-and-seek with the Japanese and to provide services to the fleet. It was important that all of our coastwatcher units remain alert and viable.

# CHAPTER 12

# Trip to Lungyen and Chienyang

*February 1945—The first American ship since May 1942 enters Manila Bay.*

January 1945 was actually a beautiful month. However, when the thermometer registered forty degrees it was cold! This is because it was so damp. So I really appreciated the hot water Alnav brought me in the morning, and timed my getting up to his arrival. I was grateful, too, for my two wool shirts and two pairs of wool pants. I wore all of them at the same time.

In our area every farmer had a few pigs because pork was the staple meat of the common farmer's household. I always chuckled at the pigs, which were the most swaybacked animals I had ever seen. They seemed to have no spine at all, and their bellies literally dragged on the ground.

Hua'an had a salt house where the region's salt was stored. There was always a soldier on guard who carried a World War I German rifle and wore a German helmet. The rifle was always at the rest position, so the salt duty must have been a boring detail. Salt could be withdrawn only by order of the mayor, and every order was taxed by the government. Fortunately, the military, as well as authorized storekeepers, were allowed to purchase salt, so our unit was a good customer.

One day in the village, a shopkeeper stopped me and showed me several silver bracelets. Two bore simple, engraved designs and were reasonably priced, so I purchased them. The other two were also engraved, but some of the engraved miniature figures were missing, although at one time they must have been extremely beautiful. I showed my purchase to Alnav on the way back to camp, and he nodded his head in approval.

Several days later Alnav came to tell me he had heard about an old lady in a nearby village who had several fine silver bracelets for sale.

"I'd like to see them, Alnav," I said.

"I go with you," he responded.

On Sunday morning Alnav and I took off for the mountain village. The weather began to turn bad and huge black clouds closed in on us as we approached the village, which was about 3,000 feet above sea level. After several inquiries, we located the elderly woman. She was very wrinkled and looked like she had been smoked through and through. We told her the purpose of our visit, then waited. The old one sat still, then called to a young girl who appeared carrying a folded cotton quilt. Inside lay treasures!

There were six exquisite bracelets! Several were fashioned with tiny, raised, intricate silver figures mounted on thin silver wires fastened to the heavy silver bracelet band. Two of the bracelets looked perfect; I could not find any imperfections. As I examined the jewelry the storm broke with fury. Lightning flashed almost continuously while the thunder rolled deep and loud. I imagined myself in a witch's den in which she was calling on the devil or her god to put a spell on me. The storm was so loud that we were unable to communicate with the old lady for about fifteen minutes.

Gradually the storm subsided and I began bargaining, with Alnav as my interpreter. All six bracelets were designed in pairs; one pair was particularly exquisite. The figures were in panels that told a story. Her asking price was not unreasonable, so I did not bargain too long or too hard. I bought all six at about three-fourths of what she originally had asked. The girl told Alnav that the bracelets were very old, but because of inflation the old one needed money for food.

When the rain subsided to a drizzle, Alnav and I took our leave and started down the mountain. We had to wait for about a half hour at two different points until streams gushing across our path calmed down. I knew I would not forget that Old Lady of the Mountain, and I have wondered many times where she got the bracelets, for her standard of living and her house did not lend themselves to such wealth. When they saw the bracelets, everyone in camp wanted to buy them. I could have sold them for twenty times what I paid for them, but I knew a prize when I saw one; I didn't sell even one.

I began taking Mandarin lessons, which were being taught to all children in the schools. Young girls and young boys went to school together, although it had not been long since girls had been forbidden to attend school. All students wore uniforms denoting their status. The Chinese language has always been one of tones. I learned that the basis of all Chinese speech is four tones:

1. One tone is even.
2. One tone rises as spoken.
3. One tone falls and stops with a hesitation.
4. One tone is chopped off quickly.

Classes were scheduled three times a week. Unfortunately, during the second week of classes, I received an assignment that took me away from Hua'an for a couple of weeks, so I missed most of those classes.

A good mail brought me a supply of coffee, a hard salami, cocoa, and chocolate bars, to say nothing of letters from home. The navy also furnished each man with three cans of beer, a little late for Christmas, but not too late to be enjoyed. Some of the men couldn't wait to drink theirs and consumed one can after another until it was gone within the hour. I had to have a genuine desire for a beer before I could enjoy one, so I kept mine for the moments when I really wanted one.

The tangerine supply was excellent. We could buy over three dozen of the large, delicious fruits for the equivalent of one U.S. dollar. We were not so lucky in our alcohol reserve. Alcohol for our radio transmitter power plant and refrigerator was getting so low that I made plans to travel to Lungyen or Chienyang for a supply.

Before I left, an English missionary by the name of Stuart came up the river and visited our camp. He was from a retreat in the mountains, a full day's walk from our camp, but on my route to Lungyen and Chienyang. We discussed prospects of our meeting somewhere. He said he would meet me in three days at 9:00 A.M. at a certain intersection of paths on the mountainside.

He said, "We'll travel together to my village and you can spend the night at my house." I accepted his invitation.

Three days later I started my journey at 7:00 A.M. with Sergeant Chen and two Chinese soldiers. I was carrying a large sum of money to buy the alcohol. In addition to their carbines, the two soldiers carried two empty fifty-five-gallon steel drums suspended in slings and hanging from a long pole between them. The pole rested on their shoulders. In their half-filled bandoliers were accountable bullets. Unlike U.S. soldiers, Chinese soldiers had to account for every bullet issued to them.

We arrived about ten minutes early at the path intersection where we were to meet the missionary. We could see a long way up and down both intersecting paths. At ten minutes past nine there was still no missionary, so we decided to continue our journey up the mountain.

Soon we came to a tiny village and heard laughter on a hillside. Young girls were gathering branches, twigs, and dry tall grass for fuel. There were very few trees. The soldiers began laughing and kidding, but when the girls spotted us on the trail, their laughter and chatter immediately stopped. As we passed the silent maids, we waved to them and called out a greeting but received no sign of recognition. Several girls, carrying massive bundles of fuel on their backs, started down the mountainside. After we passed I heard them explode into merriment.

It was nearly noon when we reached the mountain pass and descended into a small valley with a village at the far end. We stopped for tea and asked if the missionary had passed through the village that morning. I found that I could make myself understood only if I talked to a young boy who was learning Mandarin in school. He translated to his elders who, in turn, said that we were the only visitors to enter the village that day. While we were having tea a large hawk soared slowly overhead. Several of the small boys, who admired my carbine, pointed to the bird and asked me to shoot it.

They finally persuaded me to take a shot at the majestic bird, which was sailing smoothly on the air currents. I had an audience of perhaps a hundred people. I waited for the hawk to return from one of his grand circles, then led him about a foot and squeezed off a shot. We heard the bullet go "clack," after which a few feathers flew. The hawk flapped his wings quickly three or four times, then fell, landing at the edge of the village. Several small boys raced to get him. It was a lucky shot, of course. When the boys returned with it, I handed the hawk over to the head man of the village.

We continued on our way for another hour and dipped down into a slight depression that was filled with banyan trees and other lush plant growth, as well as heavy ground vegetation. Our path was entirely covered overhead by arched trees and hanging vines. Hundreds of apple-green orchids grew on the lower branches. This was a rare, unexpected garden spot on our trip. We could see no human life anywhere near this tropical setting. But there was something very odd about this green and beautiful place: there were no birds!

By midafternoon our trail led us past the rear of a dozen or so houses in another village. We walked alongside a four-foot wall with sharp stones and broken pieces of glass embedded in the top. The yards were enclosed with walls, and I kept looking over them into gardens. There were also chickens and pigs in the yards. Suddenly, I saw the largest chickens I had ever seen in my whole life! In this one yard were five chickens and a rooster. In color they resembled the Rhode Island Reds of the United States, but they were enormous. The soldiers and I stopped and watched them over the wall for a few minutes. The backs of the hens were at least twenty-four inches from the ground, and the rooster's was a good thirty inches off the ground. I added another seven or eight inches for the head on the hens, and nine or ten inches for the rooster's head, and mumbled, "I don't believe it!" And if I hadn't seen them myself, I would not have.

I had seen big chickens back home in the States. When I was a kid in Pennsylvania we had some big Wyandottes, I'd seen large chickens at the Illinois State Fair in Springfield and at the Cambria County Fair in Ebensburg, Pennsylvania, but none could hold a candle to these birds! I kept thinking to myself later, "Boy, if I could transport a clutch of eggs from these birds back to the States I would have it made." It was a poultry farmer's dream world.

It was approaching dusk when we arrived at our first day's destination, the home of the English missionary who had not shown up yet. I bought tangerines for the soldiers and myself. The sergeant showed me how to pick out the juicy ones: a soft or depressed nipple indicated it was beyond its prime. I told the soldiers to eat at a restaurant one at a time, for I wanted two to guard my gear, which held the package of money, at all times.

Meanwhile, I looked for a place to sleep and finally decided on the village jail. We were trying to get settled there, at about 9:00 P.M., when a messenger arrived with a note from our missionary friend. He invited me and my men to come to his house for the night. We gladly accepted because the jail was a real fleabag.

While the missionary and I ate a fine dinner served by two Chinese women servants, he apologized for being delayed and failing to meet us on time at the junction. He explained that a friend had arrived unexpectedly the night before and he had gotten a late start. The women were instructed to feed the soldiers well and show them where they could sleep. The missionary spoke Mandarin very poorly but spoke several of the Fukien Province dialects expertly.

He said he had heard in the village where I had shot the hawk that an American who had preceded him spoke Mandarin very well. Who could have said that? Only the schoolchildren understood my limited vocabulary. "They also said you were an excellent marksman and reenacted the shooting of the hawk several times for me," he laughed.

The home in which we stayed was the missionary's summer house, a place he used to escape the hot lowland heat. "However, I am unable to continue occupying my regular home and mission because the Japanese appropriated it," he explained.

I told him how much I and the soldiers appreciated the dinner, breakfast, and visit, and we departed early in the morning, bound for Lungyen. For the most part our trail led through the mountains. Frequently I heard cock pheasants crowing, but we saw only a few in flight, those that we happened to disturb in passing. During the day we stopped several times to rest and twice for tea at crude tea stands located near small clusters of houses.

Late in the afternoon we caught a glimpse of Lungyen in a distant valley. As we made our way downward into an ever-expanding valley, I was surprised to see several small but active coal mines bordering the trail. It was just quitting time for the miners, so they joined us for the walk down into the valley. I saw no sign of a railroad track, so the coal must have been transported to Lungyen by wagons or carts, although I saw none of these that evening.

Each of the miners carried a small bag of coal on his shoulder, which I learned was for his own home use. I broke several cigarettes in two and distributed them to the soldiers traveling with me as well as to the miners who walked with us. Our group had now grown to twelve or thirteen. The soldiers and miners enjoyed their smokes, and they smiled and talked. I could not understand them, but they believed that I could, so I let it go at that.

The military headquarters in Lungyen provided my soldiers with quarters, and I stayed at the hotel where I had stayed on my other trip to Lungyen. With a military interpreter I secured a truck and visited three merchants in search of alcohol. Only one merchant had some, and he had only one drum, for which he wanted an exorbitant price.

"I must have two drums for sure, and more if the price is reasonable," I said through my interpreter.

The merchant informed us that alcohol was available in Chienyang three truck-days away. He wasn't positive I could get it, but he was reasonably sure. I asked my interpreter to come by the next morning so we could seek more information on alcohol supplies.

I was awakened about 5:00 A.M. by the sounds of the farmers' market across the street. The usual things were for sale and bargaining was already in full swing. I was almost through breakfast when the interpreter arrived. I invited him to eat, so he sat down and ordered thin rice, a bit of fried pork, and tea. He acted as though he had something on his mind. Finally, he told me that the local military was in need of three drums of alcohol and the merchants we had visited the day before would each take two drums if I could find them.

He explained the deal. "A truck to Chienyang would cost 250,000 CN. If you pay 100,000 CN, the military would pay 100,000 and the three merchants would pay 50,000 CN."

I thought briefly and replied, "I will pay 90,000; the military can pay 90,000, and the merchants must pay 70,000, since they are getting six drums of alcohol." I added that this was a firm figure, and the money must be put up by the merchants in advance. "Or I'm not interested."

He left for about an hour; and when he returned, he told me the terms were agreeable to everyone. He had the merchants' money in hand. The military promised an excellent truck, which would cause no trouble. In my own mind, if the price was right, I planned to buy three drums in Chienyang for myself. Then I suddenly decided to buy the one drum of alcohol in the village and send it down the river to Hua'an by my two soldiers; it occurred to me that the camp might run out before I got back from Chienyang. Costs for the boats and carriers to take the drum over the mountain range to the Nine Dragons River and costs for the boats were computed, and I advanced this sum to one of the soldiers whom the sergeant put in charge. It would take them three days.

Then I sought out the interpreter, who now acted in the interest of the military, and paid him half of my truck charge. "I will pay the other half when we return." This was agreeable, and he said the truck would be ready the next morning.

The next morning brought problems. Instead of a driver and mechanic, which were to be provided under the contract price, there appeared three military men attached to the Lungyen post and sixteen civilians, including two women and two small children, all of whom wanted to ride with me on my truck to Chienyang. I objected to this imposition, and they all offered me various sums of money, which I refused.

After mulling over this unexpected turn of events for about ten minutes, I said, "Oh, what the hell? Everybody get on." Everybody rode free.

They turned out to be good company; they laughed a lot and were always eager to help. One man who spoke fairly good English became my interpreter. When we arrived in Yenping he spoke to the manager of the best inn, and I was given a very nice room. The food in the dining room also was much better than average. I stopped at the little teahouse and restaurant where I had bought the white sugar earlier and ordered 200 catties to be picked up on my return trip. I was assured that my order would be waiting for me.

We arrived in Chienyang in the early afternoon of the third day, my first trip in China without truck problems. When I checked into our naval unit, I found they had been advised of my mission. We located a merchant the next day who accompanied us in the truck for about ten miles out in the country where we stopped at an alcohol distillery. We bought fifteen fifty-five-gallon drums: two for our Chienyang naval unit, one for the merchant who guided us to the distillery, and twelve for me to take back to Lungyen. In addition the truck driver personally bought a drum. We all paid the same price as the Chinese Army did, which was less than half of what I paid the Lungyen merchant for the drum I already sent down the river. Nevertheless, I always say "a bird in hand. . . ." We left early the next morning on the return trip after eating the specialty of the house at the navy mess. Yep! It was pancakes and honey.

On our return trip we were delayed several hours with engine trouble, which the mechanic fixed without any outside assistance. Traffic on the road was very light. I don't think we passed four trucks or buses coming or going. There were no passenger cars. Only in the large cities and on main highways did I see a few passenger cars. Somehow or other we had again picked up a few passengers on this return trip. I told the sergeant to put anyone off the truck who might become a problem, and to tell all the passengers to stay near the truck during a stop.

"When we're ready to go, we are not waiting for anyone; we will go immediately," I said.

As we entered a small village, a tall man was on the road's edge waving his arms. I noticed he was an American or Englishman, so I rapped on the rooftop for the driver to stop. I climbed off the truck and inquired who he was and whether he was in any trouble.

"I live nearby," he said, "and will you join me for a cup of tea or coffee?"

"Certainly," I answered. I climbed back into the truck and we followed the man's directions to his house.

"Tell the people to rest and stretch their legs," I told the sergeant.

My host was an OSS man. He had a powerful radio transmitter and a well-furnished house with several immaculate servants around. During our conversation over cake and coffee, I was aware that he was fishing for information and that he spoke Chinese fluently. He definitely wanted to learn about my activities.

"I get lonely out here," he said. "You are the first American I have spoken to in person in more than a month."

However, I felt it advisable to cut this visit as short as possible. I gave him no information, thanked him for the refreshments, and took off. I heard shortly after the end of the war that he had appropriated a jeep and a huge sum of money and then vanished. The OSS people came by our camp, asking all in our group if we knew where he might be.

I stopped on the return trip to pick up my "pei tong" (white sugar), but alas, the merchant was only able to give me 100 catties (one and one-third pounds each) instead of the 200 he had promised. When we reached Yenping, the innkeeper gave me the same nice room I had occupied before. He was very accommodating and had hot bathwater in my room by the time I reached it. Excellent-quality candles were available in Yenping at a reasonable price, so I bought 300. From this city a road led to Foochow (Fuzhou), the provincial capital. There was also a river that flowed to Foochow and the coast, but no river traffic was in evidence. The Japanese occupied an island near the mouth of the river, but the sergeant told me that the Japanese garrison never left their island for the mainland.

The next day was uneventful, and we arrived in Lungyen early in the afternoon. I released the truck and its load to the military for overnight safekeeping and checked into the hotel.

It was nearly noon when we finally loaded all the gear and alcohol drums into three small sampans. Sampans were smaller in this area because the river was shallow. The first leg of the trip was delightful because we were sailing a beautiful stretch of the river. In two hours we arrived at the portage where there were enough carriers to load up promptly, and up the mountain we went. As usual, there was a grand view from the mountaintop with the weather as clear as crystal. We rested for about ten minutes before starting down the other side of the mountain to Gansee.

It was just getting dark when we arrived at the village, and my old friend, the schoolteacher, met us and arranged for the loading of the alcohol and our other supplies. We were able to get everything into one large sampan. The river was high and I knew our boatmen were experienced, so I had no qualms about their ability to transport us safely when morning came. My schoolteacher friend and the sergeant joined me for a chicken dinner American style at the restaurant, where the owner remembered me.

We had a good start next morning, going over the breastwork of the dam and navigating the few rapids, which served as a "waker-uppers"! Then I experienced a feeling very similar to the first steep plunge of the roller coaster at Palisades Amusement Park across from 125th Street in New York City, a vivid remembrance of my youth. These were the rapids of the Nine Dragons River in China! When we stopped for the night at Yinchon, I purchased more candles. The cormorant fisherman was busily plying his trade as we passed.

The following day we made excellent headway. The current was stronger the entire length of the trip. The rapids were worse, and if conceivable, more thrilling than before. I told myself that at least I knew what to expect, but that could be good or bad depending on a person's point of view. Finally, we docked at Camp Six. How great it was to be back with friends again!

# Double Thumbs, Salted Nuts, and a Wild Pig

*February 1945—The battle for Iwo Jima takes place. It is secured on March 16, but the fighting continues until March 26. Army troops land on Corregidor, Philippines.*
*March 1945—Daily bombings of Okinawa begin.*
*April 12, 1945—President Roosevelt dies; Harry S Truman becomes president.*

**I** learned that the first drum of alcohol had come down the river safely. Now, with a good supply of candles, alcohol, and sugar, we could relax.

During my absence, Dr. Coleman had gone to Changchow and returned with the piano, which now graced our dining room. It had been carried across the countryside, loaded onto a sampan for the trip upriver, and carried over the mountain by sixteen coolies.

"It was worth the effort," I complimented Dr. Coleman, for he sure could play that old upright. Later we were lucky to get a radioman who played boogie-woogie like a professional. It was amazing how a bit of music in camp entertained us and lifted our spirits.

Our second 600-man training class for Chinese soldiers was in full progress. Because of the frequent heavy rains, classes were scheduled on a day-to-day basis. I was assigned the job of fingerprinting each Chinese recruit enrolled in the class. Actually, it was thumbprinting. In addition, I had to get the recruits' thumbprints in lieu of a signature each time they were paid. A perplexing problem presented itself with the initial class: of the first 600 enrolled, there were 38 soldiers who had two thumbs on the right hand! Which thumb was I to print? I asked Lieutenant Lovell and the commanding officer

(CO), and we decided to print the outside thumb, which, in most cases, was larger.

General Lui organized a field operation, which was intended to hit a Japanese outpost. Captain Dane (USMC instructor), Rainey (USMC), and Birr (chief pharmacist) headed a group of sixty selected Chinese guerrillas. Two days after leaving camp they made their attack at daybreak. It was to have been a complete surprise, but we think the Chinese guide became mixed up and caused them to arrive thirty minutes later than planned. Preliminary reports showed that thirteen Japanese occupied the post, but later Chinese intelligence said there were about fifty quartered there. Some were already out of bed when the attack took place. The Japanese cook had just come out of a building to start a fire when our men approached. They killed him. Two of our men entered the one-building outpost, spraying the inside with a tommy gun and throwing two grenades. Our task force hastily retreated from the building area and returned to our camp. The next day Chinese observers reported fourteen to eighteen Japanese killed and perhaps twenty-five to thirty-five wounded. The operation was intended to be a wipe-out, but in military terms it was a SNAFU because the Japanese managed to return our fire and had in all probability made radio contact with their command post.

My February 17 birthday came. And went. At thirty-three, I was the second oldest enlisted man in the unit, although several of the officers were older.

In March 1945 we received word from our coastwatchers that the Japanese who held Amoy Island had shot down one of our planes about ten miles from Amoy. Six men, including one officer, drowned, but seven others made it to shore, where friendly Chinese were waiting on the beach to help them and to guide them inland away from the Japanese. The survivors were literally plucked from under the noses of the Japanese. Among them was a war correspondent named Don Bell, who later wrote about the incident.

Our coastwatchers had monitored the crash and the route of the survivors. Shortly after the downed men set out with their volunteer Chinese guides, a navy coastwatcher emerged beside the roadway. The air group could hardly believe their eyes as they met the men.

"Hi, fellas," one of them called out. "I'm Tucker, U.S. Navy."

"We're Navy, too," the group replied. The men said they were on a PB4Y2 Privateer out of Clark Field, Philippines, and had been shot down. The pilot and copilot were in good shape, but the radioman, Warr, had a serious shoulder laceration, and Don Bell was suffering from a severe back injury. These two were in need of immediate treatment. They were being carried in swinging chairs by Chinese civilians.

The group was surprised to learn that there was a navy station only seventeen miles away. Bell wrote, "We were shot down about a mile away from a Japanese garrison, and in less than two hours a navy man was telling us that we were within hours of safety. When we saw Tucker with his rifle over his shoulder, you can well realize our well-being."

Dr. Coleman left our camp for Changchow, where the survivors were first taken for safety's sake and first aid. Later they all came up the river and stayed with us at Camp Six. As they recuperated, they were accompanied by several of our men to Lungyen and then to a small plane at an emergency field nearby. The plane flew them to the air force base in Kunming. Warr was with us for a couple of weeks and then taken to Lungyen in a sedan chair. All of us had scrounged around to outfit the airmen in various odds and ends of clothing. We did all we could for them and gave them each a good "gom bei" farewell party.

A few days later Levesque, Reed, and King, from the coastwatchers unit, got word of an American pilot who supposedly bailed out of his airplane. They found Capt. Eugene McGuire uninjured near his crashed plane, which had been hit by a shell while making a run over Hosan Airfield on the island of Amoy. Our men sent him on to headquarters at Changchow, guided by the Chinese. Soon after his arrival, our headquarters were buzzed by two P-51s. This was a signal of recognition, and well done! Of course, the native population disappeared in a moment. Captain McGuire said one of the plane's pilots was Colonel Rector, whom we had picked up in December and had helped back to Lungyen and Kunming. The 14th Air Force fighter group destroyed eight of ten planes sitting on the ground at Hosan Airfield.

War action in our area was picking up, and our reporting, coordinating, and rescue operations were paying off. Intelligence Area IV, which included our coastwatcher units at Changchow and Camp Six, seemed to be coordinating activities more and more. Sinks, our weather specialist, moved his heavy aerological equipment to our Changchow headquarters, where the terrain was level and not influenced by the mountain winds. After Chungking he moved to Kweilin, where he barely escaped capture by the Japanese. They were after him, for sure. He was tall, dark, good-looking, and a born promoter, with some deal always cooking around camp. His enthusiasm rubbed off on all of us. I was saddened by his move to Changchow, for he was my best buddy. Many an evening I helped him with launching and tracking his weather balloons. He had a fine voice and loved to sing.

Most of our mornings were misty, but as the day cleared, the mists lifted to the mountaintops, where they hung around until suddenly they were gone, and the whole world was bright and shining. Our cook started baking egg custard pies. I was pleased that he could make such good, flaky crusts, but I never did learn where he got his milk. Water buffalo? There were no cows in our area that I could find. We began having pork chops for breakfast twice a week. The crew thought the chops were the "bestest."

My early morning shopping trips into Hua'an with Cookie or our Number One Boy, the cook's assistant, were almost always eventful. One morning Cookie suddenly stopped and pointed to a small branch that hung over the trail. At first I didn't see anything; then I made out a small green snake. I was about to reach for it, as it looked harmless, but Cookie, horrified, yelled out. He said that the snake was extremely poisonous, and I could die within minutes of being bitten by it. I dislodged the snake with a stick, then killed it by stomping on its head. On my return I took it back to camp and Dr. Coleman said it was a bamboo snake. It rarely grew to over twenty inches, but its bite would paralyze a person in a few moments.

For weeks I had wondered who got up before us and swept the paths clean before we had a chance to start for Hua'an. Surely the sweeper should be commended for his neatness and diligence. One morning Cookie and I went into Hua'an earlier than usual. It was just at daybreak when we came upon a couple of huge pigs ahead of us on the path. These pigs were so swaybacked that their bellies brushed the ground as they walked down the trail. It was their bellies' swish, swish, swish at a gaited walk that performed the tidy sweeping every morning. Another Chinese mystery was explained.

Sometimes we met water buffalo, usually led by small children, as we walked the path. They walked in single file and were so bulky that we had no choice but to move off the path in front of them. They were truly massive when full grown, yet I never heard of any water buffalo that became wild or vicious.

An old woman regularly sat under a lean-to along our path. She was a doctor of sorts and treated patients, mostly soldiers, by gripping the skin on their chests between her knuckles, then pinching and pulling the skin. Black and blue marks appeared in a dozen or more places on a patient's chest, stomach, and arms after the treatment, but a victim always sat passively in an unflinching position while undergoing the painful treatment. There always seemed to be someone waiting to be treated by the old woman.

I was glad when the mail brought me items such as vacuum-packed cans of salted nuts; I was a nut about nuts. Sometimes we managed to get roasted peanuts cooked in salted oil in larger towns and cities, but it was a hit-or-miss affair. It was a long time before I found out that the peanuts in the shells were soaked with horse urine, then allowed to dry before roasting. By that time, however, it made little difference to me because I'd eaten so many of them without ill effects. A salting process is a salting process.

We received word through our Chinese Intelligence Network that Parsons, a radioman second class, along with Captain Lin of the Chinese Army and his boatman, had been captured on Whale Island while taking pictures of Amoy harbor, a regular assignment one person or another in the coastwatcher unit. They were taken to Amoy by the Japanese.

The details of the incident were told to me later by Lively, another radioman. He had accompanied Parsons and the others to the dock near the unit's camp on the mainland for what was to be a routine assignment. The group wanted to observe Japanese activities in Amoy harbor that day from the middle and highest point on Whale Island, a small, uninhabited island within easy range of Amoy. To reach a vantage point, it was necessary to go up a path leading from a cove on the southwest side of the island away from Amoy.

Parsons said, "Lively, stay here on the dock and keep watch."

Lively took up a point to observe with his binoculars at a distance of about 400 yards. He had a 30.06 rifle with a telescopic sight. The boat with Parsons, Captain Lin, and two boatmen crossed the water and landed on the beach. Parsons and Lin started up the path, then they were not visible because of high weeds. He saw them again as they reached the top of the island. All of a sudden he could hear shots, and through his binoculars he saw Japanese soldiers running along the beach. Quickly he opened fire with his 30.06 rifle, unluckily hitting Captain Lin in the leg.

Through his glasses it looked like the Japanese on the beach were signaling to others on top of the island. The group on top were still in his line of vision, and he saw Parsons and Captain Lin totally surrounded and being dragged away by Japanese soldiers. Lively rushed to an abandoned house on Sung-sue Point near the unit's outpost for a better view. From there he could see a Japanese patrol boat approaching the east side of the island. He couldn't see it land, but he kept watching until he saw it leaving Whale Island for Amoy. In it were Parsons and Lin.

"I think there were about twenty-five Japanese involved in the capture," Lively recounted. All he could do was return to the unit and report the incident over his radio.

Captain Lin was kept prisoner until October 1945. Parsons was taken to Formosa, and then to Tokyo, where he was released after the Japanese surrender. After the war, he went to Washington, D.C., to relate his experiences to navy intelligence.

Several of us were playing cards in my room one night when one of the men burst in shouting.

"There is something funny going on. I think the Japanese dropped a flare!"

We grabbed our carbines and rushed out. Some 200 yards from our compound at the west base of the hill, where our direction finder was located, we saw a brilliant light, hanging about five or six feet about the ground. We approached within 100 feet of the large ball of white light and watched it shining in every direction. There was no flame; just a cold, chilling light. No one reported hearing a plane fly over, so we concluded that it was not a flare. The intensity of the light transfixed us.

"What in the name of God is it?" a man near me asked. There was silence, as we all were at a loss to explain its origin.

Soon Chinese came from all directions, looking as bewildered as we did. The brilliant silver ball continued to float clear of the ground in a fixed position. It lit up the whole valley. There must have been thousands of candle powers sending out beams of light that pointed and darted around in the night. We figured the center of the light must have been between twelve and twenty inches in diameter at its most dense center. It was so bright it was difficult to look at it from less than 100 feet away; none of us approached any closer. This unearthly phenomenon lasted at least a half hour; then, as we continued to watch, we noticed the intensity of the light begin to fade. Gradually, over the next thirty minutes, the white light assumed a gold color, then it began to turn a red-hot-coal color. In about an hour's time it had faded to a soft glow. We returned to our quarters, totally baffled, talking in somewhat hushed tones of the eerie apparition.

I could hardly sleep. At daybreak I was up and over to the site of the mysterious light. A ring of scorched earth measuring thirty feet across could be plainly seen. There were also some fine cracks in the earth, none wider than one half inch, but running everywhere almost like a spider web. In the center of the ring was a small hole about one and a half inches in diameter. I touched the ground. It was warm, and the warmth extended out almost five feet from the hole.

Later, with an interpreter, I visited several farmers within viewing distance of the ball of light.

"Did you ever see a light such as this before?" we asked.

One old man replied, "My father once said that he had seen such a thing." No one could explain it.

My interpreter thought that conceivably there might have been a lost burying ground or graveyard at the site and the decomposed bodies gave off a gas that eventually seeped out and ignited when it came in contact with the air. I could not accept his theory because there was no sign of a graveyard and the quantity of gas needed to fire such a ball of light for the length of time it shone would have required a real gas well. Perhaps it was a gas well that gave off some new kind of gas, I thought. Yet all of us who saw it agreed that there was no flame at all to the light. The incident provided a conversation-starter for a long time.

Warr, the air force radioman who had recuperated at our camp, made a sudden appearance one day when he persuaded his pilot and crew to fly over our area. He was working out of the Philippines again. As we looked up, down came a parachute bringing a number of needed items plus a few personal luxuries. We were all pleased by his thoughtfulness.

A Japanese plane began flying frequently over our camp. We named it "Photo Joe." Just before Easter, Photo Joe passed over us; then, according to radio reports, crashed into a mountain about ten miles up river. Four of us started almost immediately for the crash site. We were about two or three miles from the crash when we met several Chinese carrying the severed head of the pilot on a stick that had been pushed through the throat. Blood was still running down the stick and all over the carrier's hand and arms.

"Ding bu hao," (very bad) I said.

"I wonder if they did this before he died?" asked Hank Irwin.

The group continued on down the path with their grisly prize. We found the plane on the mountainside. It did not appear to be a complete wreck. One wing had been torn off and was about a hundred yards away. The pilot's body was still in the cockpit, covered with drying blood and flies. The flies made a heavy humming sound. We searched the pilot's pockets, as I supposed the Chinese had done before us, but found nothing. A bloody map lay on the cockpit floor; we took it back to camp. General Lui was informed of the circumstances, and he assured us he would have the Japanese pilot buried before nightfall, with his head!

On March 28, a week before Easter, I was having lunch in the dining room when our commander asked for four volunteers for a special mission. I was one of the four. Then he explained that General Lui would like to have a group from the camp come to his church on Easter morning to sing!

"I have selected you four to represent the Navy," said the CO. He explained that it would be a Christian service conducted by a Chinese person; there would be no minister or preacher.

What a moan went up! We all voiced our protests, insisting that we could not sing, and did not know any Easter hymns or songs. It made no difference to the commander.

"Do the best you can," he said.

Easter morning was beautiful as we four volunteers walked into the Christian church in Hua'an. The men sat on one side of the church and the women on the other. The only exception was that General Lui's wife sat next to him on the men's side. She was a lovely lady, and I admired her open, democratic attitude toward all the people she met.

The services began when a Chinese woman with a beautiful voice sang a hymn. There was no musical accompaniment. During her song a youngster about three years of age walked from his seat to the platform and proceeded to embrace the singer's leg. With unusual control his mother continued singing. Holding the hymnal in her left hand she cupped her right hand, palm down, on the small boy's head and gently turned it, pivoting his whole body away from her. It was like screwing a lid on a Mason jar. Although this amusing action was repeated several times there was no fuss and no interruption in the performance.

Finally, it was our turn to sing. The four bearded foreign devils sang "Easter Parade" with gusto, if not finesse, dubbing in a number of words we did not remember. It seemed to please the audience. Then we sang "America," which thankfully most of the people in attendance knew. I was glad when this mission was completed. I told myself that I would never volunteer for anything again.

This Easter day did not end happily. While returning to camp, Ensign Mattmiller, who was an exceptional athlete, asked us to carry his clothes so that he could swim down the river to camp. It was about three miles. When he arrived he had a message waiting for him: his brother had been killed on Iwo Jima.

On April 10, 1945, four bodies washed ashore on the coast. They were U.S. Army Air Force men whose plane had been shot down. Our commanding officer asked General Lui if the bodies could be brought inland and buried next to our camp. He consented, and in a few days the bodies arrived in four crude coffins, each one transported by twelve Chinese carriers. Each carrier had placed rags in his nostrils because the stench from the decomposing bodies was revolting. The dog tags normally worn around their necks were missing.

The bodies were examined and measured for identification purposes by a navy dentist and his pharmacist helper, who happened to be visiting our camp at the time, together with Dr. Coleman. I stood around watching them force open the mouths of the dead men so the dentist could record all dental work and oral characteristics of the mouths. In about five minutes I gagged and sought outside air, losing every little particle in my stomach. I thought about going back to help the examining team, but in seconds my stomach revolted again. This was not for me. The odor was unbearable! In fact, I carried the smell of death with me for several weeks. Psychologically I had had it. I do not know how the team managed to complete its examination. A week later the missing dog tags were delivered to General Lui's headquarters and then to our CO. Since we had no way of matching tags with bodies, we in turn forwarded the tags to the U.S. Naval Group in Chungking.

Meanwhile, a group of Chinese soldiers and a number of citizens of Hua'an came to camp to clear a piece of land next to our compound for a cemetery. A waist-high bamboo fence was erected around the graveyard. White crosses were made for each grave. The day the bodies were interred with grave site ceremonies the entire camp's complement and hundreds of Chinèse paid their respects. That same day we learned that President Roosevelt had died, which intensified the mourning. During our assignment at Camp Six, we were to bury a few more American bodies in the new cemetery. I was moved to write the following poem one night:

DISTURB THEM NOT

Neath the sod, somewhere out there,
Rest those who fought and died.
Let them rest where they have fallen,
With their comrades side by side.
Why disturb their peaceful slumber?

For those at sea, we know they dwell
Within a field of blue.
The question does not enter here,
Can they be brought to you?
Would you, if you could, have them return?
When a man has fallen at his task,
A halo must be visioned.
The ground becomes a hallowed shroud

And not an earthly prison.
Would you unwrap the fold?

Men have fought and died for freedom,
Stories old have been renewed.
Now's the time for justly thinking,
Let them sleep where sleep is good.
Why rouse those who sleep so soundly?

About two weeks later a group of fifteen traveling Chinese actors and actresses arrived in Hua'an to present a show for us. They brought several small pigs and a number of chickens as presents. The play was just so-so, and I did not really enjoy it. The group hung around camp for several days, supping tea, then bundled up their belongings and left.

We were running low on candles again, so I decided to visit shops in several coastal towns northeast of camp. I took two Chinese soldiers with me. The second day I found a fair supply in a small town, and purchased all the merchant had.

"Do you know of any other shops that have candles?" I inquired of the merchant. He told me that Anch'i (Anxi), a town forty li (about thirteen miles) to the north might have a good supply. We asked him to hold our purchased candles until we returned.

The next morning we climbed another mountain and arrived in lush flatland country patterned with many large farms. This land was occupied by the Japanese, so we had to be extremely careful where we went. We kept a constant lookout for Japanese patrols. We stopped before we got into Anch'i, and I sent one of the soldiers into town to look around and make inquiries. He returned to report there were no Japanese in the town at the moment, but they had been there "ho, ho-tien" (the day before yesterday). He also said there was an old "Mei Guo" (American lady) in the town who could speak English.

We proceeded into town, where I bought a fine grade of candles, but not in the quantities I had hoped for. It was lucky shopping for me, however, since I bought a good supply of excellent peanuts and some better-than-average-quality sugar. I left the soldiers to guard our purchases and looked up the elderly woman who could speak English. She was a charming missionary who had been warned by her church to leave the area but had refused. She also had been warned by the U.S. diplomatic people to leave, but again had refused.

"I am eighty-two years old and have lived in Anch'i for over forty-five years," she explained. "I love the Chinese. They are my people and I will not move for anyone. I will stay here until I die."

The Japanese patrols that came through town once or twice a week had never bothered her, she explained. She had a milk cow and a fine patch of strawberries within the mission compound, plus a supply of "young yee" (white potatoes). When she invited me to stay for the night, I accepted. The soldiers with the supplies slept at the village inn. For supper that night I enjoyed small new potatoes browned in butter. They were superb. For dessert we had strawberries liberally endowed with good heavy cream. The missionary had two Chinese servants who managed everything with a grace and serenity that left me impressed. I talked with the woman far into the night.

When I told her about President Roosevelt's death, she said she had read about it in a Chinese newspaper. She indicated she would never consider returning to the States because most of her old friends and relatives were dead and her friends now were other missionaries in China and her Chinese friends. She wrote a letter that night after I went to bed, and I promised to take it with me and mail it with our next mailing from camp. She also gave me a small mesh bag of her new white potatoes. For breakfast I had a large glass of milk, another bowl of strawberries, and some fried pork chops. I tried to pay her, but she would not hear of it. She just implored me to visit her again and stay longer next time. I was sorry that I never saw the dear soul again. China had indeed claimed her for its own.

I hired two carriers to accompany my two soldiers and me back to camp. It was a good return trip, although we did spot one Japanese patrol from a high mountain path. They were far below us and were unaware of us because we remained motionless until they passed from sight down the coastal trail. When we picked up our first purchase of candles, the merchant told us there had been reports of Japanese in his area that day, but he had seen none.

Back at camp, more and more men were coming through, bringing large stores of weapons and special equipment. They were all headed for the coast-watchers unit. There was a tenseness and anticipation in the air. One day a B-25 crashed near the coast, but fortunately all the men survived. Lieutenant Plank, a mine specialist, salvaged two air-cooled, .50-caliber machine guns from the wreck, which were welcomed by our coastal units.

Payday for the Chinese soldiers was a big day. Everyone looked clean and fresh. It was the custom for approximately 600 men to form a line and proceed to our porch, which was set up for the monthly task. General Lui was always on the porch with us, and Lieutenant Lovell supervised the event. Brandwein, a storekeeper third class, was now relegated to taking the thumbprints and passing the soldier on to me. I paid each his monthly allotment, which resulted in big smiles. There was a rumor that General Lui collected a certain amount of money from each soldier to pay for their food.

All about us now it was spring. Wild roses covered the hillsides, but the land was very dry due to the light spring rains. At night we could see fires on the mountains, and in daylight hours we found ashes falling around us. Burning bamboos exploded like giant firecrackers. We learned that some of these fires were deliberately set by farmers so that the ashes would help fertilize their meager crops.

There was a time when the supply of chickens was scarce. Our needs, with the camp's continued visitors, had multiplied and we were eating more and more chicken, pork, rice, eggs, and anything else we could purchase. Before long we were reduced to eating only sweet potatoes and rice; to change the menu a bit we ate rice and sweet potatoes. We couldn't eat the fish from our river because they tasted muddy and were bony. It would have been good if I had known how to fillet a fish in those months. I was sorely tempted to eat my emergency can of beans that I had carried for almost a year, but I resisted.

The fleas attacked me again! I was lucky to get a fresh can of flea powder from one of the new men passing through camp. One day my back condition was aggravated by my helping to set up a huge metal temple bell in our compound. The bell was struck for chow time in the evening and for any emergency. It was about two feet in diameter and nearly four feet tall. I could hardly sleep because my back was so strained.

Late in April our camp had a mail delivery, and I received seventeen letters! The new men that brought the mail also brought a volleyball and net. Everyone turned out to build a volleyball court, and everyone became a volleyball player.

The days became quite warm. Simon, our Indiana pharmacist, dug up a piece of ground outside the compound for a garden. A relative had sent him several packets of seeds, and Simon was a farmer at heart. Chinese farmers and people from the surrounding area came by to watch Simon tend his garden. They offered advice, and he kidded with them. For all his bigness and rough appearance, he was a very gentle, likeable guy. Simon harvested very little because our camp moved in June.

For a change one day I asked for permission to take the mail out. I walked seventy li (about twenty miles) the first day. This many li is a little misleading because the Chinese reckon that it is farther up a mountainside than it is down. Their reasoning is based on the amount of energy expended in traveling a distance. Since it takes more energy to go up a mountain than down, they figure the distance is greater. I acquired three bruised toes the first day, and they were turning black. Later on I lost the toenails.

The second day I hired a chair and four carriers, although I got out and walked up steep inclines and down sharp drops. At the end of the second day I arrived in Lungyen, where I hired a truck to take me to the emergency Army Air Force field for the mail dropoff. The army had a great mess set up there with about a dozen personnel. I relished roast beef for the first time in over a year! This outfit had heard a lot about our Camp Six because the airmen we had helped had been routed through their emergency airfield. There was no sign of an air base during the day; all incoming and outgoing flights were made at dusk. Only then did the place come alive.

When navy supplies and equipment were routed through the air base, the navy assigned a storekeeper to cover our materials. This storekeeper became friends with one of Generalissimo (nicknamed "the Gismo") Chang Kai-shek's sons, who was with the military in Fukien Province. The son was sent to Fukien to discipline a Chinese general who was dealing in opium. When the Gismo's son arrived, he spent some time learning the facts of the case and then he had the general shot. This caused a hell of a commotion in the Chinese military headquarters in Chungking, and the Gismo ordered his son to return at once. The son refused. Stronger orders were issued. Finally, when Chungking learned of the friendship that had developed between our storekeeper and the Gismo's son, Commodore Miles sent our storekeeper a message requesting that he exercise his power of persuasion to get the son to return to Chungking. The storekeeper succeeded, Commodore Miles sent a navy chartered plane to the emergency field to pick up the son, and our store-keeper promptly received a commendation from the commodore and a promotion.

Flights from the base generally were made only to take out emergency cases or to fly in army, OSS, or other priority personnel. Usually when coming to take someone out, the plane would also bring someone in. Mail always went out. During my visit another navy man arrived with ten tommy guns and ammunition. He had been attached to another of our camps and knew my friend, Gebraad.

I spent the night at the air base, then scrounged a couple of cans of Treet lunchmeat from the U.S. Army Air Force. The new man and I headed back to Lungyen but were stuck there three days during heavy rainstorms. I worried about what the rain would do to our river, but we made the first river stage fine and went over the mountain to Gansee, where we stayed overnight. The boatmen were reluctant to leave the next morning at 5:00 A.M. because the river had crested during the night. I let the boatmen decide when to begin our journey. At 8:00 A.M. we hired two more boatmen to supplement our three, and finally at 9:00 A.M. we started down the millrace. My new companion was scared as all get-out when we went over the dam and down the sluice. Actually, there was so much water going over the breast of the dam that a stranger would not know there was a sluice or spillway there. After passing the dam the boatmen went to work with a will.

We heard the roar of the rapids. In a few minutes we were in white spray that leaped high about us. Our sampan swung about, sending us in and out of whirlpools. A large wave broke over the bow and drenched all of us in the front half of the sampan. One boatman began bailing. For a few minutes we straightened out and passed through a dangerous section of jutting rocks and boulders. Several times we felt a strong bump as we scraped a rock. Boulders seemed to be everywhere, so the boatmen used their long oars to continually fend the boat away. Some of the rocks just broke surface; others stood out like giant fingers trying to clutch us. Things were going so fast and furiously that I didn't have time to console my companion, and I had some moments of apprehension myself. All in all we shot four more rapids, each of which challenged our survival. As on my first trip, I shed all extra clothing. My new friend did everything I told him to do without questioning me.

The trip from Lungyen to Camp Six usually took the better part of three days, but we made this trip in two days. The high water made rowing unnecessary, except to control the boat. Our boatmen were truly superb in their handling of the sampan. When we landed at Camp Six I gratefully gave each of them an extra 100 CN. It had been a day of wild water, and our new crew member was much impressed with the ride, as well as the camp's excellent accommodations.

Not far from our compound was a moonflower tree, whose fragrance permeated the air for more than a mile. As soon as the sun went down the thick, creamy flowers opened and stayed open until the sun rose. We collected several branches and found that the beautiful flowers would open in the evening when put in a jar of water. The flower was special to all of us, and the young girls in the village liked to wear them in their hair in the evenings.

It was now mid-May 1945. The cook found a flavorful yellow fruit called a "pea paw," which grew in clusters of eight or ten to a branch. About the size of a small plum, the pea paw was half fruit and half seeds. The cook made jelly and a dessert that tasted like apple pie from the meat of this fruit.

At the end of May our third training class graduated. During this class we had an incident that should never have happened. One of our instructors, with his class on the firing line as usual, was giving the "Conduct of the Man on the Firing Line" lesson. The lesson was repeated several times through a Chinese interpreter. Basically, the lesson taught that the carbine (or some other weapon) was *always* to be pointed in the direction of the target. If there was a malfunction or a question, the student was instructed to place his weapon on the ground aimed toward the target, then call for the instructor.

In this specific case the student's carbine would not fire. It might have been because of a bad bullet. Without thinking, the student turned around with the carbine still in his hands. At first the muzzle was pointed at his classmates down the line, then at the instructor watching from several yards away.

As the student got up, the instructor slapped the carbine to the ground and then slapped the soldier smartly across the face. Of course, the incident was witnessed by the Chinese soldier's peers on the firing line, by several Chinese officers, and by some of our other instructors and officers. The student was ordered from the line, sent back about ten yards, and told to stand there until the class was concluded. The next day our commander received a message from Chungking to transfer the instructor back to Calcutta for further assignment. The speed with which the Chinese had notified headquarters in Chungking and the discussion of the incident with our commander resulted in the decision to transfer the instructor. It was done fast. The unthinking trainee, who had lost much face, was also transferred out of the class. Slapping the weapon to the ground would have been acceptable, but not the slapping of a student in front of his classmates. That was "ding bu hao" (very bad).

Heavy rain continued throughout the latter part of May. We had postponed the beginning of the new class for 600 guerrillas a number of times because of the rain. The last Sunday in May it stormed all day. Wild streams of water cascaded down the mountainsides, and the hill in back of our camp was sending down a heavy stream that missed our compound by only about 200 feet. The Nine Dragons River overflowed and by night the valley was inundated. The people sought shelter in our dry quarters. Our roofs were new and well thatched or tiled. By night, our mess hall and kitchen were filled with the old and young, mainstream Chinese and soldiers, as many as could crowd inside. They were a stoic lot who voiced no complaints. Each of our rooms slept an extra ten or twelve Chinese on the floor. The heavy rain lasted three days. On the fourth day, the Chinese began leaving a few at a time, and by the fifth day they were all gone. We had managed to feed the small children and the oldest people, but the rest of us fasted for about four days. (I still did not open my emergency can of beans.) It was another ten days before we were able to provide even a half-ration mess to our men.

When the rain ceased I made a trip downriver to Changchow. After descending the 500 steps over the mountain, the path led to the river's edge and along the river for about 400 yards to the village and its wharf. Along this path were thousands of Easter lilies in full bloom. Among the lilies swarmed tens of thousands of dragonflies (*Odonata Anisoptera*). They were every color imaginable; the brilliant sun reflected off their shining wings in dazzling blues, yellows, coppers, deep reds, blacks, oranges, greens, and purples. As I walked through the swarms, they would take flight and separate before me. It was like walking through a living rainbow! As a kid I used to call dragonflies snake feeders. Their color just added to their remarkable ability to fly in any direction, perhaps because of the tandem set of wings they have.

The trip down the river was negotiated on a family sampan. There were three men, three women, and three small children, all very clean. A baby was fastened inside a basket; the next child was in a halter that was tethered to the mast so he could go only a certain distance forward or backward, which prevented him from interfering with the oar's sweep or falling overboard. The oldest child helped as best he could. Sometimes two of the women worked with the men at the oars or the tiller. The third woman was evidently ill, for she lay covered with a blue cotton blanket. Even the sun-bleached floorboards of the sampan were well scrubbed. The trip was uneventful, and we did not have to look for channels because the river was running high.

Our Changchow unit was a beehive of activity. Rumors and observations were cause for setting up contingency plans. The foremost scuttlebutt was that a possible Allied landing in our immediate area was in the near future. Also, there was a strong possibility that the Japanese Army would move in our direction. We had a fine naval officer in charge of operations, and we had a very good Chinese network working with us. Much information was being received and sent to our submarines, ships, and planes in the Pacific theater.

When one of our photographers visited a small town near Changchow he was cautioned about a bomb the Japanese had dropped that did not explode. It had crashed through the roof of a public building, where it had lain for several days. Our photographer examined the bomb, then successfully defused it. He became the town hero. They brought him presents of chickens, ducks, bags of rice, and other items, a few of which he brought back to the unit.

We were hit hard by malaria, but I continued to be lucky and free from the disease. A new officer arrived in Changchow, a specialist in malaria control. He sent several of the very ill men to a naval hospital in Calcutta for intensive care.

Word came that our two marine sergeants had completed their eighteen-month tour of duty in China; they were ordered to report to Kunming for further transfer to the United States. They left in a pouring rain with two full days of walking before them. They said they didn't mind, they just wanted to be on their way before headquarters changed its mind.

One night in Changchow I was asleep with the mosquito bar positioned over me when I was suddenly awakened with the sense that someone was near me. I could hear breathing. Slipping my hand under my pillow, I grasped my .45. I detected a slow lifting of the netting . . . and at that moment, I jumped up, throwing the netting over the person while cocking the pistol.

"Mish! Mish! It's me, Ski." I had almost killed one of our crew. Ski said he was just trying to slip three letters under my pillow without disturbing my sleep. He called my name several times, he explained; and when I didn't answer, he figured I was in deep sleep. He realized how close he had come to being shot.

We were blessed with lots of fresh fruit in this early part of summer. There were litchis, bananas, peaches, apricots, and plums. In addition, a squash, much like a pumpkin, was available, and it could be mixed with eggs to make a strong custard. It did not, of course, have the smoothness of a custard made with milk.

Finally I obtained some typewriter carbon paper, which I was told had been smuggled out of Amoy to the mainland. This saved me hours and hours of unnecessary typing, but I couldn't believe the price: eighteen American dollars for one box. Later in the summer I found a supply of good paper made from bamboo. I had been using white rice paper, but it was not as good a quality as bamboo paper, which was slightly yellow.

I left Changchow and returned to Camp Six at Hua'an in mid-June. Shortly after I arrived, another aircrew we had rescued, one that was back in operation against the Japanese, flew over and parachuted a number of boxes of goodies. There were cigarettes, candy, playing cards, chewing gum, toothbrushes, toothpaste, shaving cream, razors and blades, toilet paper, pipes, tobacco, books, hand mirrors, combs, and knives. I was appointed to make equal distribution; but we had so much extra that we sent the balance to our navy brothers in Changchow. Candy was the big thing for me, while others were happiest with cigarettes. I bartered what I could of my spoils for candy bars.

Rain began again, incessant rain. My shoes would mold overnight, and either I or Alnav had to wipe them off daily. Still, my clothes, writing paper, the walls, and woodwork also molded. The gurgle and dripping of the rain lulled me to sleep. The good thing about the rain was that it kept the temperature down about ten or fifteen degrees, but oh boy, the humidity was something else!

One humid morning, I was being rowed across the Nine Dragons River by a Chinese boatman when a Japanese plane flew overhead. The pilot circled and came back to drop a small bomb. It landed about 200 feet from the boat, sending up a low geyser. One of our men on the bank took a picture of the plane at just the moment when the water shot up from the bomb explosion. It was a great photograph! The boatman began rowing for shore, and when we got there we scrambled up the bank as fast as we could. The plane did not return, and we wondered why the pilot wasted a bomb on a small boat with only two people in it.

Our table of organization (TO) called for five storekeepers for Camp Six. We had two. Thank heavens for Mr. Yip, the "lao-yeh" (old one), who performed well as a desk man. I also was assisted by Harry Brandwein, who worked for the *New York Times* for many years. He was a good, conscientious worker. One time the Changchow unit sent us a storekeeper first class who turned out to be a real screwball. He had married a Chinese girl with all the ceremony that went with such a marriage but could not bring her with him to our camp. This was his second marriage to a Chinese girl. Chungking then transferred him to another camp, and later we heard he had married a third Chinese girl before the war ended. He was sent back to the States after the third nuptial enterprise.

By this time many of us in Pact Mary (our term for SACO) had seen numerous Chinese and American military men. We appreciated the Chinese soldiers (bien), but had less and less respect for most of their officers. Most officers were fatuous, vain, and pompous, and only a few were genuine and worthy of a salute. After some consideration, we found this was also true for a number of our own officers. However, we were fortunate in having many more good officers than poor ones, which was also true of our carefully selected enlisted men.

Camp Six had one commanding officer recalled because he couldn't get along with people. He issued orders right and left; his second day in camp he ordered all enlisted men to stand at formation at 7:00 A.M. and designated our boatswain's mate to take charge. This was the first time, to my knowledge, that such a formation had been called in SACO. We lined up outside his quarters and the bosun called out for us to count off: "yi, er, san, sze, wu, liu, chi, pa, chiu, shih. . . ." The new CO heard this from his room, and issued an order that everyone who had counted off in Chinese was to have five hours of extra duty.

On his first trip to the pistol range he ordered me to go with him, as he had been informed I was the best .45 shot in camp. He wanted to see how good I was. He shot first but I outscored him. He wanted to try again, and again I shot an excellent score. From then on I was on his shit list. I was as happy as anyone in camp when the word came three weeks later that he was to be transferred. General Lui did not like him either.

"He was not a compatible person," the general told me.

Our new replacement was an ex-FBI man. When we competed on the pistol range one day, I knew I had met my match. I became the second-best shot in camp.

Generals Lui and Chen became good marksmen, too, with their .38-caliber revolvers. Graduation day was always exciting to the Chinese guerrilla soldiers. We issued a carbine, tommy gun, or a .38 to every man in the class. The Chung-Hua bien (Chinese soldier) was as proud of his weapon as we were of ours. The gala graduation day always included picture taking.

Our last training class was a special group that included about seventy-five Chinese pirates and forty other coastal Chinese. The intensive course was completed in three weeks at the end of June 1945. With the exception of six men, the class members moved off to the coast under a Chinese command.

We had a parachute drop from our friends in the sky again, including cans of condensed milk, coffee, sugar, cigarettes, and medical supplies. It was a pretty sight to watch the parachutes floating down. We waited expectantly for the key moment when a bundle blossomed out and the precalculated drift carried the parachute close to where it was supposed to land.

June and July in southeast China is typhoon season, and one day we experienced a dilly. It did not last long, fortunately, and did little damage, but it was severe.

Chinese intelligence advised us that the Japanese were getting ready to evacuate Amoy and invade the mainland, possibly to move toward Swatow (Shantou), to the south of us. Our camp became a beehive of activity. Early one morning, a large group of our men and several hundred well-trained Chinese troops slipped down the river on Operation Wild Horse. They were to conduct a raid on Wu-Su Island near Amoy. At the last minute they found there were not enough boats available to transport the entire strike force, but our leader, Matmiller, approached the island anyway. His boat came under immediate fire, as though the Japanese had been expecting our raid. The island was better fortified than our men had anticipated, and the Japanese threw a strong force into the fracas, filling the outer harbor with a hail of bullets. The Chinese boatmen decided against trying to land. Later the Wild Horse force regrouped at Gon-Way, where one of our coastwatcher stations was located.

Three other guerrilla forces were placed in strategic locations awaiting the Japanese move to evacuate Amoy for the mainland. We were all on alert every minute, day and night. The Japanese evacuation began on June 30, when approximately 3,700 Japanese landed on the China coast. They were preceded by a hundred or so men dressed as Chinese civilians. These infiltrators were the ones we were always watching out for.

This was about the time Sergeant Chen and I had destroyed the Japanese patrol on the mountain, an event that Alnav kept alive as long as possible. The morning after the fight, he had awakened me gently by touching my shoulder several times, pointed to my brass basin with the wen-shway (warm water) in it, and then smiled and play-acted as if he had a rifle raised to his shoulder. He made funny noises like shots.

When I finally got out of bed, Alnav told me that a farmer was waiting to see me, so I walked outside and listened to the farmer's story. There was a large wild boar with curved tusks on the hillside near his farm, and he was afraid it might some day attack a person on the trail.

"Will you shoot him for me?" he asked. "Yesterday he killed my best dog."

I had heard tales of the wild boars in the mountains and had seen them from a distance, but I had never encountered one. I took the 30.06 rifle with the scope, much heavier than my carbine, and left with the farmer. Alnav followed me. We walked about three miles to the farmer's house, where we heard several yapping dogs a short distance beyond.

"Go into the compound and lock the door," I told the farmer and Alnav.

I then walked slowly along the trail. The dogs' barking became frenzied. I suddenly saw the boar about 200 feet away, standing very still, facing away from me toward the two dogs. I took careful aim at his hind end because I couldn't see his front shoulder. It was easy with the scope. I squeezed off the shot; and as the bullet hit him, he charged the dogs. I could not believe he could charge like that with a bullet up his butt. He had amazing strength.

Suddenly he stopped. I could see I hadn't missed him because blood was running from his rear. He turned around to face me. My second shot went into his head, and I shot him a third time in his right shoulder. Then he slowly sank to the ground and turned over on his side.

In the meantime, the dogs rushed in, one making a big mistake by going for the boar's neck. The boar flung his head sideways and upward and caught the dog under its chin, ripping a deep, bloody gash from the dog's chin to its shoulder. I would have bet that boar was as dead as a doornail when that dog went for him. I called to the dogs, but they ignored me. I walked up to within ten feet of the big pig, put another bullet in his head, and one in his left shoulder. By then the dogs had started to calm down a bit, and I heard a "Haloo" behind me. It was the farmer, his son, and Alnav running toward me.

I said "bu hao" (bad) several times, and they nodded their heads in agreement. My dialect was poor but understandable under the circumstances.

I began making arrangements to move to Changchow. We were leaving Camp Six. General Lui ordered the mayor of Hua'an to provide all the labor we needed to carry the equipment and supplies over the mountain to the river-front village. First I emptied the godowns and stacked all the gear in our mess hall. Our direction-finder men would stay for a few days to dismantle and pack all their special equipment. It was a shame to move it because we couldn't improve on its position no matter where we moved. It was precisely coordinated with the other naval DFs in China. Our large temple bell mounted off the ground on a framework of supporting timbers was too heavy to move. I hated to leave it.

Dr. Coleman came back to Camp Six with two pharmacist mates to help him remove his valuable refrigerator and a small still that he had improvised. They would all go back to Changchow as soon as possible. He also made arrangements to move the beloved piano back to the mission near Changchow. Camp Six personnel were not occupying the coastwatcher station. Instead we had appropriated several buildings of a vacant school on the northern edge of the city of Changchow.

As usual, when the doctor was in camp a multitude of ailing Chinese showed up at the compound for medical care. For the next three days he and his assistants were busy every morning. This, too, was sad for me. This would be the last time Dr. Coleman would tend to their ailments. These good-natured, small, and tough people would greatly miss him.

CHAPTER 14

# Victory Banquet

---

*August 6, 1945—Atomic bomb is dropped on Hiroshima.*
*August 9, 1945—Atomic bomb is dropped on Nagasaki.*
*August 14, 1945—Japan accepts Allied surrender terms.*
*September 2, 1945—Peace instrument is formally signed aboard USS* Missouri *in Tokyo Bay.*

The move from Camp Six to Changchow was marred by only one mishap. Twelve Chinese carried our piano down the 500 steps to the dock, which came off all right. But when it was being loaded onto the sampan, the boat listed and the piano slid into the river. That created a big disturbance and much discussion. Finally, the boatmen and helpers managed to heave it up from the water and place it on board. At the sampan's downriver unloading point eight men carried it across the flatlands to its original home in the mission near Changchow.

While I was preparing my move from Camp Six, the Japanese evacuated Amoy and landed on China's mainland. Their force of about 2,000 soldiers and 1,200 civilians headed for Changchow and then turned down the coast to Swatow, where there was a large concentration of infantry. Their maneuver was to parallel the coastline, but the Chinese National's 75th Division blocked them, so they made some sharp directional movements, continuing toward Swatow. Our group, consisting of the 1,600 guerrillas we had trained plus about 30 Americans, were a separate force from the Chinese Nationalist Army. The Nationalists allowed them to pass, then quickly moved to their rear, between the coastline and the Japanese. We kept to the hills west of the

167

Japanese main body. The enemy was caught between the Nationalists and our guerrilla forces.

The Japanese knew exactly where we were; and they knew the position of the Nationalist force on their other side. We could easily see the Japanese through binoculars. They took cover under trees and foliage during the heat of the day. With them were several hundred horse-drawn carts and wagons, loaded with gear. Some of the officers were mounted on horses and rode during concerted movements. They marched slowly toward Swatow.

We kept in touch with the U.S. Air Force out of Henderson Field in the Philippines, and transmitted the positions of the marching Japanese to them. The second day of the enemy advance, three of our planes delivered bombs with pinpoint accuracy. We assisted the planes by placing large white muslin arrows on the ground pointing in the direction of the Japanese concentrations. The first day many Japanese soldiers, civilians, horses, and mules were killed. As the day ended the Japanese began moving toward Swatow again. Our guerrillas came up behind them.

The Japanese did not spend much time burying their dead; various parts of bodies were lying uncovered in hastily covered graves. Several large fires with bodies on them indicated that they burned some of their dead. Our Chinese soldiers were extremely cruel to Japanese prisoners. In one instance a Chinese soldier cut off the head of a prisoner, and then, holding it in his arms, asked one of our men to take a picture of him.

Pop Cannon, who had been one of my roommates in Hua'an, was our first American combat casualty. He was lying next to one of our guerrillas who was hit by a bullet. The bullet passed through the guerrilla's mouth and out his neck and into Cannon's arm. However, our Chinese guerrillas fared worse. The second day of battle we suffered 150 killed and 325 wounded. One Chinese received severe injuries to his buttocks by a mortar shell. Doc Coleman, God bless him, gave up his rubber-inflated air mattress to this man.

At the end of the third day, the remnants of the Japanese force numbered about 800. We were getting close to Swatow, so we held up, not wanting to risk running into the strong Swatow force. The Japanese were in a position to keep us fairly far away with their accurate mortar fire. We learned that when a mortar shell hit close to one of our positions, the next one would land still closer, so we always moved away from our first position quickly.

We received word that the Chinese Nationalist Army, which outnumbered us five to one, had numerous casualties, but ours had been even heavier.

Drinking water had been scarce along the marching battle route. Several of our men were very sick, and dysentery was widespread. We sent many ill men back to Changchow, and several of us returned with them.

During our second day in Changchow a plane from Manila flew over our emergency airfield and dropped several parachutes, all containing cases of cigarettes. One parachute landed in the river, but it was recovered before any of the cartons got wet. Later I was put in charge of distributing the cigarettes, giving two cartons to each navy man and ten cigarettes to each Chinese soldier we treated.

Our coastwatchers observed a large Japanese oil tanker that sat deep in the water anchored up at Amoy. This was the moment that Matmiller and his Chinese swimmers had been awaiting. Matmiller and Wong, a heavily built, powerful swimmer, were ready to put their plan into action. As soon as it was dark, a small boat rowed the two swimmers to a previously selected small island, also within sight of Amoy's harbor. After checking the tide and the time, the two men lowered themselves into the water. Secured on their backs were magnetic limpet mines, which were flat on one side, with supercharges of Composition C. They were about the half the size of a basketball and weighed about twelve pounds each.

The running tide helped them swim with the mines in the direction of the tanker. Their time, so carefully estimated, was on schedule. Swimming silently and swiftly in the dark, they reached the tanker and placed a mine on each side in a prechosen spot. If plans went right, in exactly two hours, acid-eating time pencils, broken by the swimmers, would detonate themselves, and the Comp C would blow up the Japanese ship.

The tide turned shortly after Matmiller and Wong set the fuses, so they were again aided by the tide on their return. Within two hours they were back on the small island. From there they were rowed back to the mainland. Upon their return the swimmers dried themselves and changed into warm dry clothes. We all waited, and waited.

"The explosion should be in about fifteen minutes," said Matmiller. Fifteen minutes passed.

"Damn pencils must not have worked," said Matmiller.

Then, while we were talking about it, a light flashed suddenly in the harbor. We were all quiet. Seconds later we heard a great, rumbling noise. Then nothing. Lights were going on all around Amoy and its harbor. One mine must have detonated, but there was no fire. Ten minutes later we heard another muffled rumbling sound. We saw through our night binoculars that the second charge had detonated; but unlike the first explosion, this one sent up a geyser of fire that got higher and higher, then a second flame spewed over the entire Japanese tanker. We continued to watch, totally transfixed. It took about thirty minutes for the fire to envelop the ship, causing it to blaze beautifully in the dark night.

We all yelled excitedly and congratulated Matmiller and Wong for their hazardous feat. They were as happy as a couple of kids on the Fourth of July. We waited an hour. The ship was still burning fiercely when we left our point of observation for the mainland. This episode was reenacted as a play on the Wrigley Chewing Gum radio program in Chicago shortly after the war ended. Matmiller was awarded the Silver Star for his stellar performance.

A night or two later Landt and I took time off from the war to climb into a pair of rickshaws and take a tour of Changchow. My rickshaw man had fastened an old-fashioned automobile squeeze-ball horn on the fore part of his right shaft, and he used it freely at the slightest provocation. It made a sound of "ooompa." In the darkness the rickshaws twisted and turned, avoiding people and bumps. Since it was early evening people were sitting in the front doorways of their homes, from which escaped diffused yellow light. Later, in full darkness, it was more difficult to see the people. Even with a feeble glow from the rickshaws' solitary kerosene lamps, it would be hard to say we rode in anything but darkness. Now and then a cigarette or pipe would flicker like a firefly, then suddenly it was gone.

It was a ride through a dark and mysterious land. Landt and I were intrigued by the strange smells. They seemed to be mostly food and cooking odors, but we could not identify them. At night the streets were quiet in comparison with the harried daylight hours. The evening was the major relaxation period for all Chinese families, a time for them to be together. My rickshaw's proud horn was the most pronounced sound on the streets.

In front of us, two rickshaws tangled shafts, but no harm was done, and the drivers merely disentangled their vehicles and quietly went on their ways. Sometimes in the darkness the children spied us, or perhaps smelled us, and knew we were Americans.

"Ding hao" (very good) and "O.K." they called from the darkness; and when we replied to their sallies, they laughed. They seemed happy. Lord knows, they had so little to laugh about. Finally, Landt and I arrived back at our schoolhouse quarters. I handed the rickshaw man 200 CN. He questioned me by holding his hand outstretched.

"Mayo sans chen?" (No more money?)

"Mayo," I told him. He laughed as he turned away, satisfied with the amount. He loped down the lane with his buddy, his horn continuing to honk like a goose that was lost from its migrating friends.

Our CO issued an order that I, as supply man, would be the only person to buy the camp's whiskey and wine, hoping this procedure would control the price of liquor. Our men had been bidding against each other, which drove prices sky high. My first purchase in Changchow was forty-five bottles of Red and Black Label Johnny Walker Scotch. The Japanese and Chinese did not like whiskey, so there was plenty around that I could buy cheaply. The liquor probably had been brought to Changchow from Amoy before the war, so no doubt it was well aged. When my purchases were delivered, I stacked them pyramid fashion on the steps in the school's stairwell, where several of the men had their pictures taken. Then I promptly sold each bottle to the men at cost, which was about eighty cents American.

Several of the men continued to have severe dysentery. One of them, Lupo, spent almost 75 percent of his time sitting in the outhouse. He said he had read everything he could find. His illness, along with that of others, was attributed to drinking what they thought was good, clean water during the battle with the marching Japanese.

There was a hot-spring bathhouse in Changchow. The warm water gurgled up through a hole in the ground and was then siphoned off into each of a dozen bathtubs. Young attractive Chinese girls would soap and wash the bather, so it was a popular place for Chinese gentlemen and naval personnel. We had a lot of clean men in camp! I, as well as others in camp, contracted prickly heat in the hot weather. Dr. Coleman mixed a potion to use on the itch, which uncomfortably was most prevalent in our crotches and between our legs. The preparation would give us relief for about a half hour; the warm baths offered the best and longest relief.

Mr. Yip invited me to his home for tea. The entranceway was furnished with a massive Victorian apparel rack backed with a mirror; it looked elegant. I felt quite honored to be a guest in his home. Of course, we worked closely together, and I always considered him an equal, which few others in camp did. He was polite, always neatly dressed, well shaven, and he flashed a gold tooth when he talked. I met his number one, number two, and number three wives, the youngest of whom was very pretty. It was the duty of number one wife to prepare and serve our refreshments of tea and cookies. A stiff formality was observed when guests were in Chinese homes.

Our commander received the following message one day:

FROM: COMNAVCHEC.
TO: CAMP ONE CHANGCHOW.
QUOTE SACO CAMP SIX TROOPS COMBINED WITH AMERICAN ASSISTANCE HAVE PERFORMED GALLANTLY DURING RECENT CAMPAIGN IN ANNIHILATING A STUBBORN ENEMY X EYE AM DEEPLY PLEASED AND WISH TO EXTEND MY CONGRATULATIONS X
CHIANG KAI-SHEK.

We did not know why it was addressed to Camp One, which was far to the north of us. At least it was sent to Changchow and Camp Six, for whom the message was intended.

On August 14, 1945, the local newspaper and the Chinese military headquarters reported that an atom bomb had been dropped on a city in Japan by the U.S. Air Force. This resulted in a great deal of celebrating by the Chinese that night. Fireworks and firecrackers exploded all over the place! We at Camp Six did not know what an atom bomb was, let alone its effect. So we continued our daily routines. For the first time I was catching up on my paperwork, giving me a good feeling. I noticed several times that my paste pots, small earthen containers holding about two or three ounces of rice paste, had been cleaned out during the night. Early one morning I caught the culprit in the desk drawer, a rat. When I suddenly pulled open the drawer, I caught it between the drawer and the side wall. As it screamed, I pulled harder and harder on the drawer for about five minutes until it was dead.

One day a young man who had been found guilty of dealing in opium received his sentence publicly in Changchow. About noon he was led by two black-uniformed policemen to a heavy block of wood placed on the main street. People gathered. One policeman grabbed one of the man's hands and held it down on the block. With one chop of a heavy cleaver his hand was amputated.

Changchow had many beggars, from the very young to the very old. They carried rice bowls as a token of their trade. Seldom did any business establishment entered by the beggar refuse him or her a bit of rice. It reminded me of the beggars I used to see on East Broadway in New York City, where there were a lot of Jewish clothiers. I never saw these beggars refused a few cents either.

A large wooden wagon, usually pulled by water buffalo, hauled drinking water into certain areas of the city. The water was sold to people who brought their own containers. At the marketplace, food merchants spread out their wares, tobacco, dried fish, and vegetables and fruits of all sorts, on large, woven-reed mats. Fresh fish were displayed in large wooden-staved tubs of shallow water. Wide-brimmed, woven hats were displayed for sale on yo-yo sticks. The young Chinese girls were shy; they tilted their parasols to hide their faces when a Mei Guo (American) passed them, then twirled their parasols coquettishly.

Many Chinese are fine artists. An old man did two marvelously detailed black-and-white paintings on the entrance wall of our school's compound. One depicted a fierce Chinese warrior holding a mettlesome horse by the halter. I don't know who commissioned him or who paid him for the work or why it was painted on that particular wall, but when the work was completed I gave him 100 CN. Later I had one of the crew snap a picture of it, and I took the picture home as just one remembrance of the unique folk customs of the people in China.

Landt and I visited several Chinese temples in the area about Changchow. At the entrance to one was a huge twenty-foot-high figure. It was carved out of stone and surrounded by a scaffolding. The stonework was being embellished by adding a kind of plaster to certain parts of the statue. Some black hair was implanted into the fresh plaster as it was being applied. Other surfaces of the giant stone figure were painted. All the work was done by priests who spoke only when spoken to, and then only in short, precise statements. Another beautiful temple was protected by several large ferocious-looking stone lions, who may well have been reclining there since the beginning of time. Inside was one of the happiest-looking Buddhas I had seen while in China. He smiled favorably on all those who entered.

When my eighteen-month tour of duty was up, I radioed a message to Chungking to advise headquarters of the fact. My communiqué asked, "When can I expect my orders to leave for the States?" The afternoon schedule brought the following reply: "QUOTE: MISHLER DO NOT CLUTTER UP THE AIR WITH SUCH UNNECESSARY DRIVEL UNQUOTE XX." The navy system for relief of duty arrived shortly thereafter and was posted. All personnel were busy figuring and refiguring their standings. I rated highly and was informed that I was the recipient of a navy recognition award and had been promoted to storekeeper first class.

Our Chinese cook approached me one morning after breakfast to ask if his wife could be off for the rest of the day because she was going to have a baby. She had been obviously pregnant for some time.

"Certainly," I told him. I told him to hire a temporary helper until she was well enough to come back to work.

His wife's job in the kitchen had been to set the tables, then remove the dishes after the meal and wash them. That same evening when we finished our dinner, the cook's wife came into the dining room to clear the tables. Naturally, I was surprised and went into the kitchen to speak to the cook. He was all smiles and very happy.

"My wife have a healthy boy," he boasted. "She feeling well so no reason to stay home," he added. How these Chinese continued to amaze me!

Hurrah! Peace negotiations were in progress! The Chinese immediately began a huge celebration. They held a torchlight parade to our compound with masses of people filling our schoolyard. It was a colorful and inspiring sight. What a wonderful feeling to be an American! There was much drinking and singing, but I did not participate.

Because of the casualties among the Chinese guerrillas who had encountered the Japanese, we sent a request to Chungking for a second doctor and pharmacist. The pharmacist replaced Powell, who had cut the forefinger on his right hand while opening a can of rations. The finger had become seriously infected, and Dr. Coleman had sent him to bed. He gave Powell doses of the new sulfa drug we had received from the States. By the fourth day the finger looked so terrible that Coleman feared it might have to be amputated. Powell held his hand over the side of his bunk, so that the constantly dripping fluid dripped into a can. He had planned on becoming an optometrist after his navy discharge and was heartsick at the thought of losing his finger. He kept telling me how important an optometrist's forefinger was to his proposed practice.

"How would you feel if someone was fitting you with glasses and he had an amputated finger?" he moaned.

When the second doctor arrived, he conferred with Dr. Coleman, telling him that he had learned that some people were allergic to the new sulfa drug. They decided not to administer any more of it to Powell. They used another course of treatment. Soon the finger showed improvement, the swelling went down, and Powell recovered. His morale lifted immensely. Thirty years later I almost died from taking the same drug. I didn't know then that I, too, was allergic to sulfa.

A peculiar quietness soon settled upon our camp. It looked as if it might become my duty to close this SACO campsite as I had the one at Hua'an. There was a rumor that the coastwatchers and Camp Six would soon be deactivated. We were joined by two new men who brought three fifteen-horsepower outboard motors with them. Clark, our motor machinist mate, went to work on the motors and found they ran fine on alcohol and improvised several sampan motor mounts.

The photographer who had defused the bomb in the nearby village took one of the outboards and a sampan and went down the river and into the bay at Amoy. Why he did this foolish thing, no one ever knew, for he had no orders to do so, but when he landed at Amoy at full tide he was met at the wharf by a Japanese general and about fifty soldiers. The American stepped ashore, the first American or Chinese military person to do so. He asked the Japanese general to surrender, which he did, giving up his sword and assuring the navy man of his full cooperation. "The general spoke English quite well," said the photographer.

When our man returned with his story and the surrendered sword, all hell broke loose in camp as well as in Chungking! Messages flew between our commander and Chungking headquarters. The U.S. Naval Group China had been informed that only a Chinese general was supposed to accept a sword in surrender. The U.S. Navy was to keep completely out of any negotiations, so the photographer was arrested and confined to quarters. Later he was sent to Shanghai by truck, along with the first group of SACO men to leave. This group was under the command of Lieutenant Commander Meyertholen and his seven coastwatchers. We thought they had done a fine job. They were bound for home!

A new officer arrived, bringing a movie projector. Oh, boy, we thought, now we can have some good entertainment. But as one might suspect, no film was sent along. Another SNAFU!

Everyone, including me, was getting rather antsy. My heat rash was getting the best of me. Others were uncomfortable also. Walking only aggravated the itch. I had heard that the salt in seawater was supposed to clear up the problem. I was anxious, then, for several reasons to get to the ocean once more. Our cook prepared a good thirst quencher by cutting up pineapples and cooling them in a heavy crock overnight. They were cool and delicious by morning.

I had become quite friendly with one of the prominent jewelers in Changchow. Every time I went to his shop I saw his elderly father sitting in a chair beside a raised platform. This platform held a glistening black coffin with large gold-leaf characters emblazoned on it. The jeweler told me this was to assure the old man, who never uttered a word, that he would be well buried. It was the custom to make the gift of a coffin to one who was about to die.

Chinese grave sites varied widely in appearance and usually followed the style of the area. In the Hua'an area some hillside steps were bordered by niches containing clay burial pots and urns. Many had been broken over the years so that the contents were exposed—the bones of the departed. Wealthy personages were frequently buried in tombs on hillsides, enclosed in hardened earth designed in the shape of a horseshoe and smoothed over with painted clay or plaster. An old wealthy family might have four or five such grave sites adjoining each other. Also in the Hua'an area were many graves or tombs built into smaller sloping hillsides. Heavy, square pieces of stone sealed the entrances to these tombs. Some of the graves were mutilated and torn apart by grave robbers, who sold any valuables they could find.

On one of my trips by truck, I noticed a coffin on a raised wooden platform just off the road. I asked about it at the next village and learned that the person in the coffin had been involved in a lawsuit. Until the lawsuit was settled, the body and coffin would remain unburied. When I asked how long it had been on the platform, the reply was "seven years."

In September 1945 inflation was at its highest point since my arrival in China. When I arrived in Kunming, 90 CN was equivalent to 1 American dollar; now the ratio was in excess of 3,200-to-1. I had a hunch that the CN would strengthen with the ending of the war, so I bought a sizeable amount of CN with my American dollars.

One day the Chinese jeweler asked if I would like to buy a beautiful diamond ring. I replied that I would like to see it, so he assumed the duty of consignor and said he would talk to the owner and get its price. The next day he showed me the ring, a three-and-a-half-carat stone mounted in heavy gold. He called it a tea diamond, a pale yellow diamond more prized in the Orient than a blue or a white diamond. I examined it carefully through a magnifying glass and detected no imperfections or carbon spots. Since I had a lot of CN now, I wanted to convert it to a few good tangible items. I was careful not to show too much interest in purchasing this brilliant diamond ring.

"What would the owner of such a ring sell it for?" I asked my friend.

"The owner would sell it for 3,000,000 CN," he answered.

"Too much," was my reply. "But I will think about it for a day or two and then return with what I consider a fair offer." The 3,000,000 CN was worth about 1,000 American dollars.

Late the next afternoon, I returned to the jeweler and examined the ring again. I explained that the yellow diamond was not worth as much in America because we considered the blue and the white diamonds more valuable. After a while, I said I would be willing to pay 1,000,000 CN, but he laughed and said it was easily worth 3,000,000 CN. I again told him I would think about it overnight and see him the next day. Meanwhile, word got around camp about the large diamond for which Mishler was bargaining.

The next day several of the fellows went along to see the ring. I instructed them not to express any interest or make any comments about my bargaining. At the store the jeweler explained that the owner had dropped his price to 2,000,000 CN, the lowest he would consider. I informed my friend that, as much as I appreciated the owner's drop in price, the 2,000,000 CN should have been the first bargaining price.

"Such a price in America is one that few people can afford. I am not one of them," I told the jeweler, whereupon I made my last, absolute offer: 1,500,000 CN. "I will not be interested in any further negotiations," I stated, "and I want a firm reply by tomorrow afternoon."

The next afternoon I stopped in at the jewelry store and asked if the owner had come to a decision to sell for 1,500,000 CN. He looked at me with a puzzled expression.

"I do not understand! The owner decided to sell for 1,500,000 CN, and one of the men with you yesterday came by with the money. He said you were too busy to come, so you sent him. He paid for it and took delivery."

I was furious and hurried back to camp! I discovered that one of the radiomen had made the purchase. I began cussing him and would have hit him if our CO had not been present. Later I did tear into him and would have broken him wide open if some of the fellows had not intervened. From then on, no one spoke to him. If he sat down by someone, that person got up and moved to another place. The incident was known as "Mishler's diamond deal."

On September 5, 1945, all Americans except those who were sick attended a Chinese victory banquet, the most important military gathering ever to be held in the area. Many Chinese generals attended, including General Chang of four-star rank. The event was held in an immense room filled with large round tables that seated eight.

The banquet began with a good wine. As soon as a wine cup was empty, it was refilled immediately. Next we were served shark-fin soup, followed by such delicacies as tender whitefish cooked in pineapple juice and onions, turtle soup, cuttlefish (small squid), roast duck cooked in fine broth and stuffed with small oven-roasted white potatoes, roasted monkey, eels, shrimp, eggs with water chestnuts, boiled chicken in broth, frog legs, and other delicacies. Of course, there also was boiled rice and a wonderful mold made of large peanuts, raisins, sweetened rice, and sweet-potato paste. One dish was supposedly roast dog. It looked good, so I had a small serving. Whatever it was, it was thoroughly edible.

The food was cooked in excellent fashion and served hot. Since many dishes were new to me, my good friend Sergeant Chen, explained them as we ate. It must have cost someone a fortune to throw this banquet for about 160 persons. A few were in civilian clothes and were possibly leading merchants who might have supplied some of the foods. We were served custard for dessert, after which we sang several Chinese songs. Inevitably, there were toasts to China, the United States, the Generalissimo Chiang Kai-shek, President Roosevelt, and President Truman. General Chang gave me a big black cigar from a box he was carrying. It was wrapped in cellophane and manufactured in the Philippines. I slowly smoked about an inch of it, enjoying the pleasing aroma. It was about the third time I had ever smoked a cigar, but I thought if ever there was a time to do it up big, it was now!

After the ceremonies Sinks got up and sang. He had a good voice and was well received. Later we walked back to our quarters together. Sinks was one of the few allowed to remain in the coastwatchers' compound because it was a great deal of trouble to move his heavy aerological gear. That night the camp was noisy and argumentative. Half of our men were sick from eating or drinking too much. A few were missing, so two groups went out to look for them. No problem—they were found in the hot baths! About 3:00 A.M. things at camp began to quiet down. I had been careful not to drink too much wine and not to overeat and I felt fine, but others bemoaned their overindulgence.

We received orders to move to Kulangsu, which was located on a small island near Amoy, but within a day or so another order came to disregard the moving order. This same procedure occurred three times in ten days. Several planes from the Philippines continued to drop little bundles of odds and ends for us. We were always glad to receive them, but we had more cigarettes than we could use. I was issuing them in quantity to our men and to the Chinese soldiers.

Chinese commanders were dickering over which military group would be in command of Amoy. They also were trying to determine what demands should be made of the Japanese under their respective authorities. No group—Nationalist, guerrilla army, or navy command—had visited Amoy since the photographer made his unauthorized landing. As I had hoped, the Chinese currency began strengthening. Our emergency airfield north of Lungyen closed, so mail could no longer pass through that route.

A typhoon hit Changchow and dropped water everywhere. The wind hit eighty knots! Walls of buildings washed away and buildings collapsed. It flooded for five days. Then the sun came out, the water receded into the riverbanks, the wet mud dried, and everyone was rebuilding. It was surprising how the streets were cleaned up so well within two weeks. It was time for writing letters, cleaning weapons, and playing poker. Our CO was an avid bridge player, so there was always a foursome made up of officers.

One day my ears picked up the following story: "Did you ever hear the reason why a sailor can't help following a pair of pretty legs? Because a pair of legs are a pair of limbs. A pair of limbs is something you find on a tree. Something you find on a tree is bark. A barque is a boat. A boat is a ship. A ship spends a lot of its time on the ocean. And a notion is a hell of a good reason for following a pretty pair of legs!"

One of the pleasant things I enjoyed watching in Changchow was the morning and evening parade of duck men. These were the Chinese men who took their flocks of a couple of hundred ducks to harvested rice paddies, far from the city, to eat all day. It was said that the duck men could hold conversations with their ducks, and I believed it. Eight duck men left early every morning on one of the roads leading into the country. One special flock always took the lead; their duck man carried a long thin bamboo pole, which he used to point the direction he wanted his charges to take. With the addition of a few magic words, the ducks waddled off as directed. A second flock followed, and all the other flocks did the same. They kept together as if they had a line wrapped around them. Once in a while a duck or two would begin to straggle away from the flock, at which time a touch of the bamboo pole would hurry him back to his proper place. However, the main function of the twenty-foot pole was to point the direction.

After a mile or so into the country, the leading duck man called out a command. Like soldiers at drill, his ducks wheeled off at right angles to feed in a rice paddy for the few grains lost in the harvesting process. They made soft little clicking sounds as they ate. A short distance farther out, the second flock would turn off in the other direction, seeking lost grains of rice. They scavenged until evening, when the farthest flock from town assembled at some duck words spoken by the duck man. In orderly fashion they waddled back to the road, waiting until the hundreds of ducks were gathered in perfect form; then they paraded back to town. Hardly ten yards separated the eight flocks, yet no attempt was made by any duck to run ahead or to join another flock. Before beginning the return trip, the duck men gathered the eggs their charges had laid during the day. They carried them in basketlike slings thrown over one shoulder and under the opposite arm.

On September 12, 1945, we were advised that all censorship had ended. Now, happily, I could write and tell Audrey that I was located about an hour up the river that flowed directly into Amoy harbor. The truth is, she probably already knew this because we had a secret code worked out before I ever left the States. To get around the censors, I revealed my location to her by spelling out the name of the city using the first letter of the first word of each sentence in the opening paragraph. But no sooner was my first uncensored letter in the mail than I was told that because I was one of the essential storekeepers, I would not fall under the usual point system for returning home. This was depressing news!

Now that the war was over, and I couldn't go home, I wondered how long it would be before I would at least leave Changchow. Since it was late September, the weather was perfect for traveling, and I was anxious to get along. But to where? Amoy? The ever-mysterious Shanghai? Or perhaps even Peking?

CHAPTER 15

# A Lady Named Kuan Yin

*October 1945—Wrap-up of loose ends for SACO; we turn surplus armament over to Chinese military and float downriver to Kulangsu and Amoy.*

**I** was packed and ready to go for several days before we received orders to proceed to Kulangsu, the former International Settlement Island across from Amoy. This was on October 1. The boat that was to take us across the harbor was about the size of a sixteen-foot rowboat, and when we were loaded, it sat very low in the water. With me on the boat were Irwin and Clark, navy men; Dr. Coleman; and a missionary named Dr. Dupree and his wife, who entreated me to take them along at the last moment.

We had no life preservers and were going head-on into a tide. Still, we made it to Kulangsu, arriving at high tide as planned, and stepped out of our boat onto the grounds of the Sea View Hotel. Here the tide rose and fell more than twenty-four feet. Across from our hotel we could see the famous island of Amoy (called Xiamen by the Chinese), a distance of about a mile and a half. Irwin and I occupied a small guest house on the same grounds with the three-story hotel. A high wall surrounded the hotel, with the exception of the seawall side. Chinese soldiers were placed on guard at the entrance from the street and at each end of the seawall.

Our officers, naturally, occupied the best hotel rooms. However, the furniture and conveniences of our room were nice. Hand-painted scenes adorned some of the walls. The plumbing in the hotel and in the cottages was deficient. Bathrooms had no running water, and eventually twenty men were using the four functional bathrooms. Water was carried in continually by coolies, who tried to keep the toilet tanks and the urns used by bathers filled. Only one of three drinking water boats was in service when we arrived. The coolies carried water from a good well on Amoy.

Kulangsu was about one-tenth the size of Amoy and incapable of supplying any of its own needs. The hotel had a clubhouse and a social building, which we often visited. Large thick guest books were still in the club room, along with two billiard tables with missing billiard balls. I wondered why the Japanese had not used the heavy guest books as fuel.

I learned that Kulangsu was once a showplace of China. We saw about a hundred beautiful old homes, all sorely in need of repair. The Japanese had gone into most of the houses and torn out wood floors, door frames, doors, thresholds, windows, and anything else that could be used as fuel for cooking or heating.

Amoy harbor was the best port on the southwest China coastline. Before the war, Kulangsu was populated by a mixture of nationalities well able to afford the nicer ways of living. The island also had a coastal telegraph station with its cable intact. The Japanese had a use for it so they had not cut it. The station was manned by a Norwegian who, along with his family, had lived there throughout the war without being bothered by the Japanese. They had, nevertheless, experienced food and fuel shortages. There were no Japanese on Kulangsu now, but on Amoy there were still some Japanese civilians and a few soldiers who were restricted to a specific area.

Within three days of our arrival, our radio and communications personnel were transferred to Kulangsu. There were six radiomen left in our complement of twenty men. Letter writing went on far into the night, because we were informed that our commanding officer would fly to Shanghai in two days and carry out the mail. Our airfield would now be on the island of Amoy, about four miles from the city. The western side of the airfield sloped away into a marshy area and the inland waterway. We saw a number of wrecked Japanese planes near the airfield, still in their revetments.

The bumboats and sailboats, sampans and junks, merchantmen and men-of-war made a beautiful picture in the harbor. Prettiest of all were the many-colored sails on the bumboats, vessels used to ferry people and goods back and forth across the harbor. When the tide was at its lowest we could also see wrecked ships lying on the bottom of the harbor. Matmiller's sunken tanker was at the upper end of the island. Long wharves stretched along the Amoy side of the harbor where sheds and large storage buildings known as Factors had English names printed on them. England had had the greatest shipping trade in and out of Amoy before the war.

I had developed a severe sunburn on the two-and-a-half-hour trip down the river from Changchow. It was not only the direct sun rays that bothered me but also the sun's reflection off the water. My nose and lips were swollen and blistered; my eyes wanted to close by themselves, and my nostrils were filled with great scabs so I found it difficult to blow my nose.

Before leaving Changchow, an OSS officer on his way home had given me a 12-gauge shotgun and four boxes of shells. General Lui offered me 1,000 American dollars for it, but I refused to sell it to him. Instead I sold it to Lieutenant Dealy for 200 dollars, with the provision that I could borrow it to go duck hunting. The deal was that when he took it hunting, he'd share all his ducks equally with me. It worked out fine for both of us. There were lots of ducks in the Amoy area.

Lieutenant Lovell and I worked out an arrangement with the Japanese officer in charge of the Japanese prisoners in Amoy. He agreed to have his men transport us between Kulangsu and Amoy and to other islands as we ordered. The day he agreed, he sent to our dock a motor launch that had a twin-eight Packard motor and a crew of three soldiers. The soldiers were good workers and wore their old military uniforms with the white cloth of surrender tied around their left arms. We gave our orders to the Japanese sergeant, and he passed them on to the crew. We communicated in sign language most of the time but managed a little bit of talk; it didn't take them very long to learn our universal word "O.K.," which they used a lot. Of course, there was no real camaraderie, and I made it a habit to stand in the rear of the launch where I could watch the crew at all times.

On Amoy, we helped blow up the Japanese artillery guns with Composition C. The guns had been built into emplacements, and charts had been painted on a hard surface in front of each gun, showing various landmarks in the surrounding Chinese territory and the yardage and gun elevations required to hit the targets. Two of our coastwatchers' units were pinpointed. For some unknown reason, they had fired at only one of the two points, an old pagoda, which I knew they had hit several times. None of our men stationed at the pagoda had been hurt because, luckily, they weren't on the top floor when it was shelled.

I bought a new portable Royal typewriter in a large stationery store in Amoy. It still had the original paper on the platen. It cost only six dollars—a real bargain! It was wonderful for writing long letters to Audrey and Craig.

Our CO gave us the news that twelve of our men would be sent to Shanghai for duty there or would be sent directly home. The morning they left, I accompanied them to the airfield. It took two hurried trips across the harbor in our Japanese powerboat to get them to the transport plane. I wished them well and said I hoped to see them in Shanghai soon. After their plane took off, I climbed into several of the wrecked Japanese Zeros that were at the airfield. I was especially surprised to see how plain the insides of the planes were. One of them had been strafed repeatedly, and there were holes all over the fuselage. There was not a thing worth removing for a souvenir.

The day after the twelve departed, a dispatch arrived stating that Lieutenant Lovell, Mishler, Brandwein, Irwin (pharmacist mate), and four radiomen were to remain on Kulangsu until further notice. A lot of good my fifty-one points did!

On the afternoon of October 15, 1945, Irwin and I stood on the dockside of Amoy and watched eight Australian minesweepers enter the harbor. The vessels, or "sweeps," were 200 feet long and cruised at about twelve knots per hour. As the first sweeper approached our wharf, a bullhorn blared right at us. "Are you Yanks?" a voice asked.

"Yes," we nodded and waved.

"Stand fast. We are here to save you!"

This amused us because, of course, the situation was already well in hand. The sweepers brought up a mine as they were coming into the harbor. The commanding officer said he believed there were eighteen more mines unaccounted for.

That evening Irwin, Brandwein, and I went aboard one of the sweeps to talk to the storekeeper. It was a good visit, as they broke out steaks and beer. How good it was! The Aussie commander had gone to visit Lieutenant Lovell on shore, and I knew he would not eat as well as we did.

In a number of places around the island of Kulangsu where the land dropped sharply into the sea, we discovered numerous tunnels built into the cliffs by the Japanese. They had installed small-gauge mine tracks that ran from the water's edge back into the tunnels. Loaded on small flatcars were lightweight boats with built-in engines, and in the bow of each boat we found heavy charges of explosives. These were kamikaze boats, designed to ram a ship and explode upon impact. During my exploration of the tunnels, I found four boats that were operational and ready to go. The others were coming apart at the seams and would not even have stayed afloat. Our CO gave me permission to blow up the kamikaze boats. The resulting explosions did not give the island much of a jolt because I only set off one Composition C charge at a time.

A plane arrived, and the postman placed his finger on the postal-alert bell and let it ring a long time. I received thirty-five letters and ten copies of *Time* magazine. From *Time* we learned that SACO's veil of secrecy had lifted and we had been dubbed "The Rice Paddy Navy" or "What-the-Hell Gang"! It said that our operation was one of the best-kept secrets of World War II. We also learned that the hometown newspapers of all the men in the U.S. Naval Group in China had been sent articles about the roles played by the individual men.

One day Rouse, a man I had met in Changchow, arrived in Kulangsu. He was one of the four men of the Rouse and Krouse and Rice and Price quadruplets and had told us to withdraw our deposits in local banks, which we did even though we were drawing 16 percent interest. Although English, he was the Chinese Customs commissioner for the port of Amoy; and as such, he ranked higher than even the mayor of the island. He lived in the largest house on top of the hill in Kulangsu, about 100 steps up from the wharf. The Chinese government provided him with a yacht and a four-man crew that were at his beck and call. Rouse's private U-shaped beach was hemmed in on two sides by sheer cliffs.

Rouse, with his household staff of five well-trained servants, entertained us often, and the dinners were excellent. His house featured a wide ramp leading from the ground floor to the second floor, which had six extraordinarily large bedrooms. Four beds could be put in each room. The ceilings in the home were about fourteen feet high, and the bathrooms were ten-by-twenty feet in size. The dining room, when cleared, plus an adjoining room, could accommodate a hundred dancers. A long porch on one side overlooked the ocean. It was remarkable that his house, for some reason, suffered less damage from war activity than others on Kulangsu and that he could get it running so smoothly after having to abandon it during the Japanese occupation. Another interesting question was where had he kept all the beautiful silverware and dinner china during the war.

Rouse held the same position before the war, and I once asked him why the Chinese employed an Englishman instead of a Chinese Customs commissioner.

"They trust the English," he replied. His comments about China were always very complete and frank. He had been in China for more than fifteen years and had worked his way up to this position, which paid 15,000 American dollars a year and all expenses, quite a bundle in 1945.

The first dinner we enjoyed at Rouse's consisted of a delicious soup, hot rolls, Australian butter, a pastry filled with chopped meat, fresh fried shrimp in garlic sauce, french fried white potatoes, and green canned peas with a fresh mushroom sauce. Dessert was sliced oranges and a thin, fried sweet cake with syrup. A beautiful bowl of flowers and green ferns centered the dining table, but what was really fantastic was the presence of a white linen tablecloth and napkins, and even finger bowls!

Several of us were sitting on the hotel's seawall one evening watching the Aussie mine sweepers return from their day of sweeping around the islands. They were proceeding in single file past us toward the docks when, suddenly, the *Ballarat*, which was the third in line, hit a mine! The stern rose high in the air, and the bow went down like a piece of wood thrown end-first into a pond. Then it backed out of the water, the stern slapping down on the water with a heavy splash. Finally it began to roll and settled back into its regular position in the water. Almost instantly two other sweepers drew up on both sides and launched several lifeboats. Fortunately, the damage was not severe and no one was killed. However, the *Ballarat*'s rudder and propeller were disabled and the stern section needed repairs. Below deck, sections had been sealed off so that the sweeper would still float so long as the pumps were operating.

I watched the entire episode through my binoculars. It seemed more like a movie than a serious accident. If a large ship had passed over the ratchet-type mine, it could easily have been blown in two. The short length of the sweeper almost allowed it to pass over the mine before it was activated and rose to the surface.

That evening the Aussies decided that the *Fremantle* would tow the damaged craft to Hong Kong. I learned that all the dishes and bottled beer on the *Ballarat* had been broken. Before they left for Hong Kong, I visited the commanding officer of the *Fremantle* and offered to give his ship a case of American cigarettes (fifty cartons) for two cases of canned peaches, two cases of canned pears, and fifty dozen bottles of Tooth's quart bottles of beer. I knew that he could replenish his supply in Hong Kong. He accepted and returned a week later bringing us five drums of gasoline for our radio generators, hotel lights, and outboard motors.

"It's a lend-lease deal," he smiled.

Four more of our inland naval personnel had recently made their way to our unit on Kulangsu, having been delayed by lack of transportation between the stations in the interior. When we radioed Shanghai for transportation for these men, the reply was, "Send the men to Shanghai by Chinese junk." A few of the younger, romantic men were eager for the adventure; the smart ones were not. The junks rolled constantly, and the food was reported to be terrible. I would have hated like hell to have to take passage on one. I was among those who waited for a better mode of transportation.

We were now faced with having too many houseboys on Kulangsu, so several were sent back to General Lui in Changchow, including Alnav. We had a party for the departing houseboys, and I gave Alnav a handful of CN. I also gave him a pair of cloth slippers, a toothbrush, and a pen.

We limited ourselves to two houseboys, and I found a real treasure in one named "Mickey" Chen. Mickey's father was Chinese, his mother Burmese. He was completely honest and eager to please. It was when he helped me shop that I made my best and cheapest purchases. Mickey had been conscripted into the Chinese Army when he came from Burma to visit his father's relatives. He had picked up a lot of English words and was good at making himself understood.

As in Changchow, I served as the sole liquor purchaser for our camp on the island. Most of the men preferred wine, but a few liked whiskey mixed with some of the fruit juices that were available. I bought several bottles of whiskey to take with me to Shanghai. Each one cost me about a dollar a bottle. Surprisingly, Vat 69, Johnny Walker Red Label, and Dewar's scotch were always easy to find.

On October 26, an official message informed us that two planes would be flying in on the 28th to take out 12,000 pounds of men and gear. Since I no longer had the good help of Mr. Yip in Kulangsu, I worked all night on pay records, and Brandwein assisted me. We had to scramble to get our paperwork done and all supplies ready to go in two days.

I told him, "I bet those guys who were planning to go to Shanghai by junk would have raised a real bitch if they had left on the junk and the planes had arrived after they had put to sea."

To our surprise, some of our cigarettes appeared for sale in local stores; it became our job to confiscate them. The Chinese money changers, we learned, were shortchanging the Aussies in the black market. They were giving them 300 CN for a dollar and 650 CN for an Australian pound note. When I found out about this, I offered 600 CN for an American dollar and 1,300 CN for an Australian pound note, forcing the Chinese to raise their price to mine. I then increased my exchange. I had plenty of Chinese National Yuans and was glad to make these exchanges because the Australian pound was very stable; and I had over 600 Australian pounds when I arrived in Shanghai.

I had a lot of CN on hand after not buying the diamond ring in Changchow, so I was able to buy a few American and English gold pieces. Soon Mickey was putting me in touch with a number of Chinese families who were in need of CN notes and would sell me some of their gold pieces. There was a huge amount of gold hoarded by Chinese families along the coast. I also found a number of U.S. Trade Dollars, which I bought for less than the cost of an American dollar.

Irwin had become friends with one of three Spanish Catholic priests who had a mission on Kulangsu. The priest, whose command of English was limited to what he had learned traveling across the United States eleven years before he went to China, came to dinner with Irwin many times and stayed for evening beer. One evening he told us he had always wanted to fly in a plane. On the spur of the moment, we arranged for him to fly to Swatow and back with a pilot we knew.

We all waited in our rooms until we heard the returning plane buzz our hotel; then we went out to the landing field to pick up the father. His account of the trip went something like this:

"I rented a rickshaw at the Swatow airport and rushed to visit a close friend. I spent too much time talking and was late getting to the airfield, only to find the plane going down the runway. I fell on my knees and prayed, and the pilot saw me and came back. The ride was bumpy coming back. I was standing up holding onto a bar when we flew over Kulangsu. I tried to remain standing, but a great power seized me and pulled me down until I lay on the floor of the plane. It was the force of God warning me that I should never again be late for a plane."

One night about ten o'clock, when the good father was drinking with us, we heard a tommy gun firing near the hotel. We rushed out with our guns in hand and found the sentry holding a young man and two girls against the wall, pointing his weapon at them. The sentry had heard them coming and challenged them, but they did not reply or identify themselves, so he cut loose at the sound of their voices. Some of the bullets splattered within a few feet of the young Chinese. They were lucky. We commended the sentry. After questioning the boy and girls, we released them and they scurried into the darkness.

We then continued our conversation with Father DeCappa, drinking one bottle of Australian beer after another. When the talkfest broke up at 1:00 A.M., Irwin had to help the father to a rickshaw and pay the driver to take him back to the mission.

"Mish, you know I like that son of a gun!" Irwin told me.

The next afternoon the father showed up again.

"How do you feel?" I asked casually.

He put his hands up to his head.

"You shouldn't get so drunk, father," I said.

He stopped still for a moment and, with a straight face, replied, "I wasn't drunk; I was merely confused." He then told us that the other two priests had forbidden him to come to our hotel in the evenings any more.

On October 28, after the planes took out some of the men and gear, we all had nice single rooms at our hotel.

"We're going to go soon," surmised Lieutenant Lovell.

We passed the time performing our few duties and finding interesting things to do. We bartered with the Aussies, swapping cigarettes for stateside canned goods. We now had ferryboat service between our island, Amoy, and Quemoy, and the weather was as perfect as southern California in the wintertime. Foliage around the hotel was a haven for birds, which may have accounted for the hawks that soared in the sky.

Mickey and I toured a number of almost deserted side streets in Amoy one day. We found several small but pretty parks with beautifully designed entrances and walls around them. Little ponds contained small goldfish with flowing tails. I watched small children flock around the sugarcane men, paying one yuan (less than half a penny American) for a piece of cane. This was their candy. The children would chew on the cane for a while and then spit out the pulp. This splintered pulp could be seen on any street in the city and all along the paths in the country.

In a corner of the city we passed a drugstore, although there was little to indicate it was such a store. The counters, which were bare, formed a table that opened onto the sidewalks of two streets. What attracted my attention were six glazed ceramic vases sitting on top of the closed cabinets. I began talking with the druggist, with the help of Mickey, and offered him a cigarette. I knew I should not reveal my interest in his vases. I asked him about the Japanese occupation of the city, if he had done business with them, how long he had been a druggist. He told me he had always been a druggist, as had his father and his father's father.

"I am an American soldier," I informed him.

"Yes, I knew you were an American right away," he smiled.

"I'd like to take something nice home with me as a pleasant remembrance of China," I continued, with Mickey's help. "Like perhaps one of those vases." I pointed to the six on the cabinet top.

He immediately insisted they were not for sale, but for display purposes only. He added that they had been in the shop since before he was born. I pointed to one and offered him 10,000 CN for it. He shook his head. "No, no, no. It is not for sale."

I paused a moment and pushed another cigarette toward him. He was reluctant to accept this one, perhaps because Chinese custom generally obligates the recipient of a gift to give one in return. We talked more, and I assured him that I knew the vase I had chosen was indeed very beautiful, and I could understand his reason for not wanting to part with it.

"Perhaps you would consider selling me one of the other vases that has less value and beauty," I said, "like that one." I pointed to the vase I had really wanted all the time. It was hand-painted white porcelain adorned with eighteen raised figurines of Chinese men clad in colorful robes. A red dragon encircled the neck of the vase, the surface of which was made up of three-eighth-inch swirls in bright green, purple, yellow, and pink. The odd thing was that it had numerous openings among the swirls.

When I asked him to show it to me, he climbed up on a chair and handed it down. It was a vase within a vase; the inner vase was intact and could hold water. The outer vase was fourteen inches tall and twenty-five inches in circumference. All the men's faces on the figurines wore happy expressions. It was so beautiful I had to contain myself.

I pointed to the one on the shelf and said that this one did not compare to it, but I would still pay 10,000 CN for the one on the counter.

"No, it is not for sale."

"If it were, how much would the price be?" I asked. He turned to Mickey and spoke. He was quiet for some time and then said something to Mickey that I could not understand. Mickey then turned to me and said if he did sell, he would not take less than 30,000 CN. The druggist did not remove the vase from the counter, so I thought perhaps he was considering selling it.

I told the druggist that I might get notice to leave China any day now and would like very much to have this vase if he did not want to sell the other. I felt I could not bargain any longer, but I decided to make one final offer of 15,000 CN. Again he said he could not sell it for less than 30,000, and I told him it was far too high. I could not afford it.

Then I took the balance of the pack of cigarettes out of my shirt pocket and offered it to him with both hands. He did not want to accept, but I persuaded him by telling him that I wanted him to have the cigarettes so that there would be only pleasant moments to remember of our conversation. I added that I wanted his friendship even though he did not sell the vase and that he should not feel obligated in any way. He did not reach for the pack, which I had placed on the counter as we left.

As we walked down the block, Mickey told me that the druggist was strong-willed and did not want to part with family possessions. I replied that I thought he might and had hardly gotten the words out when we heard a yell.

"Wai, wai, wai" (Wait, wait, wait). The druggist was waving to us from the sidewalk in front of his store. We walked back to him and, after a little polite talking, closed the transaction at 15,000 CN.

Later on Mickey said, "Mr. Mishler, you would make a good Chinese person." He began laughing. "I did not think he would sell."

The prized vase had cost me about five American dollars. When I worked in Washington, D.C., after the war, I took the vase to the Smithsonian Institution for an appraisal. The Chinese curator told me it had been made around A.D. 1500. He also knew the exact area where the clay from which it was fashioned could be found but would not give me an estimate of its value.

November 12 there was a big holiday celebration in honor of Dr. Sun Yat-sen's birthday. Kulangsu honored him by having electric lights for the first time in many years; not so long ago, Amoy honored Chiang Kai-shek in the same way. China has many holidays and celebrates a lot of them with fire-crackers, which are extremely popular with the children.

We were just beginning a specially planned dinner a few days later when a Chinese admiral and an American plane crew that had flown him into Amoy barged into our dining room. We neither heard nor saw the plane. It compli-cated matters because we already had the mayor of Amoy and six of his staffers seated. Our men immediately gave up their chairs and waited until later to eat a simpler repast. We had scrounged most of the dinner from the Aussies, including canned peaches for dessert. I was sure the plane's crew thought we were eating and living like kings on Kulangsu. As a matter of fact, it cost us 44,420 CN to feed our guests; but since it was Lovell's idea, we assessed him half the cost.

Next door to the hotel lived a very aristocratic Chinese lady, a widow with six children. The oldest was a boy, age seventeen; the two youngest were the prettiest little girls I had seen in China. Their musical-sounding names were Ai Yong and Ai Ling. Mrs. Ting, who weighed about ninety pounds, had no income, so she was selling her lovely possessions bit by bit. I bought a green glass vase covered with chased, silver-filigree lacework. Mrs. Ting spoke English fairly well and said she had a brother who had attended Notre Dame University and was now in Manila.

Word circulated that the Aussies would be pulling out the following day. One of our men, just for the hell of it, set off a distress flare from the roof of our hotel that night. Within ten seconds, the Aussie mine sweepers responded with flares, sirens, and brilliant searchlights beamed in our direction. Within thirty seconds they had three boats in the water headed toward our hotel. The whole thing was very embarrassing; and the officer in charge of the Aussie flotilla read the riot act to Lieutenant Lovell. Our prankster was restricted to the compound for the duration of his duty on Kulangsu.

While twiddling my thumbs on the island, I read the book *Vigil of A Nation*, by Lin Yutang. I had traveled many of the routes he described, and our unit had been quartered in the school he had attended in Changchow. In fact, Mr. and Mrs. Dupree, the American missionaries who came down the river with us to Kulangsu on my initial trip, had once been Yutang's teachers.

Several of us were invited to dinner by a Mr. Lee, who had been the Shell Petroleum representative for Fukien province before the war. The large Shell Oil tank that sat on a hillside of Kulangsu was drained by the Japanese and had stood empty for over two years, but Mr. Lee had received word that it would be filled by a tanker and that he could resume his activities.

Mr. Lee was a pleasant, elderly "lao-yeh" (old one), whose beautiful eighteen-year-old daughter had been educated in Shanghai and spoke excellent English. She was the only woman to eat at the dinner table with us; her mother stood in the kitchen doorway, from where she directed the two servants.

Two Chinese men were already at the Lee home when we arrived. They were neatly dressed in European-style clothes. Mr. Lee introduced them, and I spoke a few words in Mandarin Chinese.

They both laughed and said, "We speak English." They were doctors, one having been on the staff at Johns Hopkins Hospital in Baltimore for four years, and the other on the staff of Walter Reed Hospital in Washington, D.C., for three years. Both had been prisoners of the Japanese for more than three years and had received the Japanese bamboo fire torture. Bamboo splinters were shoved under their fingernails and set on fire. The burning splinters were allowed to burn into the ends of their fingers, and the doctors bore heavy scars. They were pleasant conversationalists with good senses of humor; and, like others who spoke English, were happy to have a chance to practice their skill and learn what was going on in the world.

Before dinner I looked around the large living room and saw several unique pieces of artwork. I asked our host the origin of a small sculptured stone head. Mr. Lee explained that it was the head of Kuan Yin, the Goddess of Fertility. He thought it might have been broken from the body of the goddess in a conquest or robbery of some temple. The head was about seven inches tall and was mounted on a teakwood base, carved so that the head was held erect.

After a cup of very good, warm wine, we all sat down to a dinner consisting of many different courses. At one point a servant placed on the table a large bowl of broth containing a boiled chicken, its head and feet still attached! The head was draped over the edge of the bowl, facing Mr. Lee. He stood up, reached for the bowl, and turned the head in my direction. By Chinese custom, this was to honor me, and it was my duty to eat the head. I knew that I would not like chicken head! So I quickly stood up and turned the bowl slightly to my left so that the head pointed in the direction of Miss Lee. During this bowl-turning ceremony, there were "ahs" from the Chinese diners and smiles from the Americans.

To my great relief, Miss Lee very deftly grasped the chicken's neck with her chopsticks, twisted the head off and placed it in her bowl. I will never forget how she ate the chicken's comb and sucked the eyes out of the head, eating them with the Chinese polite indrawn sucking sound. All in all, the dinner was excellent.

Early the next morning Mickey rapped on my door saying I had a visitor. I was surprised to see Miss Lee sitting on a bench in the hotel's garden. She handed me a box.

"My father sends you this gift," she smiled.

When I opened the box, I was somewhat taken back. I looked into the eyes of Kuan Yin.

"I cannot accept such a priceless gift," I told Miss Lee. I was still very astonished at this turn of events. Then I remembered from somewhere that when a guest verbally admires an item, it is the Chinese custom for the host to give it to the guest. I spent several minutes trying to convince her I could not accept such a gift. Finally she left, in tears. I was quite shaken, too.

In a half hour Miss Lee was back with the Kuan Yin head. Her father insisted that I keep it as a remembrance of him and his family.

"Well," I said to myself, "what gift could I make in return?" I ended up giving Mr. Lee twenty-five bars of Lux soap that I had saved from an air drop. Because soap was such a scarce commodity, I thought it might be well received, but it was actually a small present in return. I placed the head with the other cherished art pieces I had obtained in China: the bronze tiger, the silver bracelets, some ancient bronze coins, and the two vases (Mrs. Ting's and the druggist's).

We had a change of Chinese soldier guards. One of them asked me how long I had been in China; and when I told him, he said it seemed we might have met before. I finally remembered. He was one of a group that had loaded the truck I first took out of Kunming to Chungking on February 3, 1944. He was surprised and pleased that I remembered him. He told me that the last navy convoy of fifty-five trucks had come over the new Burma Road. Things were just getting underway for the navy in China when the war ended; and prior to the opening of the Burma Road, it was always necessary for us to beg the U.S. Army Air Force for transportation for freight and personnel from points in India.

The Australian minesweepers, the *Maryborough*, the *Fremantle*, the *Bathhurst*, the *Bendigo*, and the *Cairns*, departed for their home ports one day. The next day the *Anhai* left and carried our mail to the U.S. Naval station in Hong Kong. We were sorry to see them go, as we had made some mighty good friends among the crew.

Mickey and I made another tour of Amoy. We visited the large, open areas that were living quarters for the Japanese civilian prisoners. The buildings had a roof only; no outside or inside walls. Living spaces on the floor were marked off in sections for each family. There was no furniture. Rice-straw mats covered most of the wooden floors. The people sat in a tailor fashion (with crossed legs) or knelt on the floor when they were cooking their food or making tea in little clay firepots. These firepots also provided their only heat in cold weather. They were mostly older people and only a few had children. They did not talk to us but just bowed their heads as we passed. I had heard there was a Japanese general among these people, but evidently he had changed to civilian clothes. The prisoner enclosure was surrounded by Chinese guards.

When we were in Changchow we had a Catholic chaplain, Father Philip Shannon, assigned to our camp. He was athletically inclined and initiated baseball, volleyball, and basketball games. He found some basketball hoops and a basketball, probably because basketball is played all over China, even in the remote villages. Our guys played some good games with the Chinese soldiers. If they had been our average height, they might have beaten us every time, for they were very quick. Father Shannon did not go with the first contingent of men that left the original Camp Six for Shanghai by truck, but he did take the first available plane out of Amoy. He wanted to be paid before he left, so I made out a check for 600 U.S. dollars, as he requested, and Lovell signed it. I cautioned him about cashing it in Shanghai and carrying the large sum of cash on his person.

Three days later the father sent us a message that he had lost his check and to send another. Alas! Navy regulations did not permit reissuance of a check for six months, and then only if it had not been cashed during that period. I assume that Father Shannon had to borrow or beg from friends, and I hope that our Shanghai disbursing officer paid him the balance of his accrued pay and, perhaps, an advance. Father Shannon died on April 15, 1989. He was a U.S. Navy chaplain for nine years.

I prepared a package to send some of my valuable souvenirs home by having a carpenter cut up one of the wooden desks in our office in the hotel. I packed a Chinese doll, a flying bronze dog from the Tang dynasty, several small vases, the stone head of Kuan Yin, and some tiny black-and-red silk shoes once worn by a Chinese woman when the custom of binding women's feet was still practiced. The latter were very old.

One day one of our interpreters took me with him on a sampan to shop in a small village upriver named Haitsung. I shot three ducks on the way. In the village I bought some water-buffalo meat that we cooked back at the hotel. It was a little tough but tasted more like roast beef than anything we could find.

On December 1 a flotilla of English minesweepers arrived to replace the Aussies. They spent most of their time sweeping for mines between China's mainland and Formosa. The Limeys were a sad lot, completely different from the Aussies. They were dirty and unkempt when they came ashore and proceeded to get drunk and lie around in the streets. They fought with the Chinese as well as with each other, and I avoided them as much as possible.

One day Lovell, Irwin, and I received a dinner invitation from a man named Blount, the newly arrived manager of the Hong Kong Bank. The bank had been closed during the war, and he was about to reopen it. With Blount was his friend, Thompson, from the Office of War Information. We were to join them at a restaurant that had been operated by the Japanese but was now managed by a Chinese gentleman. The second-floor dining room where we ate, however, was strictly Japanese decor. A small platform, about a foot higher than the floor, was covered with rice-straw mats. This was where we sat cross-legged. There were cushions we could lean an elbow on or use to help shift positions.

I suffered leg cramps a few times and had to stand up and work out leg muscles until they relaxed. Without yoga exercising, one can become very sore and stiff while eating a two-hour Chinese dinner in a cross-legged position on the floor. Every course in this six-course meal was double, and the dishes were elaborately garnished. Our meal included shrimp boiled in their shells, bird's nest soup, squid, chicken, tong solitchi (sweet and sour pork), several kinds of fruit, and much warm wine. It was a pleasant dinner, but it seemed strange that until this evening, I had not met Mr. Thompson; even stranger that I never saw him again.

Our friend Rouse left for a six-month leave of absence, with pay, to return to England. He explained that it was English custom for the first son to enter the military or diplomatic service and for the second son to secure a commercial or money-earning position. He was the second son, of course. His temporary replacement, a Mr. Newman, was very, very English and surprisingly quiet. We missed Rouse.

On December 8, 1945, a freighter from Manila tied up at the Amoy wharf. It carried tons of clothing for the poor people of China. When it unloaded, I watched bales and bales of items, packed in boxes, cartons, and bags, being carried into the large municipal warehouses. It was my firm opinion that the Chinese people were not wanting for clothing, and I wondered who would allocate these garments. Several days later I asked the mayor of Amoy when he was going to start distributing the clothing.

"There is no hurry," he said. "This clothing is for warmer weather." This did not make a lot of sense to me, since temperatures never dropped to fifty degrees or rose above eighty-five. I had a strong suspicion that one day someone would make money on this clothing and that it just might be the mayor.

On December 10, 1945, we learned that two U.S. transport ships were due in Shanghai to move 9,000 servicemen from Shanghai to San Francisco. All army men were supposed to be out of China by December 20. There was no word about air force or navy personnel.

On this day, too, Lovell gave us some concern. At heart, he was always a playboy and "Joe College" all rolled into one, which got him into numerous predicaments. Too often he put into action some of the damnedest ideas. This day he took one of the motor boats and went for a ride in the harbor. For some reason, the motor quit just as the tide was running out, and it caught him in its millrace back into the ocean. One of our men had to go after him.

Lovell was a graduate of Brown University and frequently went about singing softly, "What is the color of horse shit? Brown, Brown, Brown!" He was a hell of a nice guy, and I was glad he asked for me to be transferred to Camp Six when I first met him. He claimed I had saved his life when one of our men got drunk in Hua'an and was going to shoot him with a .45. The man,

Duncan, did not like Lovell for some reason. On this day Duncan started looking for Lovell, claiming he was going to "shoot that son of a bitch." When I
found them, Duncan had Lovell backed against a wall and the pistol pushed
into his belly.

I began talking soft, but fast, reminding Duncan that he and I were good
friends. I edged closer and closer, talking all the while about our long buddy-
buddy relationship.

"Hey, Dunc, are we good friends or what?"

"You're my friend," he mumbled, slurring his words. "But Lovell's not."

"Just think of all we've done together, Dunc," I said. Soon I was partially
between the two, and his gun was pointed at me. I just kept talking and very
slowly lay my hand on the .45 and pushed the barrel away from me. By then
some fifteen Americans and Chinese were gathered around.

"Put your gun in the holster, Dunc, please."

He reholstered the .45. The next day, when Duncan sobered up, he talked
with me at great length, thanking me for my part in the previous day's episode
and telling me about the last Thanksgiving he had spent with his family at the
old home in Moscow, Idaho. He had been in the U.S. Navy for four years without a leave to see his family, so he had gone there before being sent to China.

"I embarrassed myself and all the family," he grimaced, remembering
when, at the dinner table, he said in typical navy jargon, "Pass the horse cock"
(pass the bologna). He said his face reddened and he got up and went into the
kitchen. His mother followed to say that everyone had forgotten his remark.

"Son, we know that just slipped out," she said with her hand on Duncan's
shoulder. "Come on back in and finish your lunch."

He replied, "No, Mom, I can't go back in there! I just can't do it!"

She said, "Don't say you can't do it, son. You can do it. Now go back in
there and finish your dinner."

Then he said, "Mom, if I go back in there I'll just fuck up things worse than
ever." When he realized what he had said in front of his mother, it was too
much. He packed his clothes, hugged his parents without looking them in the
eyes, and asked his brother to drive him to the bus station.

"You know, Mish, I have never had a Thanksgiving dinner at home since
being in the navy, now six years."

Lovell, Brandwein, and our last two pharmacist mates, Irwin and Colwell,
all received orders to transfer to Shanghai. Shanghai was the magic word, for
it meant that a guy was homeward bound. Where were my orders? Was I going

to be left all alone in China? And Christmas was coming soon. I talked with Lovell. Then I wrote orders for my transfer.

"Will you sign them?" I asked Lovell, presenting the papers to him.

"Sure," he said. I might still be sitting in Kulangsu to this day if I had not written my own orders.

I busied myself with final plans for disposition of our remaining arms, ammunition, and equipment to General Chen. He, in turn, made arrangements with the Chinese admiral who had visited us the previous month and contacted Naval Group China, which had moved from Chungking to Shanghai. We received clearance to turn over our navy equipment to General Chen. Three radiomen were to be left behind to man the radio equipment, along with three new Chinese radio operators. The radiomen withdrew sizeable amounts of money without any assurance as to when they would be pulled out. I converted what they wanted into CN money. There was some scuttlebutt suggesting that our station would close down before Christmas, leaving the three Chinese operators in sole possession of the remaining radio war gear.

I decided this was not my worry and appropriated a sturdy radio-packing case in which I packed my personal possessions. The war was over; we had helped with the cleanup on the Chinese coast, and we all wanted to go home. Of course, my mind began wondering: What would happen if Naval Group headquarters found out I had written my own orders?

# CHAPTER 16

# Heading Home!

*December 15, 1945—A blessed day: the plane arrives to take us to Shanghai!*

The crew of our plane stayed overnight and took in a few points of interest. Lovell and I divided up several official boxes containing papers, vouchers, and receipts. He said he would be responsible for the large wooden box containing Camp Six's money. We also took several cases of cigarettes with us, from habit as much as anything. We never knew when they might come in handy for bartering.

I took one last look at the hotel-home-office on Kulangsu Island, then stepped onto the launch that carried us over the brief expanse of water to Amoy. We were met at the airfield by almost a hundred people, both soldiers and civilians, who gave us gifts of fruit. They wanted to say goodbye. It made me sad. I was even sadder bidding farewell to Mickey Chen. He was an extraordinary young man, and I did not know what the future held for him. I gave him things I did not want to carry with me, which he appreciated, and 5,000 CN.

After we were airborne, we began eating our gifts of tangerines and bananas, hoping that would raise our spirits. We had been waiting so long for this day, but we had not anticipated the stress of leaving all our friends. Several bottles of beer appeared, and then I decided the time had come! I opened my treasured can of baked beans, kept as a last resource and carried with me all over China. High above the mare's tail clouds, the ceremony of "the opening of Mish's beans" occurred. Everyone cheered when I finally opened them; everyone got two spoonfuls except me. I ate a quarter of the can, and, oh, how I enjoyed those beans!

The China coastline was beautiful. The water was clear and I could see the sandbars, shoals, channels, bays, rivers, and creeks in a great range of blue colors. They all contrasted with the deep blue of the ocean. I have never seen anything quite like it since. Coming into Shanghai by air was a unique sight also. The Whangpu (Huangpu) River was lined with ships that stretched far into the distance. We spotted the USS *Repose*, our U.S. Navy hospital ship with its large red cross painted on top. We landed on an airfield that had thousands and thousands of drums of gasoline piled in units of perhaps 100 drums each. I thought about how many times I had searched for a single drum or two in the mountain villages.

As soon as we landed, Lovell told me to take care of the wooden money box. "Where is the box?" I asked.

There was silence. In all the wind-up activity, in spite of his expressly saying he would take care of that box, Lovell had left it in Kulangsu. He might have been able to go home in a week; now he had to fly back to Amoy and hope for the best.

The airfield was as busy as a beehive in clover time. Armed guards on foot and on motorcycles patrolled the runways, mainly because daily there were Chinese who would run across the path of a plane as it took off, hoping the plane would kill the bad spirit that was following them. A few times, however, it was the person running who had been inadvertently killed. Moreover, several planes had been damaged trying to avoid these would-be spirit killers. Just the sight of a civilian in the open field was sufficient cause for a motorcycle cop to go racing off to make an arrest.

Some of the navy men told me that I probably would not be released immediately, so by December 18 I was convinced I would not make it home in time for Christmas. I sought out the commander of the U.S. Navy Supply Corps and asked him if he would sign my clearance papers. Without answering, he launched into a tirade, reading me the riot act. Why did I keep the men in the Sea View Hotel in Kulangsu instead of in a Chinese military encampment?

"They were drawing per diem and also free quarters in the hotel," he noted, saying as supply man I had been in charge of the quarters. He went on and on, picking at our camp's situation.

When he finally wound down I asked, "Who ever made me an officer that I was to direct the men where they should sleep?" Then I tried to explain there were no Chinese military camps on the small island of Kulangsu. If we had not taken over the hotel, we would have had to rent a private home and perhaps put in floors and lavatories.

"Why didn't Lieutenant Lovell bring Camp Six's money back?" he hacked.

"I suggest you direct that question to Lieutenant Lovell, sir."

I explained that out of the three dollars' daily allowance for quarters on Kulangsu, we had chipped in to pay for water to be carried to our rooms, to make a few other necessary improvements, and to pay the manager of the hotel daily. We finally finished our conversation, and I asked him again if he would sign my clearance. He picked up his pen and signed the document.

"But it will take several weeks before I can get transportation home for you, Mishler." This officer, Roy Stratton, compiled a book after the war entitled *SACO—The Rice Paddy Navy*.

Lovell was back in two days with the cash box, which contained about 6,000 American dollars. I was then able to change my Australian pounds back into American dollars. However, I made a big mistake in selling the gold pieces I had collected in China. A disbursing officer told me I could not take gold pieces into the States because the United States was off the gold standard. Anyone caught selling gold pieces in the United States would be arrested, he advised. Later I learned that had I carried them home as collectors' items I would have had no problem. As it was, I ended up selling them to a navy supply officer for face value.

I went into a bar frequented by U.S. military personnel and asked the bartender if he wanted to buy my three bottles of whiskey. He offered to buy them at twenty-five dollars per bottle. I negotiated a bit, and he finally opened the cash register and gave me ninety dollars for the three bottles.

Everything and everybody in Shanghai seemed to be in a hurry. There were no signs of war except for the presence of servicemen of many countries and military trucks, planes, and ships; and the lack of fuel for Chinese civilians. Food was plentiful. Buildings were intact, with no marks of bombings or strafings. On every corner were crowds of people waiting for streetcars or buses, which were always filled to capacity and beyond. People even hung on the outside. I saw military trucks being driven by hotshot soldiers, honking their horns and winding through the crowds on the streets. Some Chinese pedestrians were killed by these drivers, who should have been arrested by the military police or shore patrol.

One of the best things about being in Shanghai was that I was reunited with a number of old friends, some of whom I had not seen since my earliest days in China. We spent many hours catching up with news. One friend informed me that the guy who bought my diamond ring sold it in Shanghai for four times what I had dickered for in Changchow. Inflation was rampant in this huge, bustling city. A person with the right money could buy anything. I retained my conservative attitude in the marketplace and took very little spending money with me when I went out with the guys.

My sleeping quarters were in the Shanghai American School. All the rooms were filled, so I had to put my cot in a drafty hallway, and I soon caught a cold. Because of the cold, a navy dentist refused to do some needed work on my teeth. He made another appointment for me in two weeks, but I told him I didn't think I would be around that long.

"You'll just have to get it done in the States," he said.

My attire also presented problems for me. I had only khaki clothes, but khakis were "out of uniform." I was supposed to be wearing blues. Each time I was approached by shore patrol personnel about my clothes, I promised to get blues by the next day. I was hedging for time.

Irwin, Colwell, and I went out to the USS *Repose* one day to visit several sick friends. It was the cleanest ship afloat. Going out to it aboard an LST (landing ship, tank) was almost as bumpy as some of my rides down the Nine Dragons River. However, I had to compliment the young sailors who maneuvered the LST among aircraft carriers, cruisers, destroyers, and tankers. We once ran close to the USS *St. Paul*, a huge and impressive cruiser. We also passed a smart-looking English vessel named the *Black Prince*. They had already covered over the wartime camouflage paint with a clean, gleaming white paint.

The Shanghai American School eventually secured a room for me, a big step up from the cot in the hall. The school was located on a beautiful fenced campus, unusual for such a crowded city as Shanghai. It was so far from downtown that we always took a truck. Trucks ran about every hour, back and forth to the four-storied naval headquarters building downtown, so we could always catch a ride. On top of the headquarters building were antenna wires and a searchlight as well as a large U.S. flag.

One evening, those of us who remained from Camp Six had a beer and dinner reunion at the Enlisted Men's Club. On the way back to quarters, several of us stopped to see what was attracting a crowd on the street. The tallest man I had ever seen in navy uniform was at the center of it all. He was 6 feet 6 inches tall and weighed about 240 pounds. He was talking very loudly and betting those around him that he could turn over the car parked at the curb. As he placed his huge hands under the edge of the car, the crowd became silent. He balanced the car on its two side wheels and then flipped it over on its side! A shouted warning of "shore patrol!" broke up the exhibition.

On December 20, I checked the bulletin board at navy headquarters and found my name on a list of fifty men scheduled to board the *Orvetta*, a receiving ship, the next day. We were to be quartered on board until another ship accepted us as part of its supercargo. Another step toward home!

The same day, I was requested to appear before a board of navy officers; among them were two from Camp Six. They wanted to award me a medal to go with my battle star and asked me to recount my ambush incident with the Japanese patrol. After I finished my brief story, I told them I was not interested in receiving another award. But then I received a big surprise.

"Will you accept the commission of ensign?" an officer inquired. I thought quickly.

"No," I said, "but I would like to become a warrant officer, if such a promotion is possible." It turned out it was not. The Table of Organization was filled, and no more warrant grades were available at the moment. They continued by suggesting that if I would sign up for one more year of China duty, they would see that I made chief for sure, and maybe a warrant officer opening would come up soon. I refused this, too. I wanted to go home to establish a permanent profession and a stable home. Commander Halperin and Lieutenant Robillard ended up by wishing me well, and I thanked them for their consideration.

I spent a little time every day in the Red Cross building in the city, which had a swimming pool, basketball court, and lunch counter. One day I ran into three of our Camp Six interpreters and had dinner with them in Shanghai. They were still in the military. One of them, whose name was Gene, said his father had once been mayor of Shanghai. The other two were ill with tuberculosis but were getting no treatment for it. I wondered how any of them got along on the meager Chinese military pay. After dinner we went to an immense stadium in downtown Shanghai to witness a youth rally.

Of interest to me were the many White Russians who lived in Shanghai. The women were fair-skinned and clean-looking, and several were very pretty. They had not been bothered by the Japanese during the war, but they had a difficult time earning a living in China.

The weather was turning colder. When Irwin and I accepted an invitation to dinner from a German Jewish refugee, we took a can of ham, green beans, several pounds of rice, and a pound of coffee with us. The only heat in the home was from the cooking stove, so all of us, including our hosts, wore our outer clothing, including hats, during the entire evening. This family had been among the mass of Jews that *The Gripsholm* had deposited in ports around the world. They were highly literate people, tenaciously surviving in the face of many obstacles.

One morning at the navy operations building I recognized an air force pilot who had flown into Amoy twice and had stayed overnight with us at the hotel.

"I've got some weather equipment to fly to Peking, and if you've got nothing better to do, Mish, why don't you fly up with me? We'll go up, spend the night, and return tomorrow." After checking our draft status and seeing that we would not be called up for at least another day, I accepted. I had always wanted to see this ancient city.

We flew north along the coast and then veered northwest, passing over the large city of Tientsin before landing in Peking. Peking, better known today as Beijing, but also at one time Peiping, meant "white city" and was home to the very large Chinese University strongly supported by the Rockefeller family. I would have liked to spend a few days in the city but was disappointed because we were not permitted to leave the airfield. I did, however, have the good fortune to fly over the Great Wall of China on our return to Shanghai, where we landed just before dark.

We were caught in another SNAFU when our draft reported to the designated receiving ship only to learn there were no quarters available. We reported back to Shanghai's navy headquarters for further instructions and were assigned to an old building in the southeast part of the city, which was actually a concrete warehouse. We were given the choice of about 400 double bunk beds on the second floor. I took a top bunk the first night and went to sleep early. Nearly everyone was on liberty, and most of the men took off. I was awakened about 3:00 A.M. by definitely drunken voices, but it didn't bother me too much.

From some bunk came a voice, "Hey, fellows, keep it down. I'm trying to sleep. Didn't you see the sign near the door?" The sign cautioned all latecomers to be quiet so as not to disturb those who were sleeping.

There was immediate quiet for a few seconds, then the loud talking began again. I propped myself up on my elbow and was just getting ready to holler for quiet when the man of the first voice swung his feet down from the top bunk and implored the men to let him sleep.

"Look fellas, I told you before, and I'm telling you again. Cut out the noise and hit the sack. If I have to get down out of this bunk I'll bash somebody a clout or two."

It was fairly dark, but we could see the two noisemakers with their heads together. It was quiet again for a few moments, but then one raised his head and said, "Hey you, doing the talking, go blow it out your ass!"

Others began sitting up in their bunks, as I did. I recognized the roused sleeper as the big navy guy who had turned over the car outside the Enlisted Men's Club. He slipped down from his bunk, towering over the two others.

"Which one of you bastards told me to blow it out my ass?"

"I did," said one; and with that the big man picked him up and threw him about eight feet against a wall. But as he did so the other sailor jumped him from behind, locking his arms around the big man's neck and his legs around his body in a scissors grip. As the big man tried to pull him off, the other sailor got to his feet and waded in with blows to the big man's face. The end came when one kicked the big man in the testicles. By this time there were five or six of us on our way to the arena. We watched for a minute or two and saw the big man doubled up, taking a severe beating.

Those of us who were standing around decided to break it up and pulled them apart. Then we pushed and shoved the two sailors to the vicinity of their bunks and warned them against leaving them before the night was over. With the Japanese defeated, we had started fighting among ourselves, partly out of boredom.

The next morning when I got up the two sailors had left. I saw the big guy, and he looked terrible! One eye was swollen shut, his face had two dark bruises, and his chin was cut. The dried blood made his face look messy. When I asked him how he felt, he said, "Fine. If that little bastard hadn't kicked me in the nuts I could have taken them easily."

I came to one conclusion after this incident: two little men can lick a good big guy anytime if they know what they're doing; and those two did.

Finally I received a complete allowance of acceptable navy clothing: two new sets of blues with all the trimmings, thermal underwear (which I never wore), and three pairs of fine black navy shoes. No charge was made for this issue since I had been ordered to dispose of my original blues before going to China.

I began to get fed up with the "braid and brass" nonsense. After almost two full years of no insignia and no saluting, we were now required to observe all military regulations. I was learning to salute all over again.

The USS *St. Paul* was still anchored in the river, and our draft hoped we would be assigned passage to San Francisco on this cruiser. It would have much better sleeping quarters and food than a troop ship. Several of us walked along the Bund, which bordered on the Whangpu River, one evening. We saw two Chinese men hanging on to the two river buoys anchored in midstream. No one made an effort to rescue them. Eventually they were bound to fall off the buoy and drown. I was told that these men had been placed there as a punishment, but no one knew by whom: the official Chinese police, the Tong (a secret society somewhat like the Mafia), or the military.

Christmas Eve we were assigned to the USS *APL 44*, which was actually a floating barracks. At one time it had been a navy laundry ship. It had no power of its own and had to be towed from port to port. It could have been worse; our bunks and lockers were like new. The boat operated with a skeleton crew, so we all assumed certain maintenance tasks as we saw fit. The first thing we did was scour the area for proper Christmas dinner food. We ended up with a typical stateside celebration as a result of an "all hands" effort, during which we begged and scrounged four large turkeys, mashed potatoes, gravy, peas, olives, and several kinds of pickles and fruitcakes from surrounding ships. There were only twenty-five of us on board the old vessel, so we were stuffed on that Christmas Day of 1945.

The *APL 44* boasted a recreation area that included a library and, of all things, a piano. There were a few writing desks and reading chairs, so it was a popular place for those not on liberty. The day after Christmas a few more men came aboard while I was ashore. That evening, as I was writing a letter to Audrey, I heard someone softly playing the piano. I walked around the room divider and saw that it was the big sailor who had turned over the car and taken such a beating in the warehouse quarters!

I found a comfortable chair and listened to him for almost an hour. I could tell he loved to play the piano, and he was good, too. He just went from one tune to another without a pause. When he finished, I went over to him and told him how much I liked his music. I learned that the only reason the navy had taken him, since he was oversized, was that he was a professional diver of renown. He had done underwater work in the Chicago area for years, specializing in working on new piers and repairing old ones. He had helped raise several ships and had searched for persons believed drowned. The navy flew him all over the South Pacific for diving and for reporting underwater damage to ships. He had made two dives to retrieve large amounts of money and important code books from sunken ships.

Early the next morning a troopship made its way slowly up the river toward us. I was on deck and heard it drop its clanky anchor nearby.

"Maybe this is the one for us," we all said.

We went ashore to the Red Cross center for breakfast and a swim, but the pool water was cold because there was no fuel to heat it. Several of our Camp Six ensigns were part of a basketball team that played an army team. The score was lopsided in our favor. I enjoyed running around the track on the second floor, but time began to drag. Several White Russians, mostly girls, were employed by the Red Cross to serve as waitresses and conversationalists with the men.

A new day dawned. It was cold, but the sun soon made the day look promising. About noon we received the message! We were given orders to board the troopship that we had seen enter the harbor. Last-minute letters and a few packages were rushed into the mail. I said goodbye to my closest friends at the naval operations building and walked the streets of Shanghai smelling the food for one last time. A marvelous thought filled my mind—in two or three days I would be headed for home! It would be okay that I would again stand in numerous chow lines aboard ship and sleep on hard bunks for days.

We slipped out of Shanghai one morning pointed toward the Golden Gate Bridge and San Francisco. En route we passed the tip of Japan, which loomed like a ghost in the distance. I stood a night watch at the bow of the ship, with the express duty of looking for mines. Of course, I couldn't see much in the blackness and simply hoped we would miss any mine that was out there.

The new year came and went, and on January 3, 1946, we tied up in San Francisco harbor. The Chinese have a proverb, "A journey of a thousand miles begins with one step." I made the first step when I became a navy volunteer and a sampan sailor.

I made another when I stepped off that gangplank.

# Wrap-up

For fourteen years I corresponded with my last houseboy, Mickey Chen, whose real name was Khin McWin. He returned to Rangoon, Burma, married, and had several children who were taught in a missionary school. He employed public letter writers to write his letters to me in English. My last three letters in the early 1960s were returned unanswered. I kept in touch for several years with Gebraad, Lovell, Irwin, Coleman, Landt, Sinks, and others, but as the years went by they faded away.

I do not know what happened to Alnav. He was a fine boy. General Lui recalled him to service after the war; he was just fourteen years old. The photo I have of him is one of my most memorable treasures. No one could fill Alnav's shoes (although he wore them only occasionally).

Some of the SACO men got together a few years after the war and came up with the idea of having annual reunions. Beginning in 1955, these conventions have been held annually in cities all over the United States and in Taiwan. By 1989 Audrey and I had attended about ten of them, including three in Taiwan, which were lavish, typically Chinese, and had touches of nostalgia.

The Taiwanese menus still follow the traditional style that was a feature at the victory banquet at Changchow in 1945, with numerous courses of shark's fin soup, pigeon egg soup, sweet and sour fish, fried bamboo shoots, and other delicacies. And of course there are still plenty of red wine gom beis! SACO convention days are filled with speeches and toasts by diplomats and officials from both Chinese and American governments, by veterans of the various wars, and by members of SACO's rank and file.

For the Taiwan reunions, the Nationalist Chinese government provided new deluxe buses and escorts of military motorcycles and sports cars. They paid all our hotel and meal expenses and led us through the streets with sirens blaring and flags waving. Crowds gathered on the streets of Taipei to wave to us and cheer; even the young children applauded as we were whisked by in our beautiful buses. As always in China, the people made the difference.

# Index

# About the Author

Clayton Mishler was born on February 17, 1908, in Johnstown, Pennsylvania. Following his service in World War II, he returned to work at the Veterans Administration as a contact officer in the Detroit Regional Office and was eventually made Medical Administrative Officer. He served for several years in the Minneapolis Area Office and later transferred to the Central Office in Washington, D.C. He retired from the Veterans Administration in 1971, after thirty-one years of government service. Clayton and his wife, Audrey, moved to Austin, Texas, and spent many years traveling throughout the United States, Europe, Asia, and Mexico. He died in Austin on February 2, 1992, at the age of 83.

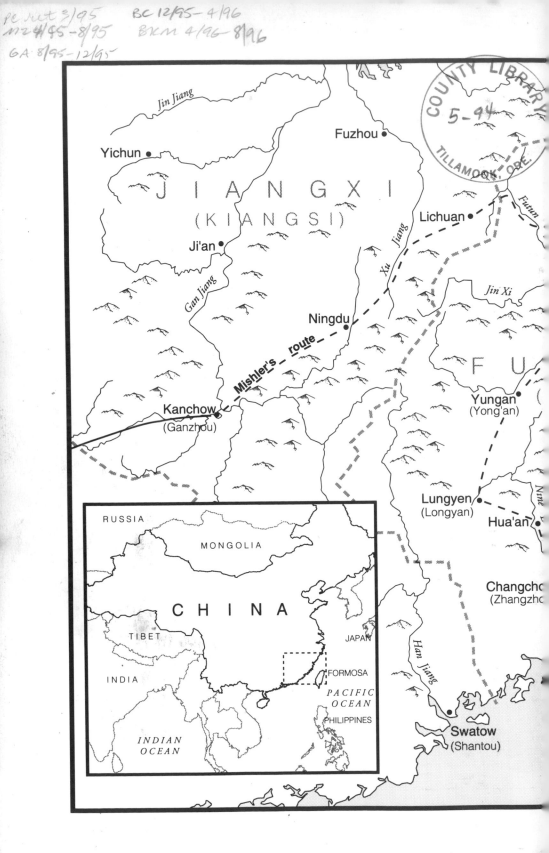

Jin Jiang

Yichun

J I A N G X I
(K I A N G S I)

Fuzhou

Ji'an

Lichuan

Futun

Xu Jiang

Gan Jiang

Jin Xi

Ningdu

F U

Mishler's route

Yungan
(Yong'an)

Kanchow
(Ganzhou)

Lungyen
(Longyan)

Hua'an

Nin

Changcho
(Zhangzho

RUSSIA

MONGOLIA

C H I N A

TIBET

JAPAN

INDIA

FORMOSA

Han Jiang

PACIFIC
OCEAN

PHILIPPINES

INDIAN
OCEAN

Swatow
(Shantou)